How my
Death Saved
My Life

Also by Denise Linn

Titles marked with an asterisk (*) are available from Hay House.
Please visit:
Hay House UK: **www.hayhouse.co.uk**
Hay House USA: **www.hayhouse.com**
Hay House Australia: **www.hayhouse.com.au**
Hay House South Africa: **www.hayhouse.co.za**
Hay House India: **www.hayhouse.in**

HOW MY DEATH SAVED MY LIFE

And Other Stories on
My Journey to Wholeness

DENISE LINN

HAY HOUSE

Australia • Canada • Hong Kong • India
South Africa • United Kingdom • United States

First published and distributed in the United Kingdom by:
Hay House UK Ltd, 292B Kensal Rd, London W10 5BE.
Tel.: (44) 20 8962 1230; Fax: (44) 20 8962 1239. www.hayhouse.co.uk

Published and distributed in the United States of America by:
Hay House, Inc., PO Box 5100, Carlsbad, CA 92018-5100.
Tel.: (1) 760 431 7695 or (800) 654 5126;
Fax: (1) 760 431 6948 or (800) 650 5115. www.hayhouse.com

Published and distributed in Australia by:
Hay House Australia Ltd, 18/36 Ralph St, Alexandria NSW 2015.
Tel.: (61) 2 9669 4299; Fax: (61) 2 9669 4144. www.hayhouse.com.au

Published and distributed in the Republic of South Africa by:
Hay House SA (Pty), Ltd, PO Box 990, Witkoppen 2068.
Tel./Fax: (27) 11 467 8904. www.hayhouse.co.za

Published and distributed in India by:
Hay House Publishers India, Muskaan Complex, Plot No.3, B-2, Vasant Kunj,
New Delhi – 110 070. Tel.: (91) 11 4176 1620; Fax: (91) 11 4176 1630.
www.hayhouse.co.in

Distributed in Canada by:
Raincoast, 9050 Shaughnessy St, Vancouver, BC V6P 6E5.
Tel.: (1) 604 323 7100; Fax: (1) 604 323 2600

Editorial supervision: Jill Kramer · *Design:* Amy Gingery

Photo Credits: Interior photos taken by family members and:
Earthquake: Alan Levi; *Australian outback:* Lynora Brooke; *fire ceremony:*
Sari Yu-Pietila; *African Zulu village:* Amber McIntyre; *Table Top Mountain in
Capetown, South Africa:* Lynette Orman; *berry picking:* Babette Hayes; *drumming:*
Ruth Toledo; *standing on the hill on Summerhill Ranch:* Jeannette Cake

A catalogue record for this book is available from the British Library.

ISBN 978-1-84850-493-6

Printed and bound in Great Britain by CPI Group (UK) Ltd, Croydon, CR0 4YY.

For my daughter, Meadow.
Your remarkable insights continue to astound me.
And for my sister, Heather . . . you were there.
You know.

Contents

Author's note: All the stories in this book are true; however, some of the names and places have been changed to protect the confidentiality of the individuals involved.

The Day the Earth Shook

This book began with a deep rumble in the earth. On December 22, 2003, a 6.5-magnitude earthquake rattled my world . . . the day I had chosen to start writing about my life.

On that morning, a chasm opened in the center of my small town, and the stone walls around my home fell to the ground with thundering intensity. Boiling mud and hot mineral water bubbled and flowed through the streets in a torrent. Sulfur fumes shrouded the collapsed shops and piles of debris. The violent wrenching movement shook me to my core, as the walls around me trembled and cracked.

I believe in synchronicity. The search for signs and portents has been one of my guiding dictates. It seemed to be an omen that on the day I planned to start writing about my life, the physical world around me ruptured, revealing fissures and rubble, much like the cycles of destruction and renewal that made up my own history. I knew that the writing process would level many of my self-imposed walls and crack open secrets locked inside me for so long. However, looking at the earthquake-marred landscape near my home, I wondered if that was what I really wanted to do.

I chose the winter solstice, the darkest day of the year, to begin the long process of introspection into the hidden recesses of my past. To start my book on the day that initiates the world's transition out of the darkness and into the light seemed auspicious. As I traveled through the dark corridors of my life, my journey helped shed the light of truth on what I'd experienced . . . but sometimes it was painful.

A friend who already had a successful autobiography under her belt said, "Don't go into any of the heavy stuff. Just make yourself look good." Yet I knew that the good and the bad, the mundane and the mystical . . . all merged and melded together inside me. How could I speak of one without revealing the other?

The aftershocks continued for months. Every tremor was a reminder of how, through recounting my life, I was stripping away my protective layers, revealing a raw vulnerability. I sometimes embraced the passionate force of the earth as our home shook from side to side, yet the widening rifts in the walls became a constant symbol of how exposed and unsure I felt.

In my search for the truth, I sought out people from my past whom I hadn't spoken with in as many as 35 years. It was heartwarming to talk to my first love from high school after so many years and to track down my best friend from when I was just a young girl of 12. Yet, in uncovering the past, old wounds were salted, and I wondered if some things were best left buried.

The soul loves the truth . . . I believe this with an ardent intensity, but as I wrote about the mysterious and supernatural events that had occurred in my life, I was tempted to tone them down, delete them, or worse, rationalize them. In the beginning, afraid that the stories would seem too incredible, or readers would think I'd imagined them, I felt compelled to dig for the facts underlying each event. I would call people I barely knew from my distant past asking, "What do you remember?"

I feared that my memory was an ever-changing kaleido-scope, and the truth could only be found in the collective memories of others. Yet I often found that people remembered events and situations in slightly different ways. So who was right? What was the real truth? In the end, I realized that the story of my life was stored in my memories, the only place it could truly be. As imperfect as my memory might be, it was the source of what was true for me, so I've scribed my life as I remember it. A kind of freedom emerged when I opened myself to the voice of my past and allowed these images, emotions, and memories to surface without censorship.

Deciding what to write about was also challenging. When I look back on my experiences, it's the turning points—the adventures, the suffering, or the rare moments of spiritual insight—that stand out. The banal, everyday happenings some-how dissolve from my memory . . . yet those moments contain the meat of my life. They're the sustenance and glue that hold everything together, even if the memories of them are gone forever.

I've come to the conclusion that no life can be chronicled with 100 percent accuracy, for the mind blurs, enhances, and alters so much. Maybe in the end, it isn't what happened that's important, but it's the wisdom garnered, the love shared, and the joy experienced that characterizes a life. And I am fortunate that I've experienced life deeply and fully, with all its scars and triumphs.

It is my hope and prayer that by walking alongside me for a few miles while you read this book, in some far and distant universe our souls will touch . . . yours and mine. I am honored that I have the opportunity to share my life with you. Even if we've never met in person, during those times when I've writ-ten into the early-morning hours, you have never been far from me. You've been my silent companion and sympathetic listener.

You've urged me to search for the truth . . . my truth . . . and you've even been my solace during dark and lonely nights. And best of all, you've shared my joy. I hope you find value in reading this book, as you have been such a big part of it.

INTRODUCTION

Why Is He Aiming
His Gun at Me?

I heard applause as I walked up to the stage—a distant, muffled sound in comparison to the roar of my pounding heart. As I stepped onto the platform and turned to look at the room, I was astonished to see more than a thousand people standing and clapping enthusiastically. Why were they applauding? I hadn't even said anything yet. I was tempted to look behind me to see who they were really clapping for. At the same time, I was also incredibly honored by the recognition.

I was the keynote speaker for the International Feng Shui Conference. My best-selling book, *Sacred Space*, was one of the first books written about the art of feng shui. Additionally, I'd written 12 other books, had traveled extensively (leading seminars in 19 countries), and had been featured on television shows and in documentaries around the world for my work in the mind/body/spirit field. However, even with a globally lauded career, I felt that my real accomplishment was surviving my life . . . making it to adulthood in fairly reasonable emotional health. Every time people clapped for me, I felt amazed that my life had turned out as well as it had.

As a child, I never thought I would live long. Given some of the violent events of my past, there was a real chance that I might not have survived. Or perhaps secretly, I'd hoped my life would end because I was so unhappy. Death sometimes seemed to be the only way out. However, not only did I make it to adulthood, but I also managed to create meaning from the senseless experiences in my life. That others found value in my work was a source of unending astonishment, so I felt immensely grateful as I waited for the applause to die down before starting my talk.

In the middle of a lecture later in the day, I called on a woman in the back of the room. She asked, "Denise, you seem to have found yourself. How did you become so grounded and compassionate?"

My mind flashed back to the humid summer of 1967. I was 17 and riding my motorbike on a country road near our small farming community. It was a warm, hazy day, and I felt carefree as the wind blew through my hair. I had just come from visiting a college that I hoped to attend and was excited about my future, as there was only one more year of high school to go. I felt content as I sailed past row after row of golden-tasseled corn on my way home.

I was so caught up in the reverie of the day that I wasn't aware of a car tailing close behind me. Suddenly, my body flew forward as my motorbike was rammed from behind. I frantically grabbed the handlebars and tried to stay upright, but the car slammed into me again. The force threw me off my bike. I slid across the asphalt and rolled off to the side of the road into a shallow, dry irrigation ditch.

As I struggled to stand up, I watched the large blue car that hit me turn around and drive back toward me. *He's coming back to help*, I thought hopefully.

He pulled alongside me and rolled down his window. I raised my head to look at the person who had crashed into me. I didn't recognize him. He was a slight man, yet there was something softly sinister about his appearance. He appeared to be young, with sallow, baby-smooth skin and limp, oily hair draped loosely over his forehead. His sunglasses gave him a cold, unfeeling appearance. His mouth was tightly clenched, and his movements were slow and methodical. With measured determination, he leveled a gun at me.

The dark hole of the gun seemed enormous, somehow out of proportion. I couldn't comprehend why he was aiming a gun at me. Everything seemed to be moving in slow motion. It seemed so unreal. *I didn't do anything to him. Why did he run into me? Why is he aiming his gun at me? Why?!*

Just at that moment, an irrational thought ricocheted across my brain. *He's aiming too low. If he wants to kill me, he's going to have to aim higher.*

A cough in the crowd brought me back to the present moment. I answered the woman as best I could, but the truth was that I didn't know how I *had* managed to become who I was. Perhaps the secret lay in my past and in the stories of my life. Maybe exploring what happened would give me an understanding of how I had evolved to be the woman I am.

CHAPTER ONE

Beginnings

(1949–1955)

Ancient people looked to the night sky with wonder and awe. These early sky-watchers recognized that the vast, ever-changing panorama of the celestial canopy seemed to chronicle and even precipitate what occurred on Earth. They noticed that the position of the heavenly bodies at the time of birth reflected the fate of the child in the years ahead. In fact, all events surrounding a birth were observed as omens and signs of what was to come. It was the power of the beginning.

All life is affected by beginnings. The position of the stars, the amount of light and dark, the lack or abundance of nutrients, the love given or withheld—everything affects beginnings. Like ever-widening circles created by a pebble dropped in a still pool, the events and the forces surrounding my beginnings have rippled through my life. The fluctuations between the light and the dark, the seen and unseen, and the known and unknown in those earliest years were portents of what was to come.

IN A RARE CANDID MOMENT in my teens, my mother told me the story of how she'd met my father and how I came to be

1

conceived. She was so exacting in the way she told the story that I've always seen the events clearly in my mind. This is the story as I remember it:

Balancing her lunch tray in one hand and her chemistry books in the other hand, Jean (my mother) negotiated through the crowded Oregon State University cafeteria. Finally she found a chair, eased herself into it, and slid the tray in front of her.

Realizing that she'd forgotten to grab a fork, she pushed her chair back, glanced at the cafeteria line, and froze. Walking toward her was a tall, striking man with startling blue eyes.

That's him! she declared to herself. *That's the man who will be the father of my children.*

The year was 1949, and at age 33 Jean had realized that if she was going to have children, she needed to find a husband . . . and quickly. She was ready to settle down. The war had been hard on her, and memories of it still clung to her like spiderwebs in the dark corners of her mind.

Before World War II broke out, she had moved to Java— a Dutch colony at the time—to live with her first husband, a Dutch Indonesian artist, on his family's coffee estate. As a woman of Cherokee heritage growing up in rural Oklahoma, the stoic acceptance of life that her parents exhibited was difficult to reconcile with her adventurous nature. As a young girl, my mother had tilled the sun-baked soil in her family's garden, milked the cows, and gathered eggs in the early dawn . . . while she dreamed of seeing the world. Her yearning to travel had eventually carried her to a new life in rural Java.

She loved the tropical lifestyle and longed to start a family. However, her new husband didn't want children, so Jean left him and hopped a ride on a freighter headed to Japan, where she had a short sojourn in a research lab at a university in Kobe.

She conducted experiments on weeds to discover which of them were edible. Since the Japanese were secretly planning on war, they hired researchers to see if weeds could be used to avoid food shortages. Catching a ride on another freighter, she made her way to Hawaii, where she did some modeling and worked as a cocktail waitress.

(It is only as I delve into my past, writing this book, that I've realized that there are more similarities than differences between my mother and myself. Despite the strife in our relationship in later years, my life often eerily paralleled hers. For my mother to hitch rides on freighters by herself in the 1930s indicates a sense of exploration unusual in a woman of that time. This wild spirit of adventure may have been echoed in my life as I hitchhiked alone through Europe as a teen. Maybe her later run-in with the FBI was reflected in the time that I found myself interrogated by Yugoslavian police. The way that she chose my father to be her mate was perhaps mirrored in the way I chose my first lover.)

Like many of the sailors who came into the bar where she worked in Hawaii, Jean was homesick. Some of the men were from Oklahoma like my mother, and they loved to talk to her about home. One night, near closing time, three FBI agents came into the bar and told Jean that they were taking her in for questioning. She sat trembling as they silently drove her to their headquarters.

"You've been talking to sailors, asking them about their activities. Why do you want to know?"

"They just come into the bar and we talk. That's not a crime. What have I done?" she asked as her voice quivered.

"What were you doing in Japan?"

"I was working in a research lab. I didn't do anything wrong," she said as she started to cry.

"What is your connection to Germany?"

"I don't have any connection with Germany!"

"You sound German. I'll repeat the question: What is your connection to Germany?!"

My mother had remnants of a speech impediment from childhood that made her "G's" sound guttural and hard, which to the untrained ear might have sounded like vestiges of a Teutonic accent.

Finally, the FBI agents let her go but kept her under surveillance. Even though American involvement in the war was a few years away, tensions were high. When the war started, Jean joined the military and worked at the Long Beach Naval Hospital in California as a scrub nurse. She didn't see the immediate gaping wounds of war, but experienced firsthand the debilitating long-term effects. She worked with men with amputated limbs and some who were in severe shell shock. The stress of treating battle-worn and injured men was so intense that Jean twice landed in a hospital herself for fatigue.

Following the war, she wanted to put those years as far behind her as she could and thus decided to go back to college. After having completed a few years of study, she was definitely ready to settle down and raise a family. But first she had to find a husband. She'd decided that she wanted four children—two girls and two boys—in that order, and each two years apart. She planned to use modern, scientific means to achieve this, but first she needed to find a man with "superior genes." Jean had studied science and had worked in research labs for years and had chosen Oregon State because of its strong chemistry department. As a result of her work, she decided that genetics was her top criterion for her future husband. On that morning in the college cafeteria, she was sure that she'd found the man with the right genes.

Dick was a towering 6'7" tall, with remarkable eyes and gleaming black hair. Looking older than his 23 years, Dick carried himself with the grace of a Navy man (he'd served on a supply ship during the war). As he stood there searching for a place to sit in the cafeteria, he had a dominating presence that filled the room, yet his eyes communicated a certain shyness and reserve.

Dick and his sister had been raised on the outskirts of Los Angeles. His father had a small refrigeration business where Dick occasionally worked as a boy. There wasn't anything mechanical he couldn't mend or fix, so he'd been a great help to his dad. After Dick left home, he joined the Navy for the duration of the war and developed a love of ships and the machinery that drives them. However, as the war drew to a close, he was glad to be out of the service and be able to get a college education. He was interested in chemistry and food technology, so he also chose Oregon State.

As she watched Dick approach, Jean thought, *Well, he certainly fits my requirement for great physical genes, but I wonder if he's intelligent.*

"Hi there!" Jean chirped as she caught his eye.

Dick looked down to see a raven-haired, animated woman. "Um, do you mean me?"

"Yes! What's your name?"

"Dick."

"Well, Dick . . . why don't you join me for lunch."

"Oh . . . okay."

"So, are you a student here?"

"Yes, I'm here on the GI bill. I'm studying food technology and the chemistry of food."

It only took a short conversation about chemistry for Jean to confirm that his "genes" were indeed high quality and that he had intelligence as well as physical prowess. Years later, Dick wrote of this first meeting, saying, "She was tall—almost six feet—good-looking, and interesting. She was nothing like the little fluffs running around campus. I was big, dumb, and inexperienced."

Their relationship developed very quickly, and soon they tossed their possessions into the back of Dick's 1936 Ford panel truck and trekked to Astoria to work in the Oregon State Seafood Lab for the summer. It was a whirlwind romance, and they decided to get married on July 4, 1949.

On July 3, the day before the wedding, Dick was at the lab in the chemistry department when a co-worker called to him, "Hey, Dick, the phone's for you. It's Jean. She says that it's urgent."

Thinking the worst, he sprinted to the phone, breathlessly grabbing the receiver. "Is everything okay?"

Jean laughed. "Yes, everything's fine. But my temperature just spiked, and you have to get here immediately because I'm fertile *now!*"

Dick stammered, "But, but . . . I really wanted to wait until after we were married. We only have one more day to wait."

"I can't wait. I'm ovulating now, and for the next two hours my chances of having a baby girl are substantially higher than if we leave it to fate."

Jean wasn't concerned about saving herself for marriage. She had been previously married and now, at 33 years old (she had told my father that she was 25), she was in a hurry to get pregnant. Dick, however, was reserving his virginity until his union was sanctified by marriage.

"Dick, we're practically married," she pleaded. "It really doesn't matter if you lose your virginity now or tomorrow. Please come now . . . and hurry!"

The pleas of his bride-to-be, plus the surprising urgency of his hormones, were convincing. Grinning, he threw down his lab coat and yelled over his shoulder to his co-worker, "See you later, Sam. I've got something I need to take care of."

The result of this hurried encounter was . . . me!

And so began the family's fable that I was conceived out of wedlock the first time my father had sex. Honestly, that was more information than I wanted to know. The idea of my parents engaging in sexual relations was monstrously embarrassing, *especially* when it had something to do with me.

More than nine months later, I was so overdue that my father drove my mother down the bumpiest country road he could find in order to start her labor. But the drive had the opposite effect on me. It must have convinced me to hold off for as long as I could. Eventually, with the collective force of medical intervention and labor-inducing drugs, I was born at 2:20 A.M. on April 16, 1950, in Corvallis, Oregon.

I was a scrawny, ugly baby; my father couldn't believe that an infant could look so unsightly. (Even from an early age, my father seemed to have an obsession with the way I looked.) My mother loved the movies, so she named me after Denise Darcell, a French movie star newly popular in America, and gave me the middle name Aleene after a great-aunt in Oklahoma.

MY FIRST HOME WAS IN ASTORIA, a rainy fishing village by the Pacific Ocean. (I was told that the house overlooked the sea and the rolling mists and fog.) Then a few months after I was born, my parents moved back to the Oregon State University area so my father could work on a master's degree.

As a baby, I was unremarkable except for my active curiosity and wiry strength. My father described me as a "whirlwind," whereas my mother said I seemed "fearless." At two months old, I was climbing out of my makeshift crib, and by four months, they couldn't keep me in any crib. When I was a year old, I scrambled up a 12-foot ladder to the top of the roof and laughed as I toddled along its crest. My mother was too pregnant with my sister, Heather, to make it up the ladder to come after me, so she just watched in alarm from below. By the time she'd decided to race to a neighbor's home to get help, I'd made my way safely back down the ladder.

It must have been hard for my mother to keep up with a child as active as I was. One afternoon my father came home after running an errand and couldn't find me. "Where's Denise?" he asked.

"I don't know," Jean replied. "She was here just a minute ago."

Dick looked through the house. With panic in his eyes, he exclaimed, "She's not here!"

"She's only two—she can't have gone far!" Scooping my newborn sister up in her arms, my mother raced out the screen door with my father close behind.

"Denise! Denise!" they called, as they looked under bushes and behind trees in their small yard.

"Dick!" The cold, hard edge of Jean's voice stopped him. He turned to see her, white-faced and trembling . . . she was holding up some clothes.

"These are the clothes she was wearing! Oh God!" she wailed. "What are we going to do?"

Suddenly, two stalwart nuns from the Catholic Church two blocks away marched up to the yard and poked their heads over the bushes that formed the boundary between the house and the street. "Do you have a toddler?" one of them demanded. Jean nodded with apprehension.

"Well, keep her home after this!"

Dick and Jean peered over the bushes and saw that standing between the nuns was a very delighted, and very *naked*, child.

"We were having our Sunday service, and your daughter ran up the aisle to the altar . . . with nothing on! Please keep track of your child!" They spun on their heels and left as my mother raced forward to hug me.

As a kid I was always happier with my clothes off, and even into adulthood I sometimes found clothes cumbersome and restrictive.

ANOTHER MOVE TOOK US TO WATSONVILLE, which was a small farming town in the Salinas Valley of California. There, my father did research for the U.S. Department of Agriculture. During my childhood we moved a lot—at least nine times—and that doesn't include the short stays that lasted six months or so. We never seemed to have enough money, and we were always packing or unpacking. As a young girl, my roots would begin to take hold in a new place, only to be abruptly ripped up once again. Nevertheless, I grew like a weed into a scrappy little thing, taking hold wherever I could.

For a few years my mother was either pregnant or carrying a baby on one hip and toting a toddler with her free hand. After Heather was born, Gordon and Brand soon followed, all in rapid succession—each two years apart. But nothing had prepared my mom for motherhood. Her desire for children was at deep odds with the reality of caring for toddlers, and she became increasingly despondent. The joy she thought kids would bring her was replaced with the reality of dirty diapers, measles, and squabbling siblings. Her free and adventurous lifestyle skidded to a halt, and she started to develop emotional problems, which disrupted the delicate fabric of our lives. Every move we made was a so-called new beginning.

When I was almost five years old, we moved into a wood-frame house in Atascadero, a small town on the Central Coast of California. It was here that my family bought its first television. This "strange box" was a source of wonder to me, especially the many space-travel shows that defined 1950s TV. The idea of mind-controlling aliens both terrified and thrilled me, but they also gave me a newfound power over my now three-year-old sister.

"Heather, I've got something really important to tell you, but you can't tell anyone," I said in a conspiratorial whisper one day.

Sitting on the edge of her bed, hugging her scraggly teddy bear and sucking her thumb, Heather looked up at me with wide eyes.

"Last night," I continued, "when you were sleeping, an alien entered your body, and it's going to spy on the world through your eyes," I declared with the authority of a five-year-old. I don't know why I told her this, but it seemed of utmost importance to me at the time.

I went on. "We can't let them get away with this. So, for a few days you need to stay in bed with the covers over your head so they can't spy on our planet."

Dutifully, Heather spent the next several days in bed with her head covered. I would periodically check in on her to make sure that the aliens weren't spying. However, I stayed out of her sight so they couldn't see me. Mother had a one-year-old toddler and was very pregnant with her fourth child, so she didn't pay much attention to the fact that Heather and I stayed in the bedroom.

MY MOTHER WAS BECOMING INCREASINGLY BITTER and angry, and she and my father began to have huge, explosive arguments. Heather and I used to sleep with our pillows over our heads because they'd be yelling so loudly. I think my father just didn't know what to do.

Their fights actually affected the speed with which I ate my meals. As a five-year-old, I ate fast. I don't mean just a little faster than most people, I mean "shovel-it-in, swallow-it-whole" fast! All of us kids ate at a furious speed for a good reason. Both my parents were very strict about proper manners, yet our etiquette lessons were punctuated by the constant battles they engaged in at mealtime. They went kind of like this:

"Denise, that's the wrong fork to use!"

"Dick! How dare you not listen to me when I'm speaking to you!" Mother would yell across the table at my dad. "Denise, wipe your mouth with your napkin."

"Jean, calm down! You're being irrational!" my dad would counter. "Your left hand should always stay in your lap, Heather!"

"Dick! How dare you call me irrational!" my mother would shriek.

Then, about halfway through the meal, a wild-eyed look would overcome my mother, and she'd pick up the peas, gravy, mashed potatoes, milk—whatever was close at hand—and catapult it toward my dad. My father was very good at ducking under the flying food; consequently, the screened window behind his seat was always caked with dried tidbits of one sort or another, which somehow didn't fit in with the middle-class neighborhood in which we lived.

The biggest problem with these nightly fights was that sometimes the arguments occurred at the beginning of the meal and then the food would end up on the walls and not in our stomachs. Afterward, my mother would be too upset to cook anymore. So whenever our parents were focusing on each other instead of us, we shoveled as much food as we could into our mouths, chewed like crazy, and swallowed in big gulps. Looking back, this seems a strange way to share a family dinner, but to a child, whatever occurs on a regular basis seems fairly normal. To this day, I have to be very disciplined not to wolf down my food.

THE FIRST TIME I REMEMBER FEELING deep shame was when I was five years old. It wasn't uncommon for my father to declare that some minor infraction had occurred that needed to be punished. This probably gave him a sense of power, which compensated for feeling emotionally impotent for losing arguments with my mother. However, I didn't know that as a kid. It just always seemed unfair to me.

"Denise, there's a sticky place on the wall," he said to me one night as he towered over me.

"But I didn't do it!" I cried.

"I think you did," he said. "Bend over and pull your pants down."

"I promise that I didn't do it!"

"Do it now. That's good," he said softly. "Now pull your panties down."

"No, Daddy, please don't!"

He softly put his hand on my bare bottom and held it there for a short moment, slightly squeezing it. Then sharply and furiously, he slapped my buttocks.

Tears squeezed out of my eyes as I whimpered, "But I didn't do it! Please don't hit me. I didn't do it."

His hand abruptly stopped, and he began to slowly caress my reddening skin. Pulling my panties up, he turned me around, held me tight, and softly whispered, "I know you didn't. You're my good girl."

Each spanking left me with a deep, searing humiliation and a certain amount of self-disgust. Even at that age, I could sense that he took a kind of shame-filled pleasure in spanking me. My mother was becoming more and more erratic and emotional, so I didn't feel that I could tell her what was happening.

An escape from my mother's rampages and my father's spankings was "flying." As a kid I loved to fly! During naps, instead of sleeping, I'd stand at the end of my bed, spread my arms, and soar up to the ceiling of my bedroom and then tumble, twirl, and roll through the air. Sometimes I'd take a moment to hover over my bed and look at my dolls, before careening wildly again. I really believed that I was flying. I didn't realize that my body was napping as I flew around the room. I didn't know at the time that I was astral-traveling.

Astral-traveling is a journey of the spirit out of the body that often occurs spontaneously in sleep. It's taught as a spiritual discipline in many esoteric traditions; however, it's not uncommon for children who are in difficult situations to astral-travel as an emotional escape mechanism. As I got older, I lost the ability to consciously fly at will. In my early 20s, however, I began to consciously do so again and was able to reclaim a degree of that skill that gave me such great joy as a child.

As a young girl, nature also offered me solace. When my parents' arguments became so high-pitched that I couldn't stand it, I would dash outside and hide behind the tree in our backyard. Then I'd peek around it and look back at the house. It was a small, two-story, wooden structure situated on a hill, surrounded by trees. When it was warm and the windows were open, even from behind the tree, I could still hear my parents' fights. I hated hearing them yell at each other, so I would turn and run deep into the wooded area behind the house. Everything there was dark, cool, and quiet.

In the woods I'd curl up beneath the branches of my favorite gnarled oak tree. Under this tree, I dug my "dirt hole," using only my bare hands and a spoon I'd taken from the kitchen. Spoonful by spoonful, I removed the soil until I'd burrowed a hole where I could hide. The earth was a rich brown. I would bring it up to my nose and inhale the fertile scent of composted leaves. I loved the way the soil felt as it slid between my fingers. When I put a spoonful into my mouth, it tasted good, really good. I was sure that there was no other soil like it in the whole world. Little did I realize how significant that dirt would be to me 50 years later.

CHAPTER TWO

The Gap Between Worlds
(1955–1959)

There is a gap between worlds. It is a still and mysterious place. In it are currents of dreams and stories from the earth and clouds and stars. It's a place that holds the elaborate weaving of life and the land. I was six years old when I first entered that place.

We had just moved to King City in the Salinas Valley of California. My father had been offered a job as a food technologist at a garlic-processing plant in the area. It was a small, dusty farming town with a large Hispanic migrant community. During World War II, a series of Army barracks had been erected on a plateau outside of town, but they were abandoned after the war. Short on money, we moved into those dilapidated barracks. My dad sledge-hammered holes in the walls between the units until we eventually had a row of apartments connected by makeshift doors.

I was happy to have so much space in which to play. Sometimes the kids from families that inhabited the other empty barracks would come over to join me. Since we didn't have furniture in most of the units, we could run through the crude doors from one end to the other. Outside we played in the military training trenches near the barracks. It was exhilarating to run in one long ditch, while other kids were running down the others trying to find me.

Inside the house, my parents' Great Food Wars continued, except now there was a wall behind my father covered in food, rather than a window screen. After we moved there, my mother got worse. She chopped her hair short; wore an ugly, old rolled-up wool cap; and had a wild animal look in her eyes most of the time. She would hold her arms over her stomach in such a way that it looked as if she were afraid her insides would fall out.

Living alone in abandoned barracks with four children proved to be too much for her, so she spent most of her time in bed reading. She said that she had a good mind and she was going to use it, rather than do housework or be a caretaker. Consequently, our home was filled with piles of old garbage and was extraordinarily dirty, but her disinterest in our welfare meant that we had an enormous amount of freedom. I used that unrestricted time to my best advantage.

I often took long walks by myself through cultivated fields of cauliflower and broccoli, and explored the surrounding hills. The sky was big, and the sun radiated a warmth that filled me with joy as I walked. On one of my adventures, I found a tall circle of cattails. Pushing my way through the reeds, I came upon a small, clear pond, completely hidden from view. At the edge of the pond was thick, black mud. I cautiously put one bare foot and then the other into the warm mud. It slowly oozed between my toes and then covered my feet. The mud looked black, but when it dried on my hands, feet, and legs, it was blue. The pond became my secret place.

It was here that I first sensed the interwoven designs that exist between the world of the living and the world of spirit. When I was sitting at the pond's shore, the invisible forces were tangible. I felt them inhale me, as I sat for hours watching the myriad living beings that were attracted to the water.

Dragonflies hovered overhead, tadpoles wiggled through the shallow depths, and tiny frogs sat in the cool shade at the edge of the pond. When I sat very still, all the life within and around the pond seemed to meld into that mysterious inhalation. And when I stepped beyond the cattails on my way home, I felt as if I were exhaled once again into the world of the living.

When it got too cold to play at my pond, I played inside. One day I decided that the empty unit at the end of our sprawling barracks home would become a theater. (My father had knocked through enough walls so that we occupied about five full units. Each unit had been a complete apartment during the war, with a kitchen, dining room, living room, and bedrooms. Consequently we had five kitchens, five living rooms, and so on, and they were almost all empty.) In that vacant unit, Heather and I strung a sheet across the living room to make a stage. One of the bedrooms became the dressing room, and the kitchen and dining room became the storage room for our "props," most of which were old, rusty pieces of abandoned Army equipment that we'd commandeered. The discarded, rusted machine parts became trees and mountains and castles on craggy cliffs in our plays. We then enlisted Brand, who was enthusiastic, and Gordon, who was reluctant, to be in our plays.

I "wrote," directed, and acted in the shows. Usually they were stories about good triumphing over evil. We all wanted to be the bad guy because they always died in the end, and we loved to reenact the dramatic death scenes. When I got to be the villain, I'd kick my feet in the air and moan with great intensity until I'd exhale loudly and sprawl out "dead" on the stage floor. Our plays were events! On the day of the performance, we'd run up and down between the barracks shouting, "Play tonight! Play tonight!" All the kids from the barracks came to watch our wild histrionics and applauded enthusiastically at the end of each presentation.

My mother didn't attend many of our plays, since she was often reading in bed, but her absence wasn't really a problem because we were having so much fun. There were times, however, when her lack of attention *was* a problem, especially during the Cat Onslaughts.

We had cats, lots of cats. I'm not sure why we had so many—maybe to rid the barracks of the multitude of mice that resided there. We had more than 30 felines—black and white ones, huge tiger-striped ones, tiny orange tabbies, long- and short-haired ones, every variation imaginable—and not one of them was spayed or neutered. So our cat population continued to rapidly expand. It was fun playing with the ever-present kittens that tumbled over themselves as they cavorted in the dirt chasing the monarch butterflies that were so numerous in the area.

The cats, however, created a problem. My mother hardly took time to feed us, let alone our burgeoning cat population. Consequently, they were hungry—very hungry.

After my mother made a meal, she would put the uncovered bowls of food on the table. She would then open the doors to air out the room—it got very hot in King City—and then absent-mindedly leave the room.

Normally this wouldn't have been a problem, except for a few errant flies that might have come in to dine on the uncovered dishes. But with 30 ravenous cats lurking outside the house, it was disastrous. As soon as the unattended door stood open, the cats charged into the house, leapt onto the table, and gorged themselves on our dinner. This occurred so many times that I made it my personal job to defend the meal against the cats. Around dinnertime I would play outside the door. When the screen swung open, I would rush forward and stand guard to fight off the horde of cats that tried to swarm into the house.

I wonder now why I tried so hard to keep the cats out. Sometimes the food was so bad it might have been better to let them eat it all. Mother would make a good meal one night, then the next, she'd take all the leftovers . . . I mean *all* the leftovers—the salad, pickles, canned peaches, mashed potatoes, meatloaf, *and the Jell-O dessert*—or whatever we'd been served the previous night—and mix them vigorously together. Usually it looked liked something regurgitated by one of the neighborhood dogs. She'd say that we couldn't leave the table until we ate everything on our plate. Sometimes I didn't leave for a very long time.

THERE WERE ALSO CHALLENGES AT SCHOOL. One day a boy came up to me and pushed me so hard that I stumbled backward.

"What did I do?" I wanted to know.

"My dad says if your family doesn't like it here in King City, then you should just get out."

"What are you talking about?" I asked, holding back tears.

"Oh, you know. Your mom keeps writing letters to the paper that say that our town isn't any good."

At the time, I didn't know my mother was doing this, but evidently she would write letters to the editor of the local newspaper criticizing the town and its citizens. We began to get threatening letters and phone calls. When I was seven years old, we were told that we were moving again. This time it would be to Chicago, where my father got a job working in management for Libby McNeil.

In later years, I asked my father why we'd moved so much. He said that my mother always cost him his job. She would call his bosses and complain that they were taking advantage of him or that they weren't paying him enough. Or, she'd complain about him to his employees, and consequently, he'd lose his position in either case.

THE TRANSITION FROM HAVING LOTS OF SPACE to play in and the freedom to roam throughout the hot, arid countryside of Central

California, to the tiny dingy apartment we were restricted to in Chicago was very hard. Everything seemed dismal and gray to me. We often rode on the subway, which was dirty and gray; and the people sitting on the subway also had drawn, pasty, gray faces. And when we'd come out above ground, everything in Chicago seemed to be covered with gray soot. (The air in the city is much cleaner today.) The houses were gray; the people were gray. I swore over and over again that when I grew up, I'd live in a house that had bright colors.

(Some childhood dreams do come true. If you visit my home now, you'll first see a bright-red front door that opens to a dining room with robust rust-colored walls and a view of an electric-blue courtyard.)

The walls were thin in our small tenement apartment near Logan Square. The winter chill penetrated the thin walls, and my hands ached from the cold. Summer, however, wasn't any better. The heat and humidity melted the tar in the sidewalk cracks. Kids used to pull it up and mold it into little babies. The sounds of the elevated inner-city train shook the walls at regular intervals during the day and night.

From my second-floor bedroom window, I could see a small, all-night "greasy spoon" restaurant below. The red neon sign from the café blinked on and off all night, making ragged red patterns scatter across my bedroom ceiling. After the lights were turned off in the room I shared with my siblings, I would tiptoe over to the window and peer down at the people entering and leaving the café.

The front window was covered with a grimy film, and an old "daily" special was advertised on a curled piece of paper covered with oil stains and stuck onto the window with yellowed, cracked Scotch tape. In the winter, the café was a never-ending source of fascination. I watched people shuffle through muddied snow on cold nights, take the last drags off their cigarettes, and toss them into the slush as they pulled open the café door. I wondered what happened inside. What did people do in there?

Once there was a fight outside the café. There wasn't much to see . . . mostly just two drunks pushing each other until they both slipped in the mushy snow and staggered up to their feet, walking off in opposite directions without looking back.

Late one night after my brothers and sister were asleep, my mother came in and asked me if I wanted to go to the café. I wonder if she'd peeked in and had seen me looking out the window. I vigorously nodded my head up and down in my eagerness to go. My father was away on business, so I guessed that she wanted some company. I hurriedly dressed and slipped on my rubber boots. Following her down the dark stairway, I stepped out to the cold, wet sidewalk.

The air was sharp in my lungs when I inhaled. As we stood outside the café door, tiny white snowflakes reflected the light that shone out through the restaurant's window. I watched them flutter down and then melt into the gray, snowy mush. I glanced up to my bedroom window and thought of how many times I'd peered down, watching people stand just where we were.

As my mother pushed open the door, we were assaulted by a burst of steamy cigarette-drenched air. Even though the small space was lit by several bare lightbulbs, it felt warm and cozy in contrast to the din of the city traffic and the November chill outside. Steam had fogged up the front window, making the space feel even cozier. We sidled up to the counter. I felt so grown up sitting there. I'd never seen children enter the café, so I knew this was an important rite of passage in my life.

I'm grown up now, I thought (I was all of seven years old), and sat up even taller on the stool. I didn't want anyone to notice I was a child.

My mother ordered a bowl of chili for me and a cup of

coffee for herself. Pulling a pack of cigarettes out of her purse, she tapped out a few and selected one. The thickly bearded man next to her leaned over to light it.

"You live around here?" he asked in a low growl.

"Oh, not far away," she replied, smiling a bit too brightly.

"That your kid?" he queried

"Yup, she's my oldest."

"Hmm," he replied to my mother, as he narrowly squinted at me.

Just then the man behind the counter, who had thick, hairy arms with tattoos on them that were so old they'd blended together in a kind of blue purplish mash, slopped down the chili. It was lukewarm and watery with hard beans on the bottom and a layer of oil on top. Much of it had lapped over the sides and onto the counter around the bowl when he'd put it down.

I looked at it and then up at my mother, but she continued to chat with the man next to us as I took a few mouthfuls of the tepid chili and stirred it a bit until it was truly cold. With a bored sigh, I began to use my finger to draw designs with the fat globules on the counter until my mother said it was time to go.

I'm not sure why she'd asked me to accompany her to the café. Maybe it was because I was awake and the others were asleep, or maybe it *was* a rite of passage of sorts. However, after that, the café held less fascination for me, and I didn't spend as much time observing it from my bedroom window.

OURS WASN'T A SAFE NEIGHBORHOOD, so we were supposed to stay indoors. I longed to play outside, and I especially missed my pond. Thursdays, however, were great because we were allowed to go out. That was the day the junk man came around with his horse and cart. It was a glorious adventure to meander through the alleys looking through trash cans, hoping to find thrown-away "treasures" to sell to him. The smell in the alley was often putrid, but the possibility of finding treasures overcame any stinkiness, as Heather and I raced from trash can to trash can.

Most items earned a nickel or a dime, which we would use to buy red licorice at the candy store. A perfectly good mug might fetch a nickel. I found a red lampshade once and earned 35 cents!

Our Polish landlords, who lived downstairs, didn't speak much English, but they made up for it by constantly pounding on their ceiling for us to be quiet. My mother didn't work, but she still spent a lot of time in bed. My father told me that if my brothers and sister and I weren't quiet, we'd be thrown out of the apartment. He told me that we didn't have anywhere else to go, so it was my responsibility to keep everyone quiet, especially when he was at work. It wasn't easy keeping myself still, let alone keeping my three bored siblings at bay.

There were also times when we didn't have any heat and our little apartment was so cold that we would bundle up in blankets and just huddle together. I'm not sure why, but on occasion, there wasn't much to eat. One day all we had was stale wheat germ. Other days we'd have plenty of food.

ALTHOUGH IT DIDN'T SEEM LIKE MUCH FUN at the time, I have fond memories of laundry day. We didn't have a washing machine or dryer, so once a week Mother would fill the bathtub with water and Tide laundry detergent, and Heather and I would take turns stomping up and down on the clothes. My brothers were too young to join us, and besides, it was the '50s, and boys weren't expected to do housework.

Stomping was fun, and we laughed a lot as we did it. The detergent made it kind of slippery, so if we weren't careful, we'd slip into the soapy brew. Then we'd let out the dirty water and jump up and down on the clothes in fresh water for a rinse cycle.

It took quite a few hours to wash all the clothes for a family of six. After we drained the tub, Heather would grab one end and I'd grab the other, and we'd twist each item of clothing until the water was wrung out and our hands were raw. Then the clothes were strewn throughout our small apartment to dry. On washing day, there wasn't anywhere to sit except the floor because the whole apartment was covered with drying clothes.

I DIDN'T LIKE GOING TO SCHOOL IN CHICAGO because of the violence on the playground. Although there were a few bullies in King City, the schoolyard was safe and fun. But Moose Elementary School seemed dangerous. Many of the kids were divided into two groups or "gangs." If you associated with kids from one group, the kids from the other one would hit you, and vice versa. At school, kids would carry around scissors and threaten each other with them. I didn't want to be associated with either gang, so I kept my head down and tried not to be noticed.

Sometimes walking home from school, we'd be surrounded by kids who saw themselves as the neighborhood tough guys. They'd grab my shoulders and push me, or grab Heather and throw our books to the concrete. To avoid going to school, I often stayed home with a "stomachache." But soon the truant officer was making periodic trips to our home asking why I wasn't in school. Then something happened that changed my perspective.

My sister came home from school one day and grimaced as she put down her books. "Heather," I whispered, "what happened?" Tears popped out of the corners of her eyes and she said, "Tom came up to me after school and socked me in the stomach real hard and said, 'Give this to your sister.'"

Evidently, since I wasn't at school that day, one of the tough guys had decided to hit Heather instead. Even though I didn't know why he wanted to hit me, I was filled with guilt. Heather was too young to defend herself. I thought, *I should have been there to protect her.*

A resolute determination filled me. No one was going to hurt my sister ever again! That evening, I took my father aside and told him about the boys and said it was really important that I learn how to fight.

"Those boys are bigger and stronger than you, and you're outnumbered, so I'm going to teach you something that will work, even though you're smaller. The next time they jump you, grab the biggest boy by the arms, then jerk your knee upwards as hard as you can between his legs. I guarantee they won't bother you anymore."

Later that night I asked my dad if he'd ever killed anyone in the war. He told me that he'd killed a number of men in hand-to-hand combat. He said that he didn't want to kill them, but he had to, and he didn't like to talk about it.

Decades later, I found out that he'd never actually left his supply ship and had never been involved in any military combat. But my father had a way of constantly creating myths about himself and his past. In later years, it was hard for me to accept that he had lied about so many things. As an eight-year-old girl, however, it was great to believe that my father was a war hero. I went to bed knowing that everything was going to be okay.

The next day as Heather and I were walking home from school, four boys suddenly surrounded us. George, who was the biggest, stepped forward with a sneer on his face and said, "Where do you think you're going? This is our territory. You can't walk here. You have to walk around."

"But that's way out of our way," I replied.

"That's tough titties! Get a move on it!" he shouted as he doubled his hand into a fist.

Remembering my father's instruction, I stepped forward, grabbed his arms and thrust my entire weight up through my knee into his groin. Instantly, George was on the sidewalk curled up and crying. The other boys looked dumbstruck as we marched past them on our way home. Periodically, I would have a scuffle or two, and my knees and elbows were almost always scabbed over from these little run-ins. Over time, though, I commanded the respect of the neighborhood tough guys, and we never had any real trouble again.

My mother's moods became more dramatic. She would either spend days in bed or get really upset over seemingly minor incidents. One thing that *really* bothered her was the treatment of Native Americans. My mother was of Cherokee heritage, and she took her ancestry very seriously. She had a sheaf of yellowed, worn pages that listed the treaties the U.S. government had broken with the Indians. She would hold up those battered pieces of paper and angrily declare, "These are the treaties that the White Man broke. They didn't keep one treaty with us!" (I sometimes wonder if the fact that my father was white didn't contribute to the constant animosity she directed toward him.)

One day when we were playing cowboys and Indians, no one wanted to be the Indians.

"I want to be the cowboy!"

"No! I do!"

"I said it first! I get to be the cowboy!"

Cowboy-and-Indian stories were popular on television at that time. The cowboys were always good, and the Indians were always bad, so naturally we all wanted to be the former. My mother thought that it was time to change that for us, though. In this, she was a woman ahead of her time. However, she had all the sorrow of her ancestors, but little access to their traditions. I wonder if the ceremonies and rituals of her people might have slowed her descent into mental illness.

When she heard us arguing, she decided that she would take her children to live in Oklahoma for a while to acquaint us with our Cherokee heritage. She was proud of being Native American, and she wanted us to be proud, too. She also wanted us to understand why she was so angry at the way Indians had been treated.

Just as my mother began packing up her kids for a visit to her native state, my father lost another job. I don't know for sure, but I imagine that my mother had something to do with it. Father decided he was going to stay behind to look for a new home and job, while Mother and the four of us went on our way to Oklahoma.

It was late summer, 1958, and we were going on a great and grand adventure! Four kids—ages eight, six, four, and two years old—and my mother, all crammed into a small car loaded with camping supplies and food. I made a big sign that said "Oklahoma or Bust" and taped it to the side of the car. On that long drive, Mother talked about the 1839 Cherokee Trail of Tears as if it had just happened. This event incited my mother's deep rage, but to me, even though it made me very sad, this story of my ancestors inspired courage.

I believe that stories about one's predecessors can be important because they serve as a kind of a guiding star throughout life. All the seemingly unconnected aspects of life can be given significance and coherence through an ancestral story. The Cherokee Trail of Tears was *my* ancestral story. Knowing what my forebears had gone through and survived helped me find courage amidst the difficulties that I was soon to face.

This event is one of the saddest episodes in Cherokee history. At the time it occurred, there were 16,000 Cherokees. They loved their land with its valleys and mountains, and they especially loved their trees. They were farmers, and their lands were so fertile that President Jackson decreed that the Cherokee land would be given to white settlers, and the Cherokees would be removed from their land. Justifying the removal, he said, "Humanity weeps over the fate of the Indians, but true philanthropy reconciles the mind to the extinction of one generation for another."

In cold, hunger, and illness, the tribe was forced to march almost 1,000 miles to Oklahoma from the Carolinas. Over 4,000 people—nearly one fourth of the entire Cherokee nation—died on that trek.

Yet like a phoenix out of the ashes, the Cherokees arose again generations later to become one of the largest and most prosperous tribes. The story of the Trail of Tears meant a lot to me. When I felt that things were almost too hard, I'd remind myself that Native American blood ran through my veins, and this made everything easier to bear.

On our way to Oklahoma, we mostly camped, but late one night after an arduous day of driving, my mother decided to stay in a motel. She pulled our black-and-white Chevy into a motel parking lot, and we all went in to get a room.

"I'm sorry, ma'am, but we don't have any rooms available," the hotel clerk said.

As we were walking out, another family walked in and asked for a room, and the clerk gave them one.

Mother stiffly walked out to the car and started to cry. She said that they didn't want to give us a room because she was Indian. Up north, she said, it wouldn't have been a problem, but in the southern states, they discriminated against Indians. I felt so bad for my mother that I wanted to go in and yell at the clerk, but we just piled back into the car and drove on.

In Oklahoma we moved in with my grandparents, who had

a big old farmhouse on several hundred acres of land. They had a large herd of cattle on their ranch, so there were always lots of ranch hands around living spartanly in the bunkhouses on their homestead. In addition to helping out with cattle drives, my uncles were on rodeo circuits, so there were also lots of saddle horses and bucking stock. (Years later, my Uncle Pat was inducted into the Cowboy Hall of Fame.)

My cousins wanted to be in the rodeo, too, but they were too young to use real cows, so they convinced me to be the cow.

"Why do I have to be the cow?" I asked.

"Because you're the girl. Everyone knows that girls can't be cowboys. Get it! Cow*boys*! You can be a cowgirl."

"Oh, all right, but you're going to have a hard time roping me," I said, as I charged out of the gate. Using my hands as horns, I raced around the ranch arena. My cousins twirled their ropes and tried to rope me. Every once in a while, the rope would loop around my middle and I'd go flying into the dirt. They said I was a pretty good cow. I told them they were pretty good ropers.

Even though my mother wanted us to embrace our Native American heritage, all the Indians on the ranch wanted to be cowboys. I wanted to prove to my cousins that I was tough enough to be one. When Uncle Ben went rabbit hunting, Heather and I begged to go with him. We both came back crying—Heather because Uncle Ben had shot and killed a sweet rabbit, and me because I didn't get to shoot it. Everyone knew that cowboys got to shoot things. Even though I knew I was of Cherokee descent, I still really wanted to be a cowboy.

Both of my grandparents—Hamp and Ginny Scudder— were Cherokee. Grandfather came as a pioneer settler to Indian Territory in Oklahoma in 1889 when he was 12 years old, and Grandmother was born in Indian Territory and was a student at Cherokee Female Seminary school until she moved with her family to their Cherokee land allotment. My grandparents' stories of their adventures on the ranch were straight out of the Old West.

My grandfather was a friend of the notorious train robber Al Spencer. Although Grandpa was a member of the AHT (Anti-Horse-Thief Society) he must have thought that robbing trains was perhaps forgivable . . . but horse thieving was a completely different matter. My relatives were always quick to mention that Al had never killed anyone.

One day the posse came looking for Al at my grandparents' ranch. My grandmother wouldn't let them, under any circumstances, into the house to search for him. The posse came back with the local banker, who was a friend of my grandparents.

"Now come on, Ginny, you've got to let these men look for Al," persuaded the banker. Reluctantly, she let them in and they scoured through everything.

"I told you he's not here," she said defiantly, looking stony-eyed. She didn't like the posse, and she didn't like them coming onto her land.

"Let's go look for him at the power station!" said one trigger-happy man as he tossed his gun back and forth nervously from hand to hand. They all charged off to the power station, and when they got there, they asked the attendant if he'd seen Al Spencer. The man said, "Hey, you're just in time. I just saw Al! He just went roaring down that road." And he pointed down the road for emphasis. "I sure hope you catch that son of a bitch."

The posse all jumped in their cars and tore off down the road. After the posse left, the "attendant" (Al Spencer) peeled off his uniform and later met up with my grandfather, who was down the road. They had a good laugh at how Al had fooled the posse by impersonating the power-station attendant.

My grandparents' homestead wasn't far from Will Rogers's ranch. Will was also of Cherokee heritage, one of the nation's most popular radio commentators, and the star of 71 cowboy movies. Will and my grandfather were good friends and made a pact that the first one of them to die would leave a horse waiting on the "other side of the river." They believed that to get to the "happy hunting grounds," you had to cross a river to get to the spirit world. Not many years later, I actually saw that "river" and lived to talk about it.

Will Rogers was the first to die. He was killed in 1935 in an airplane crash, so it was his job to leave a horse waiting for my grandfather. The second part of the pact was that the last one of them to die would arrange to have an escort of mounted horsemen accompany the body to its grave. My grandfather died last, so he received a mounted escort to his final resting place. Although he was proud of his Native American heritage, Grandfather was so intent on being a cowboy that his grave marker simply says: "Here lies a cowboy."

It took some time for my father to find another job, so we lived in Oklahoma with my grandparents for quite a while. We attended a one-room schoolhouse that housed students from kindergarten to eighth grade. It was the same school that my mother and her siblings had attended. It was on the family land, and thus named Scudder School after my grandparents.

It was cold in the mornings at the school, so we had to keep adding wood to the stove. The older kids helped teach the younger ones, and ranch wives came at noon to prepare home-cooked food. It was such a different experience from my school in King City, where most of my school friends were children of Hispanic migrant workers, and also very different from the dingy, violence-ridden school in Chicago. The only thing I didn't like was the outhouse. It had a knothole in it, and whenever a girl went in to use it, the boys would fight to peek through the hole. I used to push toilet paper in it, but that never worked very well.

Christmas for us had always been very quiet and even sparse. But in Oklahoma, the holidays were incredible. We cooked for days and days. All the ranch hands and a variety of friends and family showed up, and it took a whole day just to open the presents. Most of the gifts were practical items like socks, but my grandmother gave me a beautiful doll with eyelids that opened and closed. I loved the smell of it. To this day, when I sniff that particular plastic smell, I'm transported back into a kind of bliss.

After a number of months living in Oklahoma, we bundled up into the Chevy and headed back north. I was used to moving, so it just seemed that we were off on another adventure. This time my father had found a nice house in Northfield, Illinois, which was a suburban community outside of Chicago. I never quite understood how our standard of living could rise and fall so dramatically, but it was great to have a tree to climb, grass to run in, and best of all, just down the road there was a stream and a grove of trees. We had enough to eat and also had a heating system that worked. I quickly made a few friends in the neighborhood, and I joined the Girl Scouts. It was great! Although I sometimes missed the open land to explore in Oklahoma, this home was the nicest house we'd ever lived in. I even had my own room!

We lived next door to a neighborhood tavern, and my dad told me that it would be a good place to sell my Girl Scout cookies. Sure enough, the patrons always bought every single box. The more they'd been drinking, the more they bought. I learned that fairly quickly.

The friends I made at Girl Scouts helped offset the

challenges at home, where the disharmony between my parents had escalated. Besides the Great Food Fights, their arguing continued into the late-night hours. Once again I'd sleep with a pillow over my head to block out the screaming and the sound of crashing dishes.

One afternoon I was curled in a corner window seat in the living room, reading a book, when a bloodcurdling shriek pierced the air. I leaped out of my seat and dashed toward the kitchen, where the sound had originated. My mother was thrashing on the floor. Blood was everywhere: It was smeared across the linoleum, and red streaks slashed across the white cabinets. A carving knife lay next to her. Her eyes looked wild, and she was whimpering with small animal-like noises.

My father ran in. Mother looked up at him, struggled up to her feet, and lunged forward toward him. "This is your fault!" my mother screeched. "It's all your fault!"

"Stop moving so much. You'll lose too much blood!" my father yelled as he held off her pummeling fists.

"I don't care if I die! I don't care! It's your fault!" my mother screamed.

"You're not going to die. I won't let you!" my father yelled as he threw her to the floor and clasped her bleeding wrist to stop the flow.

As she screamed and flailed, Father shouted to me, "Call for an ambulance!"

"What do I do?!" I shrieked back at him.

"Dammit! Just pick up the damn phone and dial O."

I ran to the phone and dialed the "O" for the operator.

"This is the operator."

"Help! We need help. My mother is bleeding. Please hurry!" I pleaded.

"Stay on the phone!" the operator urged.

"Please hurry! There's blood everywhere!" I screamed,

looking at my dad who was trying to straddle my mother. He was fiercely gripping her arms while she frantically tried to sink her teeth into him.

"I think my father is trying to kill my mother!" I stammered.

"What?!" My father's head jerked up. "Denise, put down the damn phone!" he yelled. "Did you just tell the operator that I'm trying to kill your mother?"

"Um, yes, I guess I did," I said slowly, realizing what I'd done.

"Jesus H. Christ!" (My father always gave Jesus a middle initial when he was really upset.) "I didn't do anything to her!" he yelled. "She's slit her own wrist.

"Run outside and look for the ambulance!" he managed to say as he held Mother down. She kept wailing, until I wanted to cover my ears.

A few minutes later, the ambulance arrived and my mother was strapped onto a gurney. Heather, Gordon, Brand, and I stood in the yard as we watched the vehicle pull away and get smaller and smaller in the distance. None of us said anything. Everything seemed so quiet after her screams and the sounds of the ambulance had died down. I walked back into the house.

A police officer was talking to my dad. "Well, son," said the officer, "when your daughter called, she seemed to think that you had something to do with this."

My father gave me a sharp sideways glance. I looked away. His greatest fear was of people knowing our private family concerns. No matter how bad things got, he said we weren't to tell anyone because it was family business and not anyone else's.

"Actually, officer, my daughter was frightened. My wife has been having emotional problems lately. I was upstairs when it happened."

I nodded in agreement. Apparently satisfied with my father's answers, the officer drove away. I'm not sure why I told the operator that my father was trying to kill my mother. Maybe I felt that somehow he was at fault, and those were the first sentiments that came to me when I called for help.

As an adult, I came to understand that blaming one parent is not uncommon for a child in my situation. Psychologically, it's easier for a child if one parent is responsible for a tragedy, rather than assigning guilt to both. In a child's limited view, it's better to have one good parent and one bad parent, than feeling that she has no parents at all.

After he'd cleaned up the blood, my haggard father said, "Come on. Everyone get into the car. We're going to the hospital to see how your mother is doing." When we arrived at the hospital, my father said, "You kids wait here while I go in to see how she is."

My father was told that my mother had lost a lot of blood, but she would survive. The said that they were going to commit her to a mental hospital for observation. While we sat in the car waiting for our father, Heather whispered, "Do you think she's going to live?"

"I don't know. There sure was a lot of blood," I said.

My sister, who was only seven at the time, pushed open the door and started to get out.

"Heather, you can't get out! Father told us to stay in the car."

"I'll be just a minute," she said.

I kept nervously waiting for her to return. I couldn't see which direction she'd gone and kept looking around to see if Father was coming.

Finally she popped back in just before Father appeared around a corner.

His eyes were red, and his mouth was pursed. He didn't say much but began to back the car out. The car began to bump lopsidedly. We had a flat tire.

"Damn," he said under his breath, and then he got out of the car to change the tire.

I looked piercingly at Heather, but she just kept looking straight ahead. Years later, I found out that Heather had gotten out and let the air out of the tire because she was also angry with Father; perhaps she also blamed him for what happened to our mother.

Mother was only gone for a few days before she came back home with a big bandage on her wrist. The doctors must have felt that it was all right for her to come back to us. We tried to act normal, but we were afraid of doing anything that might upset her. It was hard to predict her moods. Some days everything seemed normal, and then she would suddenly get very upset by nothing at all.

On her bad days, I took refuge at the nearby stream. I'd roll up my jeans, wade into the middle of the water, and stand so still that crawdads and minnows darted through and around my legs. Sometimes I lay facedown on the shaded rock that hung over the creek; it was a hidden place of mystery and wonder. From that place I could penetrate beyond the noise of my life into the stillness of the universe. As I dangled my fingers into the cool water below, and became so quiet that even my breath was a whisper, I was sure that I could hear faint but sweet songs of the earth gliding beneath the currents of the stream.

CHAPTER THREE

The Roots Go Deepest
(1959–1962)

There are places where the currents of the earth are alive with whispered voices of the trees and stones. Whenever we moved to a new location, I searched for these secret hideaways in nature where I could hear these voices. Even as a child, I knew that the murmurs of the land provided passageways beyond my sadness and uncertainty. In the sanctity of the woods, I was carried beyond the jumble of my life into a realm rich with the music of nature. I needed that kind of refuge more than ever during the events to follow.

A short while after Mother slit her wrist, not surprisingly, we had to move again. My father found a new job working for Libby McNeill again, but this time in their food-science department in Leipsic, Ohio. Near this very small farm town, my dad found a run-down farmhouse to rent. I was happy to have new wild places to explore.

It was very rustic there. Every time we wanted any water, we had to hand-pump it. In the kitchen and bathroom were large pump handles about two feet long. We'd first have to take about a half cup of water and pour it over the shaft. This was called "priming the pump." Then we'd wrench the handle up and down vigorously until water came out. The water that spewed from the tap was almost black and smelled like rotten eggs. It felt strange to get into a bathtub full of black, smelly water in the hopes of getting clean. Luckily, we would drive into town to the Laundromat to wash the clothes, so Heather and I didn't have to do the laundry stomp-dance in the black sulfur water.

Our farmhouse came with an overgrown orchard and an old barn with lots of hiding places. Down the dirt road behind our home was a wood lot that became my magical domain. In the summer, just after breakfast, I'd slip into the trees and stay there all day. It was the only place where I felt safe. I sat nestled in the roots of the big old maple tree in the center. I loved the humus smell of the earth at her base, and the way the light filtered through her leaves overhead. She would "talk" to me. I could hear her voice inside my head; it was tender and sooth-ing. I also heard the voices of the other trees, the flowers, and the birds. When I was there, the tension between my parents disappeared as the voices of my forest friends soothed me.

When I wasn't in the woods, I'd spend time in the over-grown orchard next to our house. After climbing the apple tree just to sit and peer through the leaves at everything below, I'd shimmy up the pear tree to pick the ripe fruit. I loved it when the juices ran down my face. My favorite tree was the mulberry because we used to use the berries to make jam. One of my best memories of my mother was making mulberry jam with her. She was happy, and laughed often as we worked together. I ended up completely covered with purple stains, and by the time we were done, everything in the kitchen was splattered purple. But she didn't seem to care, and I was thrilled to have a few jars of jam to show for it.

EXCEPT FOR OCCASIONAL MOMENTS OF CONTENTMENT, however, Mother was becoming increasingly erratic. As she retreated into herself, the house became more and more chaotic. She would barricade herself in her room or she'd come out to yell wildly at us for some minor offense. My father had enough trouble trying to cope with a new job, so he wasn't up to doing much when he came home. But he didn't hire anyone to help. He didn't want anyone to know that things weren't okay.

Leipsic was a very conservative community and was different from Chicago in many ways. Here, girls didn't fight to resolve differences. They also weren't rough-and-tumble kids, like my cousins in Oklahoma. Leipsic was an old, established town, unlike our suburban home in Northfield. In this place, we were very much outsiders; almost everyone's relatives had lived in the area for generations. At school, the girls gossiped in low conspiratorial tones when I walked by. I didn't quite know how to fit in and make friends. I felt more comfortable in nature than I did with people.

Every day as I sat alone at lunch, I'd watch all the girls at the other tables laughing and joking together. I wondered what was wrong with me. One morning as I sat alone on the long bus ride to school, I made a conscious decision to make friends in this new town. I wasn't sure how to do it, so at the schoolyard, I secretly observed the most popular girl to see what she did differently from me. I noticed that she was always smiling. Every time she did so, everyone around her acted friendly in return. *That's it! All I have to do is to smile a lot*, I thought with determination.

That night, after everyone went to sleep, I locked myself in the bathroom and stood on my tiptoes to see the mirror. I turned up the corners of my mouth. It was a weird sensation; I wasn't used to smiling very much, so it took awhile to get it right. Frankly, I thought that smiling made my face look stupid. The next day on the playground, I contorted my mouth into the big smile shape. I felt really silly doing it, and I was worried that kids would laugh at me. It was incredible, though . . . instead of laughing, kids smiled back at me. It was like magic. I'd discovered how to make friends. It was much later that I realized I didn't need to always smile and be nice, and that people could like me for who I was.

But despite mastering the smile and making a few friends, I hated school. It felt like going to prison every day. Mrs. Reich, my teacher, was tough . . . very tough. Her forearms were the size of hams. When she marched back and forth across the front of the room, she looked more like a general pacing before a battle than a fourth-grade teacher. She believed that if you spared the rod, you spoiled the child. A large heavy wooden paddle hung in the front of our classroom. It seemed that almost daily someone got hit with it. Usually it was a boy named Kenneth. I'm not sure why she picked on him so much.

Mrs. Reich would make him slowly bend over a desk, and then she lifted one large arm and started whacking Kenneth's backside as hard as she could. Kenneth would try so hard not to cry, but she kept hitting him until he did. Only then would she stop. With a satisfied look on her face, she would hang up the paddle. I felt so helpless. I always defended the underdog when I could, but I couldn't see a way to help Kenneth. I don't think Mrs. Reich was an unkind person; in fact, I think she genuinely cared for her students, but she came from the old school of thought that children were best taught through discipline and hard work.

It wasn't until I was diagnosed with dyslexia as an adult that I understood one of the reasons why Mrs. Reich's class was so hard for me.

"Denise, what is the answer to the third math problem on your paper?" she would demand.

When I looked down, the numbers seemed to lift up off my paper and move around. I couldn't focus on them because they were all shifting. I couldn't speak.

"Answer me now!"

I'd start to cry. "I'm so sorry, Mrs. Reich. The numbers are moving around."

"Tell the truth!'"

"I'm not lying," I'd sob.

"Denise, you have to stay after school today."

"But I'll miss my bus."

"You should have thought of that before you lied."

The shame of this event is seared in my memory.

I do, however, have one great memory of Mrs. Reich's class. It was during the "Fart Dance." Well, it wasn't really supposed to be a "Fart Dance." It happened during Mrs. Reich's music class. She taught us all subjects, including music. For that class, she was teaching us a kind of dance where we were supposed to walk around in a circle, and every fourth step kick to the side. One . . . two . . . three . . . kick! One . . . two . . . three . . . kick! However, every time that Dwight kicked, he also let loose a huge monster fart.

Mrs. Reich furiously tapped on her desk with her music baton. "Stop laughing, everyone, right now. Dwight, stop that!"

"I can't help it," he said. His face was red with embarrassment.

"We're going to start again, and this time you will *not* pass gas," she said sternly.

Dwight looked dubious, but we began again. Dwight was right in front of me. I watched as he desperately tried to tighten his buttocks, and he barely kicked, yet those farts just kept squeezing out anyway. One . . . two . . . three . . . fart! One . . . two . . . three . . . fart! But this time the farts were bigger and louder.

Mrs. Reich vigorously rapped her baton again and marched up to Dwight, who was looking down at the floor. "Look up at me, Dwight!" she commanded.

Miserable, Dwight slowly looked up. Suddenly, an

enormous, rolling-thunder fart erupted out of him. It was the most awesome fart I'd ever heard. I don't remember what happened to Dwight, but I hummed, "One . . . two . . . three . . . FART!" to myself for weeks.

A few months after the "Fart Dance," as I stepped off the school bus singing "one . . . two . . . three . . .", I noticed that our black and white Chevy was parked in the driveway. *I wonder why Father is home so early. He's never home at this time*, I thought. As I looked at the house and then back to his car, I suddenly felt cold and afraid.

I dropped my schoolbooks on the grass, ran up the steps, and swung open the front door. Heather, who had also just gotten off the bus, was close behind. Gordon and Brand were already home, both just staring blankly out the window. Father was sitting on the couch, holding his head in his hands.

I looked around suspiciously. "Where's Mother?" I demanded.

"She's gone."

"Where did she go? When is she coming back?"

"She's gone to a hospital that will help her to get better, but you won't be able to see her for a while."

"I want to see her! What did you do with her?" I cried out.

"We were worried that she would harm you kids. We had to do it."

"She wouldn't harm us! She loves us! Bring her back!"

"She's not coming back for a long time," he said quietly. (I was ten years old at the time. I didn't see her again for two years.)

I turned and ran out of the house, slamming the door. I raced down the dirt road, tears streaming down my face, and fled into the woods. Branches whipped at my face and my clothes. I curled up at the base of my tree and sobbed.

I don't ever remember feeling that my life was in danger,

but my father and my mother's family did. They gave that as the reason why they decided to have my mother committed to a mental hospital. Evidently, she was frightening people in town. They said she was acting "like a zombie." They saw her erratic and sometimes violent behavior at the Laundromat and at the grocery store, and they began to complain about her. She was the only mother I ever knew, so her behavior didn't seem that unusual to me. Looking back, perhaps we were in danger, but at the time, I just couldn't believe that about my mother.

Police had arrived that morning with the papers to commit her. When my mother saw them, she ran and hid in the barn, but the deputies chased her and found her crouching behind some bales of straw. They yanked her out, handcuffed her, pushed her into the patrol car, and took her to a commitment hearing.

That night, I lay in bed looking out the window at the silhouette of the apple tree against the darkening sky. *Mother, I want to see you. Where are you? Why did he send you away?* Once again, I blamed my father, perhaps unfairly. He was doing the best he could, given a very difficult situation. However, I certainly do blame him for his subsequent actions.

A few nights later I was awakened by the noise of the bedroom door slowly creaking open.

"Shh. Denise, it's me," my father said as he looked over at the bed where Heather slept soundly.

"It's cold up here, so I'm just going to carry you downstairs. It's warm in my bed. You'll be more comfortable there."

"I'm sleeping. Let me sleep."

"It's okay."

"But I'm not cold," I said.

"It's okay. Come on. Don't make any noise. Don't wake up Heather."

He carried me downstairs and tucked me into his bed.

Slipping in beside me, he wrapped his arms around me. "Here. I'll make you warm."

"I'm not cold. I just want to sleep."

"It's okay. I'm your father."

I tried to scoot over to the far side of the bed, but his hands reached over to my chest and squeezed. I held my breath in shock.My breasts were just starting to develop. He kneaded and massaged each small mound, and twisted my nipples between his fingers.

"Doesn't that feel good? Women like to have their breasts massaged—it feels good."

"It doesn't feel good to me. I just want to sleep," I said as I tightly clenched my fists and started to cry silently.

Every night he lifted me out of my bed and carried me downstairs into his bed. He would grab and rub my chest, tell me how good it felt to *me*, and then hold my body tight against his, moving his hips slowly and methodically against mine. Sometimes his hands would grab other private parts of my body, and he would moan softly as he squeezed and released them with his hands in an increasing rhythm.

I would try not to move, pretend to be asleep, and try to think of other things. I imagined I was sitting by myself in the woods, finding pawpaws (a fruit that grows wild in the Midwest), watching a bird build a nest, anything but allow myself to experience what was happening. Finally he would fall into a deep sleep, his arms wrapped tightly around me. I'd wait until he was asleep and try to get out of his bed, but his arms would grab me even more tightly.

I listened to his ragged breath as he slept. *Mommy! I want my mommy. Where are you? I miss you!* I missed my mother so much.

At first, maybe my father convinced himself that he was offering comfort to me, or to himself. As he had such a strong belief that sexual activity should be confined to marriage, it would have been intolerable for him to seek conjugal comfort outside of that institution. So somehow, if he was with his daughter, it must have seemed to him (in a convoluted way) as if he wasn't really going outside the marriage. After a while, he told me not to tell anyone. Given the era, I don't think anyone would have believed me anyway. My father didn't seem like a child molester. Everyone thought he was a nice man who had a difficult wife.

The emotional wounds from those nights in his bed cut deep into my being. Even though my father didn't physically penetrate me, my body and my spirit were violated. When I eventually developed breasts, my nipples were inverted. I think it was as if my body was trying to protect me from his groping hands. It was only after a substantial amount of therapy that my nipples finally extended.

Someone once said, "Denise, that was a long time ago. You should forget about it." The problem is that although *I* can forget, my body can't. There are times, even now, when my husband touches me in a particular way, that an instant feeling of revulsion is triggered. There are still places on my body that are forbidden territory. A touch . . . a look . . . and it all comes back in vivid detail. I have forgiven my father, but my body just can't seem to forget.

ONE DAY THE PHONE RANG. It was my grandmother in California, my father's mother. She said, "Dick, it's a lot for you to take care of four kids and maintain your job. Why don't you let some of the family help you? We've got a small house, but we can take two of the kids, the oldest and the youngest. Denise is ten now, so she can help take care of Brand. He's four years old now, isn't he?" she said.

It was decided that we would all be split up. Heather would go to New Jersey to my mother's sister, Gordon would go to

Oklahoma to Mother's brother, and Brand and I would move to California.

It was a rainy, cold day as we drove to the Chicago airport to catch a plane bound for California. The windshield wipers were broken, and they sloshed back and forth in a dreary, fragmented rhythm as we slogged through the slush-soaked road. As I got out of the car at the airport, freezing needle-like jabs of rain stung my face and hands.

When Brand hesitantly got out of the car, I took his hand in mine. "Don't worry. Everything's going to be all right. I'll take care of you." I wasn't so sure that everything would be okay, but it felt good to tell him that.

The plane was ready to board. As we walked down the corridor, I kept turning to wave good-bye. Father, Heather, and Gordon looked smaller and smaller in the distance, until we turned a corner and they were gone.

We'd never been on a plane before. Brand was really excited, especially when he was given a pilot's-wings pin to wear. (The stewardesses kept checking on us, since in those days, it was highly unusual for children to travel alone.)

As the plane began to surge down the runway, I tightened my grip on Brand's hand and said, "It's going to be okay." I was actually reassuring myself, because as the plane soared off the ground, Brand yelped with delight.

"Look, Denise! There's a road. And look over there. The cars are so small!" he squealed in joy.

As we looked out the window, the wet, cold world dropped away. The plane went higher and higher. Suddenly it burst through the clouds into sunlight. All we could see were the tops of the clouds in all directions, bathed in golden sunlight. I clutched Brand's hand. Everything really *was* going to be all right.

Brand told me recently that the stewardess coming toward him with the plane pin was his earliest memory. He doesn't remember anything before that flight, but he said that he would never forget how magical the lights in the cities at night were. Even though he was only four, he remembers that the plane was a TWA Constellation Three Tails. He's had a soft spot in his heart for TWA ever since.

Brand eventually grew up to own his own plane and earn a Ph.D. in astrophysics. I sometimes wonder whether the joy he experienced that day somehow didn't help spur on his later interest in aviation.

Our grandparents were waiting expectantly at the airport gate. I'd met them before, but it had been many years prior. My grandmother, a round, short woman, was wearing a flowery dress and sparkly earrings. My grandfather, a tall (6'2"), stocky man, was dressed in his Sunday-best clothes. As soon as my grandmother saw us, she ran forward and threw her arms around us. She hugged us both very hard, at the same time. We weren't used to displays of affection and were taken aback by her excitement. She then hugged me so tightly that I was burrowed into her round, soft body, and was saturated by her sweet, floral perfume. No one had ever embraced me so warmly or had been so thrilled to see me. Finally releasing me, she grabbed Brand and embraced him so hard that I thought he would disappear into her voluminous dress.

As Grandpa silently negotiated his big Buick through the Los Angeles airport traffic, Grandma chattered excitedly about our new life in Southern California. We finally arrived at their very small bungalow in Temple City, just on the edge of the town of El Monte.

Everything was so different at my grandparents' house compared to our home in Ohio. Our farmhouse was always a tumble of garbage, clutter, and newspapers. I remember one time that the trash was piled up so high in the kitchen that it touched the ceiling. I worried that it would crash down on me, so I avoided walking by it. And the kitchen wall always had lots of dried spaghetti noodles stuck to it. To see if spaghetti noodles were done, Mother said to throw a noodle at the wall. If it stuck, it was done. It was fun to throw spaghetti at the walls (and we ate a lot of spaghetti, so there were a lot of noodles on the wall), but we never bothered to clean it up. Plus, there was always other types of food on the walls, which was left there from all the times that my mother threw our meals at my father.

In Ohio, when it was cold, we put a bare mattress on the living- room floor in front of the wood-burning stove, but that bed was never removed, so there it stayed—a heap of blankets, pillows, and toys—throughout the warmer months as well.

At my grandmother's house, everything was meticulously cleaned every day. She dusted relentlessly, attacking every surface with a vengeance. When she vacuumed the thick velour pile carpet, she was careful to vacuum only in one direction to make a concise pattern, and we were then forbidden to walk on it because we would leave footprints. Only guests were allowed to walk on the carpet with impunity.

Grandma's furnishing style was lace, lace . . . and more lace. Everything was covered in it. The couch had lace doilies on the arms. The side tables had even larger lace doilies, which were covered with small ceramics of cute dogs and little angels. And even the toilet roll and all the Kleenex boxes were covered with lacy fabric. The towels in the bathroom all had lace sewn in pretty rows across them and were starched to attention. We were told that we could never use those towels because they were for guests; however, I'm sure that my grandmother's guests would have preferred to wipe their hands on their pants rather than mar the perfection of her towels.

I'm quite sure that no one ever used those towels, because

25 years later, the very same ones, slightly faded, were still neatly strung across the bathroom towel rack. My father was always concerned with appearances and wanted everyone to think that we had the perfect life. I wonder how much of that attitude came from living in a home that was always ready to be on display for guests.

There was lots of food jammed into the refrigerator and the cupboards. I mean *lots* of food. My grandparents had lived through the Depression, so Grandma always made sure that there was plenty of food. My mother's cupboards, on the other hand, were usually bare. When Mother did the shopping, we would have groceries for a few days and then there would be almost nothing to eat. Mealtimes in Ohio were either a kind of a feast or a famine. At Grandma's, I think we could have lived for five years on all the cans of food that were socked away in every spare cupboard. And Grandma liked to cook.

Somehow she managed to make food look like it was lace-covered as well. She made radish roses, carrot curls, and mashed-potato florets. On top of the meatloaf, she would lay thin slices of carrots, radishes, and beets to create lacy flower designs. She decorated every dish in some way.

At dinnertime, Grandpa, Brand, and I would sit at the table in anticipation, in great contrast to our usual trepidation about my mother's leftover concoctions. Then when Grandma brought forth the evening meal, a dish at a time, we always felt a sense of awe. It was akin to the moment that the priest brought forth the wine and wafer at communion. It always seemed sacrilegious to cut into any of her nightly offerings. (Although my parents didn't believe in religion, they did take us to the Episcopal Church on holidays and for an occasional service.)

Grandma was famous for her dinner parties and especially for her appetizers. One Saturday when she was preparing to host her bridge club, we spent the morning carefully preparing her special mushroom canapés. We were almost done when she exclaimed, "Oh no! I'm short one pastry bottom. This is terrible. That means that one person won't get a canapé."

I didn't know what to say. If Grandma said it was terrible, then it must be.

Suddenly she was elated. "I know what I'll do! I'll take a piece of cardboard and put the topping on it. No one will be able to tell that it's not a canapé. Then when I pass them around, I'll take that one and pretend to eat it, and then toss it when no one's looking."

It sounded like a great plan, and I was happy to be included in the secret. We carefully positioned the cardboard canapé so that it would be closest to her on the tray. When all the guests arrived, my grandmother proudly walked around, serving her delicacies. There was exactly one canapé for each guest.

She smiled graciously as each person delicately bit into the morsel and exclaimed how good it was. After everyone had been given one, Grandma picked up the last one, smiled at everyone, and lifted hers up and took a tiny nibble as well. A look of horror fell over her face as she turned and escaped into the kitchen. I ran after her. I glanced back into the living room. No one seemed to have noticed my grandma's quick departure.

"Grandma! What's the matter?" I asked.

"Someone else got the cardboard canapé. When I bit into mine, it wasn't cardboard!" she lamented. For my grandmother, a disastrous dinner party was the end of the world. I peered into the living room. No one seemed to be clutching their heart or having trouble breathing as they nibbled their appetizer.

Then Grandma's face blanched. "I don't know how it could have happened. I was so careful." Then, replaying the event in her mind, she was horrified to realize that my grandfather had taken the cardboard canapé. We peeked back into the living room. Grandpa just popped the rest of the canapé into his mouth and started chewing. Our eyes got wide as we looked at each other and then turned back and watched him gulp it down. Never taking our eyes off Grandpa, we cautiously walked back into the living room. Someone said, "These are great canapés, Gladys!" and there was a general assenting murmur.

"Uh . . . thank you," she stammered.

"Honey, that canapé was really delicious. Did you do anything different?" asked Grandpa.

Grandma's eyes got really wide, as she said, "No . . . it's the same recipe."

Grandpa loved Grandma's cooking so much that even when he ate cardboard, he thought it tasted good!

MY GRANDFATHER ADORED MY GRANDMOTHER and would do anything to make her happy. When she developed a fascination with cemeteries, my grandpa was happy to accommodate her. Every Sunday we packed a sack lunch, piled into his big Buick, and drove to different cemeteries. As soon as we drove through the gate, a hushed stillness would fill the car. Grandma began her narrative as Grandpa drove as somber as a hearse driver along the meandering roads. He rarely said anything.

"Ooh! Look, kids," she said. "Aren't those flowers beautiful?"

Brand and I pressed ourselves against the right rear window of the car to view the newly laid flowers on a grave. We then enthusiastically agreed that they were beautiful.

"Slow down, Roy," Grandma insisted whenever we came to a funeral in progress. Grandpa was so devoted to Grandma that he always did as she asked. He'd slow down, and we'd all be silent and suitably reverent for the occasion.

"Oh, the poor dear!" Grandma would declare. "I wonder how he died. I hope he didn't suffer." Brand and I would solemnly shake our heads and "Tsk, tsk" because a life was cut short. If it were a large funeral, Grandma got Grandpa to drive by it several times. "Roy, turn around. Drive by it again."

After we'd pass by the funeral, she'd use the event as a teaching tool for her grandkids.

"Denise, did you notice that woman wearing red? You should never wear red to a funeral! Occasionally, in the summer, you can get away with a medium blue, but never red."

"I'll never wear red to a funeral, Grandma!" I'd declare. And she'd reach back and pat my hand.

Grandma got most excited when we'd visit the Rose Hills Memorial Park and Mortuary. It was the mausoleum in which my grandparents' ashes were to be placed after they died.

Approaching the mausoleum was kind of like a pilgrimage. As we stood before the huge door, Grandma would hold my hand on one side and Brand's on the other. We would stand in awed silence for a moment until Grandpa swung open the doors and we entered at a dignified processional speed. Grandma glared at anyone there who wasn't acting in a reverent manner.

On the far wall were small, inscribed panels called *niches*. In a worshipful manner, Grandma would touch the numbered plaque. She'd whisper, "This is where our ashes will be. We wanted to have a beautiful place for you to come and visit us when we're gone." It was a weekly ritual. We knew exactly where the niche was and what it was for, but Brand and I just nodded each time, like it was the first time that we'd heard her say it.

School and especially the clothing styles in Los Angeles were very different from Mrs. Reich's strict classroom in Ohio. In El Monte, all the girls wore skirts with layers of petticoats. The goal was to have your skirt radiate out horizontally from your waist. Of course, this wasn't possible, but three stiff petticoats went a long way toward inflating my skirt. My petticoats were so voluminous that I had to battle with them to shove my skirt under the desk at school. My grandma had kindly taken me shopping to get the same kind of clothes that the other girls at the school wore. The clothes that I had worn in school in Leipsic would have been laughed at in California, as they were very out of date.

All the girls at my new school teased their hair—even ten-year-olds like me—the higher the better. To get maximum height, I teased the top of my hair, lacquered it with Aqua Net hair spray, and then teased it some more. Eventually, I was able to add three inches of height to my head in this manner. To create the "beehive" hairdo, we used a special method that involved wadded-up newspaper soaked in water. We squeezed the excess water out and positioned it on our heads. The teased hair was then layered over the damp newspaper.

EVEN IN THE EARLY '60s, gangs were beginning to be a part of the Los Angeles social landscape, but they were different from the gangs in Chicago. Somehow these were edgier and more aligned with older gangs. They were more like distinct social groups with specific rules of conduct. There were the Hispanics, the surfers, the greasers, the jocks, and myriad splinter groups. There were often after-school fights between the various groups, with girl groups often aligning with the boys.

The first week I was at El Monte School, a girl named Peggy came up to me at recess. She was tall, lean, and tough, and wore a wide, shiny metal belt that cinched her waist. Her hair was teased into a perfect beehive.

Smacking her gum, she said, "You can join our gang, but you have to tease your hair higher, and you have to get a rat-tail comb."

"Okay," I murmured. She spun away and marched off. I didn't want to say no to Peggy. I don't think anyone did.

Everyone had heard that a girl at a neighboring school had a black-widow spider make its home in her hair. When the black-widow babies were born, they swarmed over her face and she was bitten so badly she died. I know now that this was an urban myth that spread all across America, but at the time I really thought a girl had died because of spiders in her beehive hairdo. I mean, that's why they called it a beehive, right? I seriously wondered if Peggy had black widows living in her hair.

After school, I asked my grandma if I could get a rat-tail comb.

"Why do you need one?" Grandma asked.

"All the other girls have them."

That seemed to be a good enough reason for Grandma, so the next day I showed up at school with a shiny new rat-tail comb. Living with my mother and father, I would never have been able to get something just because it was in style. Our clothing was often secondhand, and every item needed to be practical and durable—never what was trendy or in style.

During recess, Peggy pulled me aside. "Well, let's see it," she said.

I pulled my comb out of my book bag. Peggy took it in her hand and turned it over.

"This will do," she said. She then opened her book bag and pulled out a coarse emery board and began to file the end of my comb.

"What are you doing to my new comb?" I cried.

"I'm making a weapon."

"A weapon?!"

"Yup. See, you can keep it poked into your hair like this," and she reached her hand up to her hair and pulled out the biggest, sharpest rat-tail comb I'd ever seen. The end was filed to a stiletto point.

"See, if anyone ever messes with me, I just stab 'em," she said, lunging forward at me to make her point.

I knew then that I would never "mess" with Peggy.

"Come on," she said as she handed me my comb, which I clumsily poked into my hair. In one corner of the playground, a group of girls waited for Peggy to show up.

"Hey, everyone, this is Denise. She's going to be joining us."

I smiled wanly.

"First, let's show Denise how we use our combs." Like professional gunslingers pulling their pistols out of their holsters, ten hands reached up and grabbed their combs out of their hairdos and thrust them toward me. I jumped back.

"It'll take some practice," Peggy said, "but you'll learn it eventually."

"Denise, you're new, so you have to go to the end of the line."

At recess, all the girls in each "gang" would hook arms with each other in a line of six to about twelve or so and march around the school grounds terrorizing the other kids. Everyone else had to get out of the way. The girls would yell, "Coming through!" or "Get out of the way!" and all the kids would scramble. There were quite a number of these terrorizing lines of girl gangs roaming the schoolyard at recess.

When you were new to the gang, you were at the end of the line, which wasn't great. Peggy (who was in the center) sometimes would walk near a swing set or the teeter-totter. Being at the end of the line meant I would either be banged into the swing set or I'd have to let go, which was definitely not cool.

I didn't like terrorizing little kids or being a part of the gang, so I decided to quit. I really don't think Peggy would have let me do so except for the fact that I had a run-in with "Hairy Eyebrows," which increased her respect for me.

Hairy Eyebrows was my teacher, and no one liked him.

Of course that wasn't really his name, but that's what the kids called him behind his back. He had huge eyebrows that grew together above his nose, but also grew straight out, creating a kind of shelf above his eyes. He had dandruff that used to collect on this shelf of thick, black eyebrow hair.

Hairy Eyebrows used to pick on Maria, a small, shy Hispanic girl who didn't speak English very well. He would always single her out and humiliate her in class. Fairness has always been important to me, so I decided to do something. One morning before school started, I walked into the principal's office and asked to speak with him. I told him my concern about Maria. He said, "Thank you for coming to see me. Please feel free to come again." After that, I noticed that Hairy Eyebrows left Maria alone. Someone must have told Peggy that I wasn't afraid to talk to the principal, because she didn't give me any problem about quitting the gang.

ONE AFTERNOON, GRANDMA SAID, "Denise, there's something that I want to talk to you about. Let's go into your room."

My room was actually the den/family room, and every evening we watched television there. *The Lawrence Welk Show* was my grandparents' favorite program. Grandma also did her crafts in there, and Grandpa's desk was tucked in one corner. It was a small room, but at night I pulled the couch into a bed, the den became my bedroom, and Brand slept on a daybed tucked in the hallway.

I sat on the edge of the couch. Grandma had such a solemn look on her face that I began to worry. "When you were younger, your dad told us that we could visit with you, but we were forbidden to ever tell you about our beliefs. When he was growing up, he was a very practical child and was always interested in science. He was never attracted to anything spiritual or religious. He said that religion was for people with weak minds. So whenever we visited, we never said anything to you kids. However, now that you're here with us, I want to share a few things with you."

Grandma continued, "I'm an astrologer. I did your chart the day you were born. You are a double Aries . . . I think you needed all that fire energy just to make it through your life so far."

She then handed me the astrology chart that she'd done the day of my birth, and said, "Astrology is a map of probabilities for your life. It's a method that has been used for thousands of years." She then took the chart in her hands for a few minutes, looking at the intersecting lines and symbols on it. I was fascinated that she'd known about my life, even when I was just a few hours old.

"It's important for you to know that although you've had some difficult experiences—and there are some more ahead—everything will turn out all right. Remember this, Denise—the roots go deepest when the wind blows the strongest.

"You see, in nature, a tree that survives hard times, such as droughts or strong storms, will often be stronger than a tree that has grown in perfect conditions. During a drought or high winds, for example, the roots will go deeper into the earth to reach water or to add stability to the tree. The trees that have the deepest roots are usually the strongest. The difficult experiences that you've had and will have in the future will build your character and allow your spiritual roots to go deep," she explained.

She and my grandfather trained with a man named Manly Hall, went to see spiritualists, and also attended the Science of Mind church. As I continued to sit on the edge of the couch, my grandmother continued, "In addition to astrology, we also believe that death isn't the end of life. We believe that the spirit goes on, and we also believe in angels."

In that moment, my whole life changed.

I trusted my grandmother, and I believed whatever she said. As she told me about spiritual dimensions, suddenly an immense, mystical realm of life opened up for me.

"Denise?" Grandma asked, looking concerned. I had looked off while she was talking.

"I'm sorry, Grandma," I murmured. It was hard to focus on what she was saying, as my life had suddenly become so much fuller.

"Grandpa and I also believe that you have 'abilities.'"

"What do you mean?" I asked, suddenly very alert.

"Do you remember last Sunday when I lost my offering envelope?"

The memory jumped into my mind. Grandma had been getting ready for church, and she'd misplaced the offering envelope that she was going to put in the collection plate at church. "Denise, have you seen my church envelope? I've looked everywhere for it," she had asked.

I'd just woken up and was still in that soft, blurry place between sleep and wakefulness. An image arose in my mind of the envelope behind the lettuce in the refrigerator. Sleepily, I answered, "Try looking in the refrigerator behind the lettuce."

A minute later, Grandma came into my room with a strange look on her face, clutching the envelope to her chest. "You were right. I must have absentmindedly left the envelope in the refrigerator when I was getting the casserole out for the church social. How did you know it was there?" she asked.

"I dunno," I yawned. "I just saw a picture in my head."

Until my grandmother mentioned the envelope, I'd forgotten about the incident. She continued her explanation. "Well, the picture you said that you saw in your head means that you have the 'Sight,'" she continued, whispering the "Sight" as if it was a hallowed word.

"Grandma, I was just guessing."

"No, you've got the 'Sight'!"

I didn't know what the "Sight" was, but I figured that it must be good because Grandma seemed excited about it. Then one day when I came home from school, she was lying on the couch with her feet up and a cold washcloth on her forehead.

"What's wrong?" I asked, concerned.

"I have a bad headache, and my feet ache," my grandmother said dismally. "Do you think you could rub my feet?"

I sat down next to her and began to massage her feet. Suddenly she sat up and peered at me and said, "That's amazing! My headache is gone! There's heat radiating out of your hands! You've got the 'Touch'!"

Wow! I thought. *I have the "Sight," and I have the "Touch"!* I didn't know what having the "Touch" was, but obviously it was as good as the "Sight," because Grandma was so excited. During her Bridge Club nights at the house, I'd overhear her bragging that her granddaughter had the "Sight" and the "Touch." After that, whenever she had a headache or wasn't feeling well, she'd have me massage her feet and would tell me that I'd healed her.

BRAND WAS ALSO HAPPY TO BE LIVING with our grandparents. He spent lots of time with Grandpa helping him with his refrigeration jobs. Although his grandson was only five years old, Grandpa took Brand on almost all of his jobs. They would leave in my Grandpa's big blue-paneled truck loaded with tools, to fix a broken refrigeration unit in some small market. When they came back, Grandpa would boast about what a great help his grandson was, and Brand would beam with pride because he'd helped his grandpa.

As for my other siblings, Heather was having a good experience with her aunt in New Jersey, but Gordon, who was shy and introspective, didn't fit very well into the working-ranch atmosphere of Oklahoma.

Then, one evening my grandparents received a call from my dad saying that he was ready for all of his kids to come back to live with him. After she hung up the phone, Grandma asked Brand and me to come into the living room. *The living room is for guests. Why are we going in there?* I wondered.

Grandma plopped down on the lace-covered sofa and looked down at the rug. A solitary tear slowly ran down her cheek and dropped to the carpet. It was immediately absorbed into the fibers. I held Brand's hand as she quietly told us we would be going back home. My body stiffened as I thought of returning to my father. I'd never told my grandparents what he'd done to me. Somehow I believed that we would never have to go back.

I looked at Brand. He just stared out through the lace-curtained window and steadfastly wouldn't look at me. *It's not my fault, Brand. I don't want to go back either,* I thought sadly.

Grandma told us that she and Grandpa loved us very much, but they wouldn't be able to contact us because it might upset our mother. I held my breath when she said this. *No contact! Noooo! I don't want to go! I want to live here forever!* I wailed within myself, but I just silently nodded my head and accepted the fact that we had to go back. Two weeks later we were on a plane back to Ohio.

CHAPTER FOUR

When the Wind
Blows Hardest

(1962–1967)

I had a love/hate relationship with Nordon, Ohio. It started
with love and ended with hate and despair.

My mother's psychiatrist said that Mother might be ready
to get out of the mental hospital, but she'd need a big house
so she wouldn't feel closed in. My father wanted to be ready
for her when she was finally released, so we flew back to Ohio
to live in a huge house that he'd bought in Nordon, where he
had a new job. Finally, after two years, we were all going to be
back together again. I was 12, Heather was 10, Gordon was 8,
and Brand was 6.

Nordon was a small farming town on a meandering, muddy
river. Our new place was a historical house and one of the biggest homes in town. It had three stories plus a full basement,
huge stained-glass windows, hand-carved wooden walls, and
antique chandeliers. Compared to my grandparents' small
bungalow, it looked like a mansion to us. To this day, I have no
idea how my father managed to purchase such a home.

I was so happy to see Heather and Gordon again that I
pushed the events that had occurred with my father in Leipsic
to the back of my mind. After our arrival, Father took me aside
and said, "I've just talked to your mother's psychiatrist. It looks

like she'll have to stay in the mental hospital for awhile longer. She's not ready to come home. Since you're the oldest, you're going to have to take care of everything while I'm at work. I'm going to need you to look after your brothers and sister."

At my grandparents' house, I had watched June Cleaver in so many episodes of *Leave It to Beaver* that I was sure I knew how to do it. I fervently jumped into my new role as homemaker. In the morning, I made a hot breakfast—eggs, toast, bacon, pancakes, everything—just like on television. When Father came home from work, I had a steaming meal ready. After he ate, he'd have a few beers, relax in front of the television, and fall asleep while I did the dishes and cleaned up. I didn't really blame him for that because we were all living in an era where women did the housework and men brought home the money. Also, I somehow felt it was up to me to keep things together.

We had arrived at the beginning of summer, so after Father went to work, I'd clean the house, cook, make lunches, do the laundry, mow the lawn, and get the groceries. For a while, I was able to keep up with everything. After all, on television it looked effortless. The TV housewife was always smiling while she mopped the kitchen floor in her high heels.

I saw my life in terms of a television show. In some ways, it was easier to pretend to live in a TV world than to experience the pain in my own life. I *was* June Cleaver . . . but it wasn't always easy. *What was I doing wrong?* I wondered. I was exhausted and cranky most of the time, and I certainly didn't feel like squealing with delight about my squeaky-clean kitchen floor.

One day I had an epiphany while grocery shopping. It was one of those moments when enlightenment strikes with lightning brilliance. Suddenly I felt as if I knew the secrets of the universe. I know this sounds dramatic, but honestly, that's how I felt.

Every few days, my father left money for me to go shopping; the grocery store was walking distance from our house. The day of my shopping epiphany, I was pushing the grocery cart past the Campbell's soup and the Ritz cracker aisle and into the frozen-food section. As I passed by, the words "Swanson's TV dinners" seemed to glow. I stopped and slowly turned to stare at the sign. TV dinners? Oh wow! TV dinners!

I picked one up. The picture showed a cute tray with various foods in different compartments. One section had pieces of fried chicken, another had fluffy white mashed potatoes, yet another had bright green peas, and there was also a piece of apple crisp! On the label, I read that all I had to do was put the dinner in the oven, and 25 minutes later there would be a hot, nutritious meal ready. I hugged it to my chest as if it were a long-lost child.

That day the TV dinners were on sale for $.25. I pulled my money out and counted it, and then filled my entire cart with them. I was so excited. There were so many different kinds— meatloaf, enchiladas, meatballs, Salisbury steak (which is really just hamburger, but it sounds better). I couldn't wait to get home and try them.

I *loved* TV dinners. I loved how easy they were to prepare. I loved how they tasted. I loved that there were no dishes. I just threw those cute little trays away after meals. To this day, I'm grateful to the Swanson company for this great invention.

Then I went on a craze, discovering lots of other instant meals as well. Instant mashed potatoes were great—just add hot water and stir! I made tasty meals with pork and beans in a can; I just chopped hot dogs, added them to the beans, and I'd made dinner. And instead of making my own salad dressings, I bought dressing in a bottle and poured it over iceberg lettuce to make a salad. Jiffy cake mixes were my specialty. All I did was add water, stir, and bake. Now I knew the secret of the TV housewives. And not only that, but everyone seemed happy with my meals. My father was so tired that I don't think that he cared as long as everything was running smoothly. And anything was better than the Jell-O concoctions Mother made in King City.

There were times, however, when June Cleaver stepped aside and the girl who was the Rat-tail Comb Slinger stepped in. I was very protective of my brothers and sister, so one day when Gordon, who was eight years old at the time, came home and said that someone had shoved him, I grilled him. "Who shoved you?!"

"Max," he said.

Max was a strapping 13-year-old who lived on the next block. My face flushed red as I hollered, "I'm gonna get him!"

"No!" Gordon pleaded. "Don't cause any trouble!"

"He's not going to get away with pushing my little brother!" I yelled over my shoulder as I tore out of the house.

Max's yard was perfectly manicured, with a picket fence around it. Flowers lined the path to the door of his white-shuttered, wooden house. I swung open the gate to Max's yard, stomped up the walk, and knocked on the door. The door swung open and Max's mother looked down, smiling sweetly. "Oh, you must be the new girl," she said.

With a knowing wink, she said, "Max, there's a girl here to see you." I tried to smile back at her as nicely as I could. Max came to the door and closed it behind him; he seemed embarrassed by his mother's words. But then he straightened his broad shoulders, flexed his muscles, and swaggered toward me with a glint in his eye.

"Yeah, well . . ." he said.

I looked him straight in the eye and said, "You may not know it, but today you messed with the wrong kid!"

"What . . . what are you talking about?" he stammered, as his male bravado suddenly collapsed.

"That kid that you shoved today . . . he was my brother," I said. "And I'm going to make sure that you never touch him again—I'm going to beat you up!"

I don't think a girl had ever talked to Max that way. In fact, girls my age in Nordon baked pies, tried new kinds of lipstick, and hung out at the Dairy Queen—and they definitely didn't beat up boys.

Upon hearing my words, Max looked shocked. I doubled up my fist and stepped toward him. He looked at my fist and then up at my hostile expression, pushed past me, and started running down the sidewalk. I went charging after him, yelling, "Run, you coward! Don't you ever touch my family again!"

People stopped mowing their lawns and watering their grass in shock as they watched my scrappy figure chasing Max and bellowing at the top of my lungs. I didn't catch Max, and I actually don't know what I would have done if I did, but he never bothered my brother again.

JUST BEFORE SCHOOL STARTED, we all piled into our car to go to Bargain City and Goodwill to buy our school clothes. The quality was poor, but the price was right. Even though we had one of the biggest houses in town, we still couldn't afford nice clothes.

Once school started, my homemaker routine was a bit different. In the morning, I'd make breakfast for everyone. (I'd also discovered boxed cereals.) All I had to do was put out a box of Cheerios and milk, and I'd "made breakfast." It sure was a lot easier than whipping up pancakes or scrambled eggs and bacon. When we all walked home for lunch, I'd make peanut butter-and-jelly sandwiches, and, of course, I'd heat up TV dinners at night.

I was so pleased with myself. I'd found a way to keep the

household running smoothly, meals on the table, clothes cleaned (the house came with a washing machine), and the housework organized, as well as help Brand and Gordon with their school-work and finish my own. I did this for about five months.

ONE NIGHT MY FATHER ANNOUNCED that our mother was coming back home. "I'm going to pick her up, then I'm moving out," he said matter-of-factly, but I could see that he was sad as he spoke. "I don't think it will work if we're both living here. We'll also be getting a divorce. You won't be seeing me because I'm moving to another state."

Father had finally come to the realization that the marriage would never work. I think he'd also convinced himself that by leaving, he was doing the best he could for his kids.

I rarely saw him after that. However, at the time, I was so glad to see my mother again that I wasn't really sad to see my father go. (Memories of my anguished nights in his bed still lingered in the corner of my mind.)

During the time that my mother had been in the mental hospital, I'd built up an idealized image of her. I often imagined how much better things would be if she were home. In my mind, she was a kind, generous, loving mother, and I convinced Heather, Gordon, and Brand how wonderful it would be to have her home again.

We all waited eagerly as the car pulled up with Mother. I'd stayed up late the night before making a big sign that said "Welcome Home." It hung on the front porch swinging in the breeze. It was decorated with drawings of flowers and birds. When she stepped out of the car, I was shocked. She looked so much older, and her hair had gone from shiny black to stark white in a little over two years. Yet her eyes sparkled to see all of her children lined up to greet her, Von Trapp style. She stepped forward and embraced each of us. We all went into the house, and she seemed very pleased. I sighed in relief. Everything was going to be okay.

A little later she pulled me aside and asked, "What have you been doing while I was gone?"

I was bursting with pride. I was so excited about how I'd managed to get the housework done, make the meals, keep up with my grades, and help Brand and Gordon with their homework, too. I thought she would be so proud of me. As I chirped away telling her of everything that I'd done, I wasn't aware of the storm that was brewing . . . until she started screaming.

"How dare you! I'm in charge here, not you! You've been trying to usurp my authority while I was gone!"

"No, Mother! No! I was just trying to take care of things while you were gone. I'm really glad not to do it anymore," I said, shocked at how quickly her mood had changed.

"Are you saying that you won't help out? You damn well *will* help out! And you'll do what I tell you to, and when I tell you!" she shrieked.

"Mother, please! Of course, I'll help out! I'll do anything you want!" I cried. I was desperate for things to go well for her homecoming, and they weren't going well at all.

"You will follow my orders! And I demand respect from you at all times!"

"I thought you would be happy with everything that I've done," I said trying hard not to cry.

"I'm definitely not happy, and I'm not happy with you either!" Her eyes got that wild look that would become so familiar in the future. We used to call it her "crazy eyes." She always reminded me of a trapped animal as her eyes quickly darted back and forth, as if looking for some kind of escape. In that frightening moment, all the rage toward my father that had been stored up in her for more than two years metastasized and suddenly shifted its focus to me.

As a 12-year-old, I didn't really understand mental illness. (My mother had been diagnosed as a paranoid schizophrenic.) All I knew was that I had must have done something wrong, and I wanted to do whatever I could to try to make it right. I'm not sure why she was let out of the hospital. She seemed much worse than when we had lived in Leipsic. Now, instead of believing that my father was plotting against her, she thought that I was. I reasoned to myself that if I tried hard enough, I could fix it, but no matter what I did, I never could.

OVER THE MONTHS, MY MOTHER'S MOODS turned violent. Sometimes in the middle of the night, she would flip the light switch on in my bedroom, rip the covers off my bed, and begin hitting me as hard as she could while screaming at the top of her lungs in hideous animal-like shrieks. My response was to curl up, brace my hands over my head, and wait until she'd exhausted herself and left. Later, I discovered that it was easier to sleep in the bathtub with the door locked. When I was in the bathroom, she would scream and bang on the door, but she'd eventually leave. I didn't know what was worse—the secret shame-filled advances of my father, or the rages of my mother.

I never knew when my mother would explode. Her moods would come on quickly . . . sometimes without warning. If it happened when we were in the car, she'd start screaming, pull the car over, and demand that I get out and walk. It wouldn't matter how far from home we were or what time it was. One time we were driving on the highway late in the evening about ten miles from home when one of her moods came on.

"Get out! Get out!" she screamed as she pulled over to the side of the road.

"But, mother, it's nine o'clock and it's dark. Please don't make me get out."

"Get out now!" she said as she started punching me.

As soon as I got out of the car, she sped off down the highway. I knew it was going to be a long walk. After a while, a trucker pulled his rig over and jumped out.

"What are you doing out here?" he asked.

I explained that I was walking home.

"How about I give you a ride?"

"No, thank you. I can walk. It's okay." I knew never to get in a car with a stranger.

"Aw, come on. It'll be all right," he said.

"No, thank you."

He then grabbed me by the shoulders and started to push me down to the ground. I desperately tried to stop him. In the struggle, I accidentally yanked off his necklace. As soon as I pulled it away, he let go of me. He looked at my clenched fist with the chain dangling out of it. Then as I opened my hand to reveal a crucifix of Jesus, he looked at me and said, "I'm sorry. I didn't know what I was doing." I silently handed him his necklace, and he got in his truck and drove off. Who knows? Maybe Jesus had something to do with it, because uncharacteristically, a few minutes later my mother came back and picked me up without saying a word.

WHEN MY MOTHER WASN'T IN A PARANOID STATE, it was wonderful. My father sent money to support us, so she didn't have to work, and she had a free spirit that I loved. Most of the other mothers in town went to the beauty parlor once a week to have their hair coiffed, but my mother had long hair that spilled down her back and blew wild in the wind. While most mothers made cakes for bake sales, mine spent her time reading Sartre and talking about existentialism. She wore outrageously colored shifts, brightly adorned beads, and big hoop earrings. She was into modern art, jazz, Jack Kerouac, and Allen Ginsberg poems. Although her mood could change in an instant, she could be joyous and carefree . . . but those times with her were few and far between.

Mother was in a good mood when she said that we were going to Oklahoma again. A neighbor said she'd watch the house, so once again we all squeezed in the Chevy and drove to Oklahoma to stay on the ranch. I was excited to go back. While I was there, I had a profound experience.

It was still dark, in the early-morning hours, when I crept down the stairs of my grandparents' old farmhouse. Every step creaked so loudly that it seemed to echo through the house. The smell of gas from the kitchen stove was strong as I tiptoed past the butter churn. As I walked outside, I closed the screen door carefully so it didn't squeak. I didn't want to wake anyone. The air was crisp and sharp. To the west, the full moon was about four fingers above the horizon.

I walked swiftly to the barn. The horses were uneasy with someone there at that unusual hour. They flicked their tails nervously. I wanted to go riding, but I wasn't allowed to use any of the ranch hands' horses. However, there were some extra saddle horses that weren't used for rounding up cattle. I thought it might be okay if I rode one of those. Resolutely, I picked out the sandy-colored horse, grabbed his mane, and pulled myself up. He flinched and snorted, but settled down. I dug my heels into his side and he moved forward. Bending over, I reached down to open the gate and then latched it behind me. As I leaned forward and threaded my hands into his mane, he took off galloping. I hung on like my life depended on it.

We raced up hills and down valleys and splashed over streams. He whipped through woods and across fields. Finally, he slowed down to a trot, and then came to a stop on a knoll covered with tall grasses. As he bent over to nibble, I slid off his back and sat in the grass to watch the sunrise.

Just after the sun rose, something happened. I don't know

how else to describe it, but everything just stopped. The breeze stopped. The birds stopped singing. There were no sounds. Even the horse was still. I could hear only my breath and my heart . . . nothing else. It was like everything was frozen in time but me. I slowly became aware of an immense and powerful presence. It encompassed both me and the surrounding area. It was wise and awesome at the same time. "Safe" is the best way to describe what I felt—absolutely safe and serene. I felt safer than I'd ever felt in my dirt hole in Atascadero, or hidden among the reeds at my secret pond in King City, or in the wood lot in Ohio, or at the creek in Northfield.

A voice in my head said, *Denise, you are at a crossroads in your life. There are some very difficult times ahead for you; it is your destiny. Just know that you are not alone.* As I "heard" those words, I remembered what my grandmother had said about my astrology chart, when she told me that there were going to be some hard times ahead, but that they would make me stronger. I don't know who or what was speaking to me, but it was comforting. Suddenly the presence withdrew. Birds began to sing, the breeze picked up, and the horse neighed.

THIS TIME WE WERE ONLY IN OKLAHOMA for a few weeks, and I was sad to be returning home. As we drove back to Ohio, I had the feeling that the premonition about challenging times ahead was going to be accurate. Once we got back, Mother's fits of anger became much worse. She thought that I was too strong-willed, and sometimes she had special sessions that she said were to "break my will." During these bouts, she'd draw a line on the wooden floor with chalk and tell me to stand on one side of the line. She would stand on the other side of the line with a belt.

"You're going to learn to obey me. Step over this line!" she'd yell.

I would never cross the line right away. When I didn't

move, she took the belt and started hitting me with the buckle end, yelling, "You will obey me! Step over the line!"

I felt that crossing the line was a kind of death. It meant that I would lose myself, so I wouldn't budge. Somehow, by not giving in, I felt that I still had some control over my life. It was silly to give the line so much significance, because by the time I finally stepped over it, I would have huge, bleeding welts on my arms and legs.

One time, when I was 13, I felt so desperate about my situation with my mother that I swallowed a whole handful of aspirins. I didn't take enough, because all it did was make me sleep for a very long time.

I CAN SEE NOW THAT MUCH OF THE WAY I perceived myself as an adult had its roots in my early years. Even though I had moments of courage and tenacity as a child, I also developed an extreme lack of self-respect. For most of my adult years, I felt a deep shame about who I was. I felt guilty about almost everything. Even when I was teaching worldwide, I still harbored a severe lack of confidence, which surprised some people. I'm not sure how I was able to create such phenomenal results helping others to love themselves when I was suffering so much myself. However, I believe that you teach what you need to learn yourself, so perhaps I taught about feeling worthy and developing self-esteem because that was exactly what *I* needed to learn.

The depth of my guilt probably had its source in the fact that just after she returned, Mother started to tell me that everything was my fault—I mean, *everything*. She said it with such certainty that I believed her. When my brothers and sister misbehaved, she said that it was my "psychic" influence on them, that I made them do it. For example, one time Gordon tracked mud into the house.

"Denise! Come here at once. There's mud on the floor," she said.

"But I didn't do it!"

"You didn't have to physically do it. You brainwash people around you. You're continually usurping my authority."

"But Mother, I didn't do it!"

"Don't talk back to me! It's your fault. Clean up the mud and Gordon's shoes. You're confined to your room for the afternoon."

I was constantly in trouble because of my so-called psychic influence or because I had "brainwashed" people. I didn't actually know what either of those things was, but I knew it was bad because Mother continually told me that I was trying to sabotage her.

If Heather talked back, I was punished because Mother said I'd made my sister do it. She would then misbehave even more, and Mother would say, "Heather, it's not your fault. You can't help yourself. Denise brainwashed you. You're Denise's spineless puppet." Mother always called her a "spineless puppet." Heather hated this and would glare at me as if it was really true.

I can understand now why my sister would get so angry with me. It was as if I was taking credit for her actions. She needed to misbehave to prove her own free will, to prove that she had control, and, unwittingly, I was taking that away from her. No matter what my brothers or sister did, I was the one who got in trouble. My mother's paranoia was empowering for me and very disempowering for them. In a convoluted way, she was programming me to believe that I could influence people.

HAVING A PARENT WHO WAS MENTALLY ILL was a personal hell that I didn't know how to escape. I was afraid to let anyone know what was happening because I desperately wanted people to think we were a normal family. Divorce had a very negative stigma in Nordon. Everyone knew that we were from a "broken" family, but we really didn't want anyone to know about the mental illness, too. It would have been considered much worse than divorce. However, once when I felt scared about the escalating violence and I was worried that Mother might try to take my life at night in one of her rages, I tried to talk to the mother of one of my friends about it. She told me that my mother just had a "nervous disposition," and I wasn't trying hard enough to get along with her. I didn't talk to anyone else after that.

I tried to compensate for the lack of love at home by excelling at other things and gaining the approval of others. I became an overachiever at school. I was a cheerleader, on the student council, a reporter on the school paper, and I did well on the debate team. I also won blue ribbons at local fairs for my paintings, excelled at sports, did volunteer work at the senior center, and got good grades, which wasn't easy, since I had trouble reading. However, the more I accomplished and the more awards I earned, the angrier my mother became. I mistakenly believed that if I accomplished enough, I would finally gain her approval.

"You can fool everyone else, but you'll never fool me. I'm your mother, and I know what you are. You're a fake. If people like you, it's only because you've fooled them. If you win any awards, it's because you've tricked them," she said over and over, no matter what I achieved.

"That's not true," I'd say. Yet at the same time that I denied her accusations, I began to adopt her view.

I really wanted her to love me and to approve of me. I mistakenly thought that I just wasn't trying hard enough. I needed to try harder to get her approval. *She's my mother. She must know me better than anyone else. She must be right . . . there isn't anything of value within me. Although lots of people like me, I must have fooled them into liking me,* I thought.

But no matter what I accomplished, in her eyes it was

because I'd fooled people. Later, in the greater arena of my life, I tried to gain everyone's approval. However, when anyone liked me, I didn't have any respect for them because obviously I'd fooled them into liking me. I only respected people who *didn't* like me because obviously they were discerning enough to see the truth. I eventually realized that the person I really needed approval and love from was myself . . . and until that occurred, no one else could ever fill that void.

WHEN MY SCHOOL'S DRAMA DEPARTMENT staged Thornton Wilder's play *Our Town*, I was given a lead role. When my mother said she would come, I was excited. I kept looking out into the audience to see if she was there. Finally, peeking out from behind the curtain, I saw her silhouette at the back of the audience. My heart pounded. She liked theater, so surely when she saw me, she'd be proud of me.

When I got home, I was flushed with enthusiasm. We'd received a standing ovation, and I knew that I'd done a good job. As soon as I saw Mother's face, however, I knew that I was in trouble.

"I've never been so embarrassed in my life!" she lashed out.

"But Mother, everyone said I did well!" I pleaded.

"I couldn't even listen to you. All I could see were your shoes. They weren't polished. Everyone in town must be laughing at me. You didn't polish your shoes just to humiliate me!"

"No, honestly! I'm so sorry. I wasn't trying to embarrass you. I just forgot to polish my shoes."

After that, I tried to win her approval through art. I won some awards at the county fair, and I even sold some of my paintings to various people in town. I once worked for a month on a realistic landscape of a water mill and a pond. I thought it was the best thing that I'd ever done. A professional artist saw it and said that I had talent and maybe should even consider a career in art. When I showed the painting to my mother, she said it wasn't good art because it was realistic. She said good artists had "unfettered minds" so they never did realistic paintings; they only did abstract paintings. When I did abstract ones, she said they weren't any good because they weren't realistic.

Living with someone who is a paranoid schizophrenic is kind of like living in a science-fiction alternate universe where reality is constantly shifting. Sometimes I'd do something and it would be good, and another time I'd do the same thing, and I'd be punished. I never knew what the rules were.

When I was 16 and feeling particularly defeated, I decided to run away. One crisp autumn day, I surreptitiously packed some food and tucked $20 of my savings into my pocket. (I'd started babysitting when I was 12 and had saved almost everything I'd made.) After school I took off on my motorbike, which I'd bought with the money I'd saved. I didn't know where I was going or what I was going to do when I got there, I just knew I had to get away.

I rode past miles of corn and soybean fields, farmhouses with chickens running around in the yard, and a field that a farmer was mowing. The mown grass made the air smell fresh and clean. The freedom felt delicious. As I rode up a small rise, I spotted a small, overgrown cemetery perched on the top of the hill. I parked my bike and pushed opened a rusted ornate gate. Poking through the tall grasses were lichen-covered gravestones too weatherworn to read. It looked like no one had visited for a very long time. It was so still and serene, and I suddenly understood why my grandmother liked cemeteries so much.

I felt comforted by the headstones. The people buried beneath them had once been alive and maybe even struggled in life in ways that I had, but now they were at peace. I looked forward to that kind of tranquility. At the center of the cemetery was a large marble monument. I walked up to it and put my hands on its sun-warmed surface, then sat on it and bit into my peanut butter-sandwich. I felt so peaceful as I leaned back and watched the clouds float overhead. I thought about the person who was beneath the monument. I imagined that he probably liked my company.

I lay there for a long time and even napped for a while. When I awoke, the sun was setting and I started to feel cold. Getting back on my motorbike, I kept going down the road, looking for somewhere to spend the night. I wasn't dressed very warmly, and the temperature was dropping.

As soon as the sun fell beneath the horizon, I knew I had to quickly find somewhere to take shelter. In the distance was a big old barn. By the time I reached it, dusk had settled and it was hard to see clearly. The barn was in disrepair and didn't seem like it saw much use. I pressed myself through an opening between two loose boards. Rusted farm equipment was piled up and scattered over the floor. There wasn't anyplace I could sleep. In the corner a ladder led up to a loft. It was rickety, but I climbed up it. Straw was strewn haphazardly over the loft floor, but it was softer than sleeping on the ground, and the roof provided shelter. I was beginning to see my breath as I labored to pile some straw over me to keep warm. I lay in the straw, curled up tightly to maintain warmth, and gazed at the stars through an opening in some of the boards. I was cold, but I was free.

The next morning I was awakened by the sound of someone in the barn below me. Evidently, the barn wasn't abandoned. I could hear my heart pounding in my ears, and I prayed that no one would come up and find me. I could see the end of the ladder where it leaned up against the loft. I watched it, fervently praying that no one would climb up. *What if they see my motorbike?* I thought. *They'll know I'm up here.* My motorbike was leaning against the back of the barn, but it wasn't completely out of sight. The person below must have bumped against the ladder, because at one point, it wobbled slightly. I stopped breathing while I watched to see if he was climbing up.

Finally, I heard the barn door creak open and close. *What if he's still down there?* I thought. I was scared and wanted to leave, but I waited awhile longer. Then I heard a car drive away. Brushing off the straw and dirt, I scrambled down the ladder, raced out to my motorbike, and set off back home. I was afraid to run away. I didn't know where to go or what to do. Although it was difficult living with my mother, I wondered if running away would be any better. It was early when I got home. No one seemed to have noticed that I'd been gone all night. I jumped into the shower, dressed, went to school, and never told anyone what had happened.

I KEPT JUGGLING MY SCHOOL LIFE and my home life, but it got harder and harder. Mother would call the track coach and say, "How can you allow someone as devious as Denise on the team?" Then she would call the head of the chamber of commerce and spit out, "How can you let someone as underhanded as Denise represent Nordon at the art show?" She'd also call the mothers of my friends to tell them that they should know the kind of girl their daughters were hanging out with. Even though her actions hurt me, I didn't want to tell anyone that my mother was mentally ill. She was often cruel, but I felt protective of her. She was my mother.

Children in abusive homes usually adopt one of three survival modes. They can become rebellious, reclusive and withdrawn, or be people-pleasers. Brand and I became the latter, Heather was rebellious, and Gordon was withdrawn. Instead of clinging to each other for comfort, we each found a niche with our peers at school.

I was super "nice" and was even voted "nicest" in a high

school student poll. The smile I'd taught my face to form while living in Leipsic paid off. But I had two completely separate lives. In one I was a normal teenager interested in boys, music, makeup, and clothes, and in my other, I was trying to survive my mother.

Being "nice" helped me be elected a cheerleader. I loved jumping in the air and yelling, "Go, Wildcats, Go!" and "Fight! Fight! Fight!" at the top of my lungs. It was probably great therapy, as I could yell as loudly as I wanted. I especially loved Game Day, because I could wear my cheerleading clothes to school for the pep rally. It was my only good outfit, and I felt so pretty in it.

I didn't think anyone noticed that my clothes were secondhand or from Bargain City, so I was shocked when the teacher who was in charge of the cheerleaders took me aside to talk to me about my attire.

"Now that you're a cheerleader and you represent the school, you should do something about your clothes," she said.

I nodded but didn't say anything. I didn't know what to do, so I didn't do anything. I didn't have any extra money to buy more clothes, and I knew my mother would get upset if I asked her. I couldn't ask my grandmother for help, and my mother forbade contact with my other grandma in California, so I did nothing and hoped that the teacher wouldn't notice. Every time I saw her in the hallway at school, I ducked until she passed.

A few weeks later, she handed me an envelope to give to my mother. When I got home, I handed it to her. I got worried as I watched her scowl as she read it. She then took the letter and ripped it into little pieces.

"Your teachers have taken up a collection for your clothes!" she roared. "Take it back! Take all of it back! We don't need their charity!" she said as she thrust the envelope into my hand. Inside was a thick pile of money. The next day, I returned the envelope. Nothing more was ever said about my clothes.

There were so many times when I yearned to talk to my grandmother or write to her, but I was forbidden to do so. Mother hated Grandma as much as she did my father. She blamed her for everything from manipulating my father to "usurping" her authority while taking care of Brand and me. Calling my grandmother wasn't really an option. In those days, making a long-distance phone call was a big deal. It was expensive, and my family, like many others during those years, only used such calls for emergencies or for hurried greetings.

Boys were my savior. I don't mean that they were like knights in shining armor saving me from the evil stepmother (well, in my case, my *real* mother). What I mean is that my *preoccupation* with boys was my savior because it took my attention off my home life. Even in the eighth grade, at 13, boys liked blondes, so Susie Foster, my best friend, and I began coloring our hair. At first we used lemon juice and sat in the sun to lighten it. Susie and I then progressed to hydrogen peroxide, still thinking that we could claim to be natural blondes because we thought hydrogen peroxide was natural. Somehow our hair still wasn't blonde enough, so we used Nice 'n Easy every two weeks. It was years before I discovered that indeed, blondes didn't have more fun, and I reverted back to my natural dark color.

The sexual revolution was slow to hit Nordon. Anyway, I was a sexual late bloomer. I probably would have bloomed early, but the repressive atmosphere of the Midwest in America in the early '60s meant that "good girls" didn't have sex. The emotional scars left by my childhood also no doubt contributed to my reticence to explore my sexuality. In that era there were mixed messages sent to a girl who was curious about her sexuality. You were judged as "cold" if you didn't "put out," but if you did, then you were called a "slut." I decided that being cold sounded better than the alternative.

I GUESS THAT EVERYONE REMEMBERS his or her first kiss. I hope it wasn't as traumatic for Randy as it was for me, but I think it probably was.

One day Brand, who was ten and liked to tease me, hollered, "Denise, it's the phone for you! It's a boy." He strung out the word *boy* so it sounded like "boooooooy."

I made a face at him and grabbed the phone out of his hands. "Hello?"

"Denise?"

"Yes?"

"Um. This is Randy."

"Hi, Randy." Even though I was 16, I felt shy talking to boys I liked. I often didn't know what to say.

"Um. Do you want to go to the movies with me on Friday?"

"Sure," I answered.

"Okay. I'll pick you up at 6:30."

"Okay."

"Bye."

Randy's family had been farming for many generations. He was 17 and not very good-looking, but he was tall, wholesome, and kind. I was really looking forward to going out with him.

I was so excited that I spent hours getting ready. Although I already had straight hair, I spent an hour ironing it to make it even straighter. All of my friends did it. I carefully laid my hair on the ironing board, placed a piece of wax paper over it, and then ironed over the paper. It was a challenge not to burn my head. After my hair was done, I began to put on my makeup. I applied and reapplied black eyeliner. I wanted to get the line perfect.

When the doorbell rang, I raced for the door yelling, "Bye!" and was out the door before Randy could meet my mother. I never knew what kind of mood she'd be in.

The line at the theater was long. We finally found our seats and settled in, but I was so nervous that I couldn't concentrate on the movie. Randy's hand started on his lap, but I kept noticing that little by little, it crept closer to mine, but he never actually held my hand.

After the movie, Randy drove me home. He pulled up into the driveway, then jumped out of the car to run around and open my door.

"I had a really nice time, Randy."

"I did, too," he said as he leaned forward.

My heart was beating so hard as he moved closer and closer. Suddenly he reached forward, pulled me toward him, and locked his lips onto mine.

I screamed and jumped away.

"What's wrong?" He looked so worried.

"Well, it's just not what I expected. I mean . . . oh, I'm so sorry, but it was wet—like a fish," I said, wiping my mouth. "I didn't know that kisses were so wet. I thought it would be like when my grandma kisses me . . . you know, dry."

"I'm so sorry," he said, backing off and looking frightened. "I should have asked you. I'm sorry."

"It's okay. I just didn't expect it to be so wet," I said, as I turned and ran up the steps into my house.

On that night of my first kiss, I would have been shocked at how quickly I embraced the sexual revolution of the '60s a few years later.

CHAPTER FIVE

The Land of Golden Light
(1967)

I loved my motorbike. She was a sweetheart—a little Honda 50, with about as much power as a push lawnmower—but I just adored her. I spent every weekend cleaning her with a toothbrush. When my life became too hard, I would get on her and drive until I found a wood lot. These small copses of trees were remnants of the great forests that once covered Ohio before they were chopped down for agriculture. The smell of the dank earth of the woods, the way the wind blew through the leaves, the sudden rainstorm that flattened the grasses and made the air tingle with freshness . . . all of this brought me solace from my mother's tirades.

In the summer on early mornings, I used to ride my motorbike out of town where I would hide it at the edge of a grove and spend hours alone under the trees. Lying on my back, I opened my arms to welcome the warmth of the sun that filtered through the leaves above. As my mind wandered, I saw images and visions woven into the design of interlacing branches. Through holes in the treetops, I watched clouds float by, and I made up stories about cloud dragons. Sometimes I lay facedown to smell the earth up close, and to observe the moss and ancient lichens. My motorbike brought me the freedom to escape to the trees, but in the end, she almost brought me death.

I ONLY HAD ONE MORE YEAR of high school. I knew that I wanted to continue my education, but I wasn't sure which college was right for me. I found a small school in Ohio that seemed like a good fit, but I felt that I should visit first before I applied. My mother didn't have the time or the inclination to take me around to look at it, but she agreed that I could ride my motorbike there. I had an easy journey, and once there, talked to professors and administrators. I spent the night with some students I met while visiting, and the next morning started back for home.

As I puttered along on my motorbike, I dreamed about how, in only one more year, I'd be able to move away from home, away from my mother. However, that feeling shattered instantly as a car jammed into my bike from behind and threw me into the shallow ditch next to the road. Stabs of pain jolted through my body, but I watched the driver turn his car around. I thought he was coming back to help me. Horror overtook me when he pulled out his gun and aimed it at me through his open car window.

With methodical precision, he squeezed the trigger. I heard a loud explosion, and for a split second I wondered if I'd exploded. The pain was piercing as I fell to the ground. Every breath was excruciating, and my lungs burned with the intensity of raging flames. The bullet passed through my abdomen, shattering my spleen and adrenal gland. It ricocheted off my spine (I still have a bullet-sized hole in my spine) and then passed through my small intestine, diaphragm, and stomach. The bullet then nicked the aorta and penetrated my left lung, collapsing it. (In subsequent surgeries, I lost my left kidney, and a six-inch tube was inserted to replace part of my aorta.)

All I thought about, as I lay bleeding on the ground, was how mad my mother was going to be that I got shot. I learned later that Mother *was* furious when she first heard. She was angry because she thought that people would judge her for letting me go on my own to the college. I was right to worry about her rage . . . it lasted for months.

The next thing that happened was blocked from my memory for 15 years, until it spontaneously flashed back to me in vivid, wrenching detail. Finding out what happened during those missing minutes helped me understand so much.

My eyes were closed as I lay on the gravel. Every breath was painful, and every sound was exaggerated. I heard a car door open and close, and then I heard footsteps coming closer to me. Next, I heard a sound that seemed like a gun cocking. I forced my eyes open and looked up into my assailant's eyes. They were wild and frightening, betraying his fear and heightened excitement. To this day, I don't fully understand what happened next. Maybe I was in so much shock that my natural reactions were suspended for a while. I don't know, but I'm certain that what happened at that point saved my life.

Looking into his frenzied eyes, for some unknown reason all I felt was compassion. I didn't feel fear or anger, just love and a deep understanding for his pain. A kind of internal struggle seemed to occur within him, as his hand holding the gun began to shake. It seemed as if part of him desperately wanted to shoot me again, yet another part couldn't shoot the woman who was looking at him with such kindness.

Like a balloon collapsing as air escapes, the intensity exhaled from his body. His arm dropped and, visibly agitated, he turned around, got in his car, slammed the door, and drove off.

My body wanted to give in to the relentless throbbing pain, but I knew that if I was going to survive, I would need to get help. I began to crawl slowly up toward the road. I made it a few feet and then collapsed. Then I crawled some more and collapsed. Every foot gained was paid for in pain and exhaustion, but I kept telling myself, *I've got to get to the road to get help.*

When I finally got close to the road, I knew that someone would find me. For years I thought the man who found me was a farmer, but doing research for this book, I recently discovered that, in fact, he was a salesman on his way home from work. I remember how his face suddenly became pale as he looked down at me.

"I've . . . been . . . shot. Please . . . call . . . my . . . mother," I whispered as he leaned over me. At the same time that I feared her anger, I yearned for her comfort.

At that moment, the salesman heard a vehicle coming down the road. Jumping up, he flagged down the car, which was driven by a couple of local teenagers.

"Go get an ambulance, quick! There's a girl here who's been shot! Go now! I'll stay with her. Hurry!" he said, as he watched the boys race to their car and tear down the road toward town.

He grabbed a sleeping bag out of his car and kneeled beside me. Rolling me on my back, he placed the sleeping bag over my body. As he removed his hands, he stared at them in disbelief. They were covered in blood. "Oh my God!" he whispered.

"Please . . . get . . . my . . . mother," I said, barely able to speak.

When the ambulance arrived, the medics looked shocked when they saw the bullet hole and the blood. It was highly unusual for someone to get shot in that part of the country at that time. As I lay in the back of the ambulance, I looked out the window and watched the tops of trees sail by beneath an August blue sky. The sound of the siren seemed far away and distant. Strangely, it was all beautiful. The sun was setting, and the lingering light filled the ambulance with a warm glow.

When we reached the hospital, the wailing sound of the ambulance blended into the frantic voices of the emergency hospital staff shouting, "She's been shot! She's been shot!"

A nurse in the emergency room pulled out some scissors and was about to cut my dress off my body. "No!" I somehow managed to shout. At the time, I thought my mother would be mad at me if my dress were cut. Even though it hurt to move, I sat up so they could pull my dress over my head. (Months later, I repaired the bullet hole in the dress and continued to wear it.)

The hospital lights were harsh, almost blinding. The voices of the staff sounded deafeningly loud. Each sharp wave of pain seared through me harder than the one before. As I lay back down, everything began to get dark and still. The pain subsided, and I found myself being drawn into a womblike darkness. Suddenly, the darkness burst, like a black bubble, to reveal brilliant, golden light. It was so beautiful! Everywhere around me, into infinity, was shimmering light. Infused in the luminosity was pure, sweet music. This symphony of light and sound ebbed and flowed throughout the universe and pervaded my being until I merged into it.

I know it doesn't make sense, but I was made of light and sound that flowed into eternity. And it all seemed completely natural *and completely familiar.* I was home.

I tried to look down at myself, but I didn't have a body. My "self" was everywhere, without limits of time or space. I wasn't separated from the universe. Somehow that didn't seem unusual. Everything seemed more real than I had ever experienced. It was as if my teenage life up to that time had only been an illusion . . . a dream. Just like when you wake up in the morning and your dream, which had seemed so real, begins to fade into the "reality" of the day, my entire life up to that point seemed to be nothing more than the passing whisper of the wind.

There was no past, no future, because all time flowed in a continuous, everlasting "now." I tried to think of the past, but I couldn't. It just didn't exist. The past and the future folded into the glowing light to form an infinite present.

I wish with all my heart that I could take you there, if only for a moment, because infused in this exquisite "now-ness" was a most perfect love. It was the love that lies at the very heart of our being, a love that is as natural as breathing. It was a love that goes beyond all boundaries, like a vast, unlimited ocean, penetrating every cell and molecule of my being. The love I experienced wasn't the type that you can fall into or out of. If God is love, then in those few moments beyond death's door, I experienced divine love. It was without boundaries and indescribable in its sweetness.

Glowing and shimmering as it flowed to the distant horizon, a golden river of light manifested itself at my feet. Stepping into its warmth, I knew that I would never return to my earthly life when I reached the other side. I wouldn't have to be trapped in a body that was damaged and in excruciating pain. I could escape the trials of my childhood and the abuse of my parents.

As I felt its fluid light moving gently on either side of me, I dipped my fingers into the river. As I raised my hands, the light clung to them for a moment, making them radiant and luminous.

As I walked across the river, part of me wanted to let go and dissolve into it. I wanted to surrender to that powerful current, meld my being with its greater force. Where would the river take me? To the far shores of the universe? To the center of the heart of God? I didn't care. Yet I could feel the pull to the far shore. I knew that I had to make it to the other side of the river to be free. Every step took me closer to my true home. But before I could reach it, I heard a deep voice reverberate inside my mind: *You may not stay here. There is something you need to do.*

I screamed, "No-o-o-o-o! No! No!" I felt as if I had been lassoed and was being dragged back to my physical body. "No! I don't want to go back. It's too hard. I'm not ready! No!"

I had a spontaneous memory of my cousins on the Oklahoma ranch practicing their calf-roping skills on me. I know now that the "rope" I felt around my middle was my "astral cord" that was pulling me back to my body. The harder I struggled, the more insistent that "rope" was around my midsection, steadily yet firmly pulling me back. (In ancient times, it was believed that each person's soul was connected to the body by an invisible cord. As long as it was intact, the person's soul could leave the body; however, once it was severed, the body died.)

WHEN I AWOKE, I WAS IN A HOSPITAL BED, fighting for my life. My injuries were extensive, as both the gunman's bullet and the impact of his car had seriously wounded me. The doctors said it was one of the most difficult surgical cases they'd ever worked on. They described my recovery to the newspapers as "a miracle." Day after day, I struggled not only with physical pain but also with my grief about having to come back to my life. I wanted to stay in that beautiful place.

Then came the nightmares—horrible, terrifying ones. I felt as if I'd touched heaven, and now I was experiencing hell. The daily nurse logs chronicled these nightly occurrences: "Patient has nightmares that seem to get her quite upset." "Patient awakened by nightmares again, seems very anxious." "Patient had very bad dream."

Even the local newspaper reported that I was having nightmares:

> "We are dealing with a sadist." This was the Sheriff's comment [about the gunman] concerning his

investigations of the sniper shooting of 17-year-old
Denise Fortner . . . Miss Fortner is still in very critical
condition . . . one of the problems faced by her doctors
is that the youngster has frequent nightmares about her
terrifying experience.

These weren't ordinary nightmares. They were real, and
they weren't about getting shot. Even when I was awake, I
began to see listless, gray people wandering the hospital corridors. Their faces were shrunken and ashen like living corpses.
Perhaps they were people who had died in the hospital. I didn't
know. However, they seemed to be unaware of me. I saw them
when I was wide awake. But the most terrifying were the other
creatures that also wandered through the hospital corridors.
They were smaller than humans and were grotesque in appearance. Their bodies were misshapen, almost hunched over, with
a troll-like appearance.

Even as I write about these creatures, it's hard to think of
them without being scared. Sometimes they would sit on my
bed and stare at me with craven eyes. One particularly repulsive
creature used to point his finger, and blood would shoot out of
it. The blood would dissolve in the air just before it hit my body.
He would then laugh hysterically. The entry in the nurses' log
states: "Patient crying, states that 'people' [the creatures] were
coming in her room and wouldn't let her sleep, and she had to
fight them off."

One morning I found myself having a nightmare about
these creatures. I remember thinking desperately, *This is only
a dream . . . all I have to do is open my eyes and they'll disappear!*
However, when I opened my eyes, they were still there! I quickly
closed my eyes and opened them again, thinking they'd be
gone. But no such luck. There they were, laughing in macabre
delight, as if they had pulled a great joke on me. Morning sun

streamed in the window; I could see everything clearly in the hospital room. Yet at the same time, the creatures were there, laughing mirthlessly. I started screaming, and a nurse rushed in to comfort me.

Over the years, I've had time to think about what those creatures were. Of course, there's always the possibility that as a result of my heightened fear of being attacked, I hallucinated the vacuous people and the creatures, but it was all too real for me to believe that. I think that somehow, in my moments on the other side, I became an intermediary into unseen realms. I believe that the "human" forms I saw were ghosts—lost souls not knowing where they were or how to get "home." They'd probably died in the hospital. I believe that the creatures that tormented me were astral entities or beings that reside in an unseen realm. Astral beings can be energized by the strong negative emotions that exist in hospitals as a result of the life-and-death dramas that unfold there.

My mother and Heather visited me often. Once I tried to talk to them about the creatures, but it was obvious that they thought I was just having nightmares. My Los Angeles grandparents didn't want to upset my mother, so they didn't call or visit, but Grandma sent me a card to say that her whole church was praying for me. My father visited one time for only 15 minutes. After he left, I evidently became hysterical, according to the nurse's notes. I told the nurses that I didn't like my father, but I didn't say why. I think that the memories of the sexual abuse rose to the surface and were raw and exposed in my vulnerable state.

Outside the hospital, a police guard was posted 24 hours a day. Going back into old records and newspaper reports of the shooting, I realized that there was good reason for that guard. Right after I was shot, the local paper reported:

Reportedly, Denise was able to tell her mother that she got a good look at her assailant "and will never forget his face." Sheriff C. says that when Denise is able, he hopes that she will be able to draw on her artistic talent to sketch a picture of the sniper's face.

I did get a good look at the gunman, but this was a pretty dumb thing to put in the newspaper, *especially in the same article that listed my home address!* Now my assailant knew that I could identify him. The sheriff and a number of other police officials continued to parade through my room, asking me what I'd seen. My mother had told the police that, on the day after I was shot, I told her that the gunman had wild, "crazy eyes." However, when the police asked me what I saw a few days later, I described a man with sunglasses. I couldn't remember seeing him without any sunglasses. My mother was angry with me because she said I made her look like a liar to the police.

"Why did you tell the police that you don't remember seeing him without sunglasses? Are you trying to make me look like a liar?!" she raged.

"Honestly, I don't remember saying that, Mother. If you say I told you, I'm sure I did, but I just don't recall it. I'm so sorry. I don't have many memories of that day."

It was many years later, during that spontaneous recall of the missing minutes, that I realized I actually had seen the shooter without his sunglasses. For 15 years my mind had suppressed the memory of the gunman getting out of the car and standing over me. When he pulled the visor off his glasses, I could see the "crazy" look in his eyes.

During my time in the hospital, my usual defenses were down, and the subconscious beliefs about myself that stemmed from my mother's negative opinion of me came to the surface. My mother constantly telling me I was a fake must have imprinted onto my consciousness. Once I said to my doctor, "Dr. White, I wasn't really shot. I'm faking it."

"You're not faking it. You were shot," he replied.

"No. Don't let me fool you. I faked the whole thing."

Dr. White couldn't convince me that I'd really been shot, so finally he went out and brought back the bullet to show me. (I'm not sure why he had the bullet and not the police, or maybe he used another bullet to try to convince me.)

I looked carefully at the bullet and then said, "Okay, maybe I did get shot . . . but I'm faking the pain."

He looked at me with deep sympathy and said, "Denise, not only is your pain real, but I've been amazed by your bravery and your strength."

ONE NIGHT IN PARTICULAR, I felt neither brave nor strong. Amidst the nightmares, the 24-hour police guard, and my mother's tantrums, I experienced a miracle. It was the middle of the night, and I was in extreme pain. I squeezed my eyes shut, as the slightest exertion seemed to tear me open. I couldn't get away from it; it rolled over me wave after wave. I silently pleaded for someone to help me.

I heard footsteps as someone came into the room. Then I felt a hand gently slip into mine. Immediately the pain subsided, and a wonderful feeling of safety flooded my being. I opened my eyes, expecting to see the nurse or doctor who had kindly come in to comfort me, but the room was empty!

I could still feel the warmth and texture of a hand squeezing mine, but I couldn't see anyone! A feeling of peace washed over me as I fell into a deep sleep. After that, whenever I was in pain, comforting hands came to soothe me in the night hours. Sometimes the hand felt male, sometimes female. I particularly remember a very small, childlike hand holding mine. I was so grateful for the presence of what I now believe were angels, like the ones my grandmother told me she and my grandfather believed in.

Since that time many years ago, angels have come into my life in many forms. Usually they come invisibly, as they did when I was in the hospital, but sometimes they come in a physical form, looking human but with a heavenly presence. Most of the time, though, they come as a sudden insight or intuition.

My injuries were so severe that initially the doctors had very little hope for my survival. My parents were told that I wouldn't live long, and if I did, I would be incapacitated for my entire life. However, my experiences in the "land of golden light" ignited a healing force inside me, and I recovered very quickly. (It was the same energy that I was able to call upon for my work in later years as a healer.)

Even though the gunman's assault had been terrifying and my body had sustained substantial damage, what I lost doesn't begin to compare with what I gained. Something mysterious and magical had occurred that changed the course of my life forever. My perception of life completely and irrevocably shifted.

In one way, I was a fairly normal teenager concerned about boys, the latest hairstyles, and the newest Beatles song. I still cared about these things; however, after I was shot, my view of the world changed. When I would chat with someone, instead of seeing our differences, I experienced the unity that existed between us. I began to feel a deep love for almost everyone. Sometimes this was challenging for my friends because it wasn't "cool" to say "I love you" and "I think that you're great."

I no longer thought that my life began at birth and ended at death. I realized that "I" was not my body, and "I" would not die when my body did. I knew that life was eternal. Time no longer seemed linear and finite because I perceived the universe around me as malleable and changeable. I could sense and see that everything on the planet was surging with energy and life-force. I began to realize that all life was interconnected, for every human being, deer, fern, mountain, pebble—everything—was a part of a great tapestry of light and sound, rather than each a separate object.

Although many wounds remained—not only the physical injuries from the assault, but also emotional ones from my childhood—I "knew" that nothing was an accident. I knew that my life was guided and there was a higher purpose to my existence, even if I wasn't consciously aware of what it was.

Growing up with a mother and father who believed in science rather than God, I was taught that the only true reality was the one that you could measure in physical terms. However, after the shooting, I viewed the world in a much different way than my parents did. I began to perceive radiant, glowing light around supposedly inanimate objects. My vision was altered, and I began to see light emanating from people, plants, and objects, which I later learned was known as an "aura." Every object on the planet was not just physical matter but was also infused with vibrant light and varying frequencies of sound. I had glimpses of this realm as a child during my times in nature, but this was more vivid and intense.

Once when my mother and siblings were visiting me in the hospital, I asked, "Where is that beautiful music coming from?"

"What music?" said Heather.

"Can't you hear it? It's wonderful."

Heather just rolled her eyes. I was increasingly aware that I needed to be careful not to tell people when I heard music or saw apparitions in the hospital.

Once, a nurse took me in a wheelchair to the hospital lawn to get some fresh air. As I sat in the sunshine, I began to hear a lovely, soft melody. I looked around and realized it was coming from the grass. Every blade had a luminous light around it and was emitting its own tone, creating an almost angelic chorus.

As I looked closely at a small tree, I could see light radiating from its trunk and its leaves, and I could hear the "song" of the nutrients rising from the earth. Each leaf seemed to be in a reverie as it unfurled itself to the sun. Even the earth beneath my feet pulsed with a gentle cadence. At the time, I had great difficulty understanding how the nurse couldn't feel and see the overwhelming beauty around us.

I was privileged to be able to glimpse such a brilliant world. It was a world that was natural and real, different from the one I'd known before. As I sat in my wheelchair on the hospital lawn, absorbing the sun, I knew that we were part of a vibrant, living universe, and we couldn't hurt another without hurting ourselves. It was hard to comprehend how anyone could be cruel or violent.

CHAPTER SIX

Of Roots Lost and Found
(1967–1968)

August 25, 1967: 20 days after I'd been shot, I was discharged from the hospital. The transition to my home wasn't easy. I was still weak and needed to rest. The police were covertly watching our home in the event that the gunman showed up. There was concern that he might try to find me to stop me from identifying him. My mother was upset about the surveillance, so she walked up and down in front of our home with a placard that said, "I know that we are being watched."

I think that all the events surrounding the shooting exacerbated her paranoia. Then she ran away for three days. While she was gone, Heather helped me change my bandages. When she came back, she was angry that I'd brought this into her life. It didn't occur to me that my mother's actions were irrational; I just felt really guilty about making her so upset.

My body healed quickly, and my life returned to normal—or as normal as it could be. I was glad when I was able to go to school to get away from home. However, a police guard was posted outside my classroom, which was definitely *not* normal. I think some of my classmates thought the guard was cool and his presence added some adventure to the mundane events of school life. Other students found the guard a frightening reminder that the seemingly safe haven of Nordon wasn't so safe after all. The police had no luck finding the gunman, and they eventually relinquished the guard. However, two months after the shooting, I really wished that I still had my police escort.

AFTER SCHOOL ONE OCTOBER AFTERNOON, I decided to walk to the library to do some research for a book report. On my way there, I felt exhilarated by the day. Summer had yielded to autumn. Days were warm, yet the air was crisp and fresh. The trees were aflame with red, orange, and yellow leaves. I loved the sound they made as they crunched beneath my feet. Everyone burned their leaves in the gutters along the street, so there was a wonderful scent in the air.

I felt him before I saw him. A chill ran up my spine as a car pulled up alongside of me. I glanced over my shoulder and saw the man who had shot me. He had sunglasses on and his head was lowered, but it was him. *And I knew that he recognized me!* My heart pounded as I took off running with every ounce of my strength. I didn't look back; I just ran until I was safely inside the library. I knew he couldn't have done anything to me, as we were in town, but it seemed like a warning to me. He seemed to be covertly threatening me to stay quiet.

When I later talked informally to a policeman about the event, I was asked why I didn't get the license-plate number. The policeman didn't understand that we had different goals. His agenda was to nail the assailant; mine was to stay alive. In that moment, I hadn't cared about the number. I just wanted to get as far away from him as I could.

After that, I could feel his presence everywhere—prowling like a caged cougar. Sometimes he seemed close, sometimes farther away. I could feel him lurking . . . pacing . . . waiting for the right time. I was determined that he wouldn't find me alone again. I didn't go anywhere by myself after that. I walked with my best friend, Susie, to school, and we went home together. We'd go to the library together, and we often double-dated. Susie was my constant companion for my senior year. I felt safe when we were together, and for this I'm still eternally grateful.

THE SHOOTING WAS HARD ON EVERYONE in my family. My mother got worse, and this made it difficult for my sister and brothers to put up with her moods. Heather had grown tall, intelligent, and independent, and she was doing her best to keep the household together amidst the chaos caused by the shooting. Yet Mother could instantly crumple her spirit with a few sharp indictments, repeatedly calling her a "spineless puppet" and telling Heather that she had no mind of her own. Heather and I were close in age, so I felt closer to her than to the boys, but Mother's constant blaming of me for my sister's deeds put a widening wedge in our relationship.

Gordon retreated further into himself, becoming quiet and withdrawn. He said little but watched with a wisdom and sadness far beyond his years. Brand wanted to find the man who'd shot his big sister and kill him. He got a book on karate and began practicing on his own. He was also homesick for Grandma and Grandpa, but he learned to never mention them to Mother because her reaction was swift and violent. I only remember that one quick visit from my father, and I don't ever recall him calling or visiting us again.

IN LATE OCTOBER, I received a call from the police. They said they'd found the man who'd shot me. They had an abundance of evidence that indicated that he was the assailant. All I had to do was identify him. They said it would be easy. They were wrong.

I love (and hate) our justice system. As flawed as it is, it's probably one of the best on Earth. Yet, it's an immensely imperfect system. It doesn't protect the rights of victims, and it doesn't always protect the rights of those who are accused, either. The law says that you're innocent until proven guilty, but that's only the spirit of the law. It's not the actuality. Grave travesties of injustice occurred for me and for the man who shot me. Even though I knew he was guilty, there were a number of times when his rights were trampled on. Everyone, even guilty people, deserves to be treated fairly.

As I go back into my memories of the events that surrounded this time in my life, I've been astonished that my recollection has been so accurate. After I left Nordon, I never wanted to think about what happened, and for this reason, I thought that my memory would have blurred, erased, or at least changed my remembrance of these events. I recently read court transcripts and newspaper reports for the first time in 37 years, however, and there wasn't one instance where something surprised me or differed from my memory. I discovered that my recollection of these events is vivid and specific.

The police told me that they were going to take me to the Shell service station managed by the man who shot me. "You'll be in a disguise, so you don't have to worry. And if he tries anything, we'll be close by and we can stop him. All you have to do is identify him."

My hair was tied back and covered with a scarf, and I was told to wear sunglasses. However, it was night. This wasn't Hollywood where people wore sunglasses at night. *No one* wore sunglasses after dark in small farm towns at that time, yet I was told that was to be my "disguise."

If anything, these sunglasses will make me stand out! I thought in dismay.

I was also told that he might be armed. *Great!* I told myself, *I'm going to stick out like a sore thumb, and he might have his gun on him.*

The police told me not to worry, but I couldn't see any way that I could be protected if anything happened quickly. If the gunman recognized me and tried to attack me, there was no way they could stop him fast enough. These were small-town police who usually had nothing bigger to deal with than a stolen bicycle or a domestic disturbance. This situation was way out of their league. But I kept reasoning with myself that they were adults; thus, they knew what they were doing . . . but inside myself I didn't really feel that they did. The last bit of advice I was given was: "Act normal."

Act normal! Oh sure, I normally go into a gas station at night with sunglasses on, knowing that I might get shot again, I thought, but I did try to do as they asked.

A man came out to pump gas. He had some similarities to the man who shot me, but it wasn't him. I carefully studied his features. It definitely wasn't the man who shot me. A wave of relief rolled over me.

As the police drove me away from the gas station, I told them, "That's not him." They said that I was wrong, and were emphatic that the attendant was indeed the man who shot me.

"He has some similar features, but that's not him." I shook my head adamantly. Being a people-pleaser, I didn't want to disappoint them, and they were so sure that he was the shooter. But at the same time, I wasn't going to falsely identify someone. The police were very disgruntled with my refusal to single out the service-station attendant as the gunman.

It was unfair to the suspect to ask a scared 17-year-old girl to identify someone while she was wearing dark sunglasses at night. It was equally unfair for the police to try to coerce me to agree that the man I'd seen was the one who'd shot me. To my credit, I was unwilling to identify the station attendant as my assailant in spite of the pressure. It was a good thing I didn't acquiesce, because the police had made a big mistake.

It turned out that the manager of the station, who was the true suspect, wasn't there that night and the man that I was told to identify was, in fact, an employee. That same night, the police also took Patricia, a woman who had recognized the man following my motorbike, to the Shell station for her to identify the attendant. She also wore sunglasses. I think the police had watched too much *Dragnet* on television. I kept expecting them to say, "Just the facts, ma'am. Just the facts," like Joe Friday. As we sat together, Patricia and I both agreed that the station attendant wasn't the right man. She told me that the man she had seen following me was S., a man whom she'd worked with at General Motors. Again, it's unfair to a suspect to let witnesses get together to corroborate information.

After the police discovered that they'd made a mistake, they then drove to the station manager's home and arrested him on a John Doe warrant. At the county jail, he was placed alone in a bare cell-like room and was forced to sit on a chair facing a door that opened onto a hallway. Patricia and I were taken to the jail. We were told that they'd made a mistake at the service station, but *this* was the right man.

First, they had Patricia walk down the hall to look into the room where S. was seated.

"Hi, Patricia," said S. quietly.

"Hi," said Patricia in a small, frightened voice. She turned abruptly and bolted down the hall.

Then I walked down the hall. As I turned to look into the tiny room, an instant feeling of revulsion rose up in my body and lodged in my throat. It was *him*. I knew it was the man who had attacked me. He stared at me and then gave me an oily smile, seeming to take a sick pleasure in my fear and discomfort. I felt unclean and nauseated, and I wanted to get away as fast as I could.

I was glad they'd caught him but, at the same time, the

way the police organized the confrontation was grossly unfair to S. (and to me). Whatever happened to two-way mirrors? (But this was farm country . . . police stations there probably didn't even have them.) First, Patricia and I were allowed to discuss the accused's characteristics prior to our identification. She knew him, so she could adequately describe him. Second, we were told that this man *was* the assailant. We weren't shown a lineup. Third, the identification occurred in the jail, which is not an environment conducive to the perception of innocence. Last, the suspect had no counsel.

The fundamental constitutional rights of the suspect were denied, and for this I'm ashamed of our justice system. Nevertheless, there was no doubt in my mind. The man sitting in that cell *was* the man who shot me. I knew because I recognized his features. I also knew because of the severe physical reaction I had upon seeing him. The spontaneous feeling I had when I first saw him was immediate and debilitating.

Later, I had even greater reason to decry the justice system . . . when it was turned on *me*.

WHEN THE GUNMAN WAS BROUGHT TO TRIAL, the evidence was overwhelmingly against him. I had identified him as the man who shot me, Patricia had identified him as the man following behind me, and he closely matched the description and sketch that I gave to the police artist while in the hospital. I had identified the automobile that hit me as a large, dark blue car; and he had a large, dark blue car. *The blue paint from his car was an exact match to the blue paint on my motorbike, where it had been hit*, and there was an indentation in his car that would have occurred when it slammed into my bike.

The bullet in my body matched bullets from his gun, according to a ballistics expert from the Bureau of Criminal Investigation. The defense attorneys hired their own ballistics "expert" who was paid $500—a lot of money at that time—for a perfunctory examination of the bullet and the gun. Under oath, he said he spent over two hours examining the evidence at the Bureau of Criminal Identification labs and testified that the bullet wasn't from S.'s gun. However, it was later proven that he actually spent only 30 minutes in the lab and his microscope was out of focus the whole time. In other words, he lied under oath for money. (I know this frequently happens in criminal trials, but at the time, I was severely disillusioned.)

Additionally, S. couldn't account for his whereabouts during the time when I was shot. Despite this overwhelming evidence, the man who I was certain shot me eventually was released . . . and I was vilified.

Since the defense attorney didn't have a case or supporting evidence to free his client, he resorted to character defamation—he slandered me, the victim. Because of the rumors that the defense spread about my character, the same town that had rallied to help me while I was in the hospital spurned me with vehemence.

I received hate calls. My friends' parents forbade their children from talking to me. When I walked down the sidewalk of downtown Nordon, people walking toward me lowered their heads and crossed the street rather than walk past me.

These people felt that I had betrayed their trust, but at the time it was very hard for me to cope with all the hateful energy focused toward me. I hadn't done anything wrong, yet I was the person on trial.

I was accused of being a "drug addict, a Communist, and slut" who consorted with "men of different races." After the case, I ran into a juror, and he confided in me that knowing what kind of a person I was had tipped the scales in favor of the suspect.

At the time of the defense's false accusations, I was an

honor student, a class officer, and had been a cheerleader. In some ways, I was a normal hometown girl. I had never smoked a cigarette, could barely spell "Communism," and had only been kissed a few times, let alone having multiple sexual partners.

However, even if everything that I was accused of was true (which it wasn't), it shouldn't have had any bearing on the case. Later on in my life, I came to believe that no one can make you feel like a victim unless you allow it. I embrace the words of Eleanor Roosevelt who said that no one can make you feel bad . . . only you have that capability. At the time, however, I did feel like a victim, betrayed by the very system and people sworn to protect me.

THE CHARGE OF BEING A "DRUG ADDICT and a Communist" stemmed from an event that had occurred near the college I had chosen to visit the day before I was shot. On that day, after I talked to administrators and walked around the beautiful campus, I fell in love with it all. My heart was set on attending the school. I didn't know how I would pay for it, but I figured that I had a year to work that out if I was accepted.

My motorbike, which wasn't running well, needed a bit of work before I began my journey home the next day. I pulled out my little tool kit and my owner's manual and started fiddling with it on the campus lawn next to the parking lot. Daniel, a man who used to be a student at the college, saw me struggling with my motorbike and stopped to give me some advice. He once had a motorcycle and knew about mechanics. I was grateful for his help. He looked at my little set of tools and laughed. A few minutes later, he came back with some better tools, sat down on the lawn, and took over. While he worked, I told him that I was considering going to school there and had come to visit. He said it was a good school and he thought I'd be happy there.

After he repaired my bike, Daniel invited me to have dinner with him and his girlfriend, who had also been a student at the college. I enthusiastically accepted his invitation, as it seemed a great opportunity to learn more about the school.

Before heading to Daniel's house for dinner, I checked into the college accommodations. I had been assigned a room with a student already enrolled. When I took my small overnight bag to the room and knocked on the door, the girl inside cussed at me through the door. A student passing in the hall warned me that my would-be roommate for the night was a bit crazy and had a tendency to attack people.

I thanked her for the warning. Because of my experiences with my mother, I didn't want to have anything to do with crazy, violent people. I checked my purse to see if I had enough money for a motel. I wasn't quite sure what to do, but I felt certain that Daniel and his girlfriend could recommend something.

When I arrived at their apartment, Daniel introduced me to Marianne, his girlfriend. I hadn't met anyone like her before. There was a kind of gracious depth that radiated from her. I liked her instantly. She welcomed me into her home with such warmth that I felt like I was an honored guest.

As I helped her prepare dinner, Marianne told me about the college and the surrounding area. She asked me about my interests, and I told her I wanted to study art, psychology, and biology. As we sat down for dinner, a friend showed up at the front door. After introductions were made, the conversation turned to the war in Vietnam.

I was amazed by what they were saying. In Nordon, everyone seemed to think that the President knew what he was doing and anyone who opposed the war was just plain anti-American and a Communist. (In Nordon in 1967, being a Communist was one of the worst things that you could accuse someone of being.)

Over dinner, Marianne, Daniel, and their friend discussed the injustice of the Vietnam War. They talked about wartime atrocities and illegal actions that our government was taking against protestors. I'd never heard opinions like that expressed in Nordon. My new friends had opened my eyes to a whole different way of perceiving the news. Daniel and Marianne seemed to be very caring people who were genuinely concerned about the actions of our government.

After dinner, Marianne said, "We're going to have a smoke. Would you like some?"

"Oh, I don't smoke," I said. My mother was a chain smoker, and I hated the smell of cigarettes. My clothes and everything in our home always smelled like smoke.

Marianne laughed. "This isn't a cigarette. It's marijuana." She pulled out some rolling papers and began sprinkling some dried plant matter into it. My grandfather used to roll his own cigarettes, so I was familiar with these papers. I'd heard of marijuana, but I didn't know anyone who had ever tried it. I can't imagine that it was even available in Nordon at that time.

My eyes must have gotten wide, because she said, "Don't worry, this isn't *Reefer Madness*." (She was referring to a propaganda movie made in 1936—now a cult classic—in which high school students smoke marijuana, play "evil" jazz music, become criminals, commit murder, and finally are committed to an insane asylum.)

"It's okay. You don't have to smoke it. Just try it," she said as she inhaled, held the smoke in her lungs, and exhaled slowly. She then handed the joint to Daniel.

"It won't hurt you. This is nature's gift to us. Just try it," said Daniel, as he also inhaled from the hand-rolled joint.

I wasn't sure it was a good idea, but Marianne and Daniel were so nice that I thought it wouldn't hurt to try it. Marianne handed it to me and said, "Just suck in the smoke, and then hold it in your lungs before you exhale."

Holding it between my fingers, I inhaled and gagged. I thought I was going to throw up. I had never even tried a cigarette, and the smoke made me feel sick. I was gagging so much that Marianne ran and got me a glass of water.

"I'm sorry, but I don't think I like this," I said, trying to regain my composure, handing the joint back to Marianne.

"That's okay. But go ahead, try it one more time."

Once more I put the joint in my mouth and tried to inhale and instantly gagged again. The joint reminded me of a cigarette, and I had an instant aversion to it. In any event, it wasn't a pleasant experience, and I didn't try it again. As it was getting late, I asked Marianne and Daniel if they knew of any motels or anyplace I could spend the night.

"Why don't you just stay here on the couch?" Marianne said.

"Really? I mean, I don't want to put you guys out," I said.

"It's no trouble at all," she said kindly.

When I considered my options, it seemed like a good idea. I helped Marianne with the dishes, and then thanked my hosts for a pleasant evening and curled up on the couch. When I woke up the next morning, the sun was streaming in the window. Marianne and Daniel were out, but I left a "thank you" note on the dining table and slipped out the door to begin my journey home.

WHEN THE POLICE INTERVIEWED ME in the hospital, I told them exactly what had happened on that evening. The way this event was described during the trial was very different from what actually occurred. The local newspaper reported that, according to the defense lawyers, I had been part of "an orgy where marijuana and LSD were used and consumed."

When I read those words in the morning paper, I was horrified. I wasn't at an orgy! There wasn't LSD! It sounded so lurid. It was like I was reading about someone else. I couldn't believe they had said that about me. It wasn't true!

I read the words over and over and felt like throwing up. When everyone else in Nordon woke up to read those words in the newspaper, they must have been aghast, too. People who had been my friends were no longer allowed to talk to me. No one wanted his or her children spending time with a "sex fiend, drug addict," as one person described me.

The defense used the dinner conversation about Vietnam to declare that Marianne and Daniel were Communists. Since I was there, it was assumed that I also had "Communist leanings." No one wanted his or her child to spend time with someone like that.

Somebody started a rumor that I was having lots of "interracial sexual escapades." (I later heard that the defense lawyers had started that rumor.) Nordon was a very conservative, white community and, with the exception of a few migrant workers, there weren't other races living there. Although some people in town might have given lip service to racial equality, any kind of interracial liaisons was severely judged. The fact that I had never had any sexual encounters, except for kissing, didn't seem to make any difference to anyone. Nothing dissuaded town members from believing that I was an "orgy-going, Communist-leaning, drug addict."

ONE HIGH SCHOOL FOOTBALL PLAYER did call me for a date during that time. He was someone I admired. He had been in several of my classes in school, and we had worked on homework projects together. I was happy that at least one person didn't believe the rumors. He said he had to work late, so he would pick me up after dark. After he came and got me, he drove me to an out-of-town diner for a late meal. All during our meal he kept looking nervously over his shoulder. He seemed distracted, but I was so happy to be out on a date with him that I didn't really pay much attention. On the way back to my house, he pulled into a dimly lit side road and turned off the ignition.

"What are you doing? I need to get home. It's late."

"Hey, come on, baby! Give me some of that orgy stuff you give everyone else. Don't hold out on me."

I was stunned. I felt so stupid, and suddenly understood why he had been so distracted and nervous. He picked me up late so no one would see him stopping by my house. He took me out of town for dinner so he wouldn't be recognized. The only reason he had asked me out was . . . *oh my God!*

"It's not true. It's not true! Take your hands off me!"

"Hey, it was in the paper. Everyone knows what you did. But I don't care if you're a Communist . . . just give me some orgy stuff."

My body went rigid, and I felt so cold. It was almost like I was watching the scene from above as I said in a monotone, "Take me home now."

Somehow my words must have pushed past the testosterone and made it to his pea-sized brain, because he stopped groping me. He turned the key in the ignition and took me home without saying another word. That night as I lay in bed, I burned with shame and humiliation.

I FELT EVEN MORE HUMILIATION on the day my mother was called to testify. Somehow the defense attorney had heard of my mother's extreme dislike of me, so the defense team met with her a number of times. Mother seemed to revel in the attention they lavished on her. Eventually they requested that she testify on the defense's behalf. On the stand she stated that I wasn't trustworthy and had a bad character. A couple of days after that, two women at a grocery store looked at me and then one whispered, loud enough for me to hear, to the other, "Even her own mother testified against her."

Later, I thought, *Why didn't I speak up and say that my mother was mentally ill?* It just didn't occur to me at the time to tell people that she was a paranoid schizophrenic and that her testimony might be prejudiced. Somehow the veil of secrecy about mental illness was so profound that it never occurred to me to tell anyone. Even after she testified against me, I still felt protective of her. After all, she was my mother.

In the closing arguments, the assistant prosecutor held up my dress with the bullet hole in it. These are his exact words on that day:

> "These holes were not caused by a marijuana burn, but by a bullet. In spite of the marijuana allegation, no one said, 'You naughty girl, you smoked marijuana—POW!'" He pointed his finger at the dress as if it were a gun going off. "There was no proof of any orgy or wild party. I submit that Denise has told the truth!"

He then pointed dramatically at S. "That's the man she saw!"

Holding up the bullet taken from my body, he said, "That's not pot! That's not LSD! That's not marijuana! That's a bullet!"

Although his pleas were impassioned, his closing words solidified the belief by people in town that I was at a drug-induced orgy. His words gave credence to the notion that it did happen, and the trial ended in a hung jury. A second trial eventually took place, and that jury let him go free.

Although I was shocked by the verdict, a small but insistent thought clamored within me. I reasoned that my assailant must have gotten off because I deserved to be shot. I knew that

I wasn't guilty of what I was accused of by the attorneys; however, I began to believe that I was such a despicable person that somehow I must have warranted punishment. Images of the murky nights in my father's bed swirled inside me, making me feel unclean. *Maybe I brought that upon myself, and now I'm being punished for letting it happen to me*, I thought in despair. *Mother's right—there isn't anything of value within me. I'm disgusting.*

It was years before I realized that my father's groping wasn't my fault, and that I didn't deserve to be shot. The road back to knowing that I was a worthy person was long and hard.

AFTER THE FIRST TRIAL, Aaron, one of my good friends from high school, called and asked if he could see me. I was so happy that someone—anyone—from school wanted to spend time with me, but when I saw his guilt-ridden face, my spirit dropped.

"I'm so sorry to ask this, but my mother forced me to come. She knows that we're friends, and she wants me to ask you something."

"What is it?" I asked. My heart was leaden, and my mouth was dry.

Aaron cleared his throat several times. "I'm so sorry, Denise. I'm so sorry, but my mother says the women in her bridge club want to know if it's true that you're a Communist and that you have sex with men of other races."

I knew what it cost him to ask me that, and at the same time, I felt so alone and so sad. I thought for a long time about my answer.

Finally, I said quietly, "Tell her that it's all true." I don't know why I told him that, except that I felt that she wouldn't believe the truth anyway.

Aaron looked at me in surprise. He knew that it wasn't true. He knew that I was lying to him. However, he just nodded his head once and turned quickly to leave. As I watched him walk away, I saw him reach up to wipe his eyes on his sleeve. I could feel how much it had hurt him to ask me that . . . and I knew that his mother would be happy to have something to tell her bridge club.

I WAS HAVING SUCH A ROUGH TIME that I thought it might help to talk to a priest. Also, I really wanted to talk to someone about the "angels" that had visited me, since it would have been difficult to make a long-distance call to Grandma. Even though my parents were not religious, when I was a child we went to the Episcopalian church, so I thought it would be best to talk to the priest there. I made an appointment to talk to him in his church office. As I talked to him about my experiences in the hospital, he reached across his desk to hold my hands. I was touched by his concern.

"I'm sorry to tell you this, Denise, but those weren't angels holding your hand. I know that what happened to you seemed real, but it wasn't. Many things in the Bible are metaphors, and the mention of angels in the Bible isn't meant to be taken literally. I'm sure you were probably hallucinating because of the pain medication."

This seemed a very strange thing for him to tell me. I didn't know much about the Bible, but I did know that what I had experienced was real. Angels *had* held my hand and had been at my side in the hospital.

Then he leaned forward and lowered his voice, "You know, I'm so glad that we have this time together. Being a priest, I needed a certain kind of woman to be my wife. You've met my wife. She's a nice woman. She's good at visiting the sick and attending coffee socials, but what can I say? She's not very exciting in bed."

Why was he telling me this? I began to get a knot in my stomach.

"I guess what I really want to say is, I wish I could be with a woman who's sexy like you."

I pulled my hands away and stood up. He must have believed the stories in the newspaper! I felt unclean and so betrayed. He was a priest! I went to him for help. I was just out of high school, only 18 years old. How could he say that he was attracted to me? Why did he tell me that angels didn't exist?

I turned and walked out of his office through the dimly lit church, and all the feeling drained from my body. When I pushed open the heavy church door, the sunlight felt good on my face. I turned and looked at the church, shuddered, and then sprinted out of the parking lot, past the library, past the swimming pool, and even past the golf course. I ran until I was too exhausted to go on. It was as if running hard could cleanse the taint of his words off me. I didn't talk about angels or about my near-death experience for many years after that.

I don't know what I would have done without Rich Betts. He came into my life when I was just out of high school. He was like a magnificent, winged horse carrying me high above my life. I always thought that first love would occur someplace special. I'd walk past someone on a beach at sunset. Our eyes would meet, illuminated by the glowing, lingering light, and he'd see into my soul. However, when I fell deeply and profoundly in love with Rich, it was at a tavern. It wasn't even an upscale tavern with flickering candlelight on each table. It was grimy and gloomy. In fact, it was basically a box with no windows— just a bleak building outside of town that was a good place to get drunk.

I was 18, the legal drinking age for beer in Ohio, and in the months after the trial, I began to drink a lot. Everything that had happened hung over my head like a heavy pall, and drinking dulled the pain of the trial, the incident with the priest, and being rejected by so many people. This particular day had been rough, and I felt like numbing the ache with alcohol. I pushed open the door to the bar. The smell of stale beer, cigarette smoke, and old urine assailed my nostrils. It was dark inside, and I groped my way through the crowd while my eyes adjusted to the light. From the back of the bar, I heard the voice of an acquaintance holler, "Hey, Denise, over here! We've got a seat for you!" There were a couple of people from out of town who obviously hadn't paid much attention to the stories in the newspaper.

When I got to the booth, the table was slick with spilled beer, and as I tried to scoot into my seat, it was sticky from too many years of Sloe-Gin Fizzes and Rum and Cokes. These were the drinks of choice for girls who wanted to get drunk but couldn't stand the taste of alcohol. They were sweet and slid down fast.

I ordered a draft beer. A few minutes later the bartender came back with a huge, cold mug. Ice slipped off the glass in thin sheets as I gulped thirstily.

As I plunked down the mug to take a breath, someone tapped me on the shoulder. I turned and looked up. A tall, rugged man looked down at me and smiled. I couldn't speak. I couldn't move. I had never had this reaction to anyone before.

He held out his hand and said, "Do you want to dance?"

I couldn't say a word, so I just nodded. As I stood up, I stumbled toward him. He caught me around the waist and gracefully guided me onto the small dance floor. It was a slow dance, and I laid my head on his shoulder. Suddenly everything was all right. I mean *everything*. Everything that had happened to me as a child, my suicide attempt with the aspirin, getting shot, and the trial . . . everything was okay. The bar that had looked so slimy minutes before, now seemed like a magical fairyland as we danced to song after song. I couldn't ever remember feeling so happy.

We started dating after that night. Rich was a year older than I was and lived with his family in a white wooden house in a neighboring town. His father was a doctor, and everyone respected his family. Rich was kind and strong, and he believed in me. Even when people started to tell him not to date "the girl who had been shot," he told them to mind their own business.

We never made love, but we used to go to French's Woods to "make out," and we'd fantasize about getting married and having nine boys so we could start our own baseball team. But our relationship came to an abrupt end during a November party at his sister's home. Just before we went to the party, someone called to tell me that the man who shot me had been found innocent in the second trial for my case.

"What do you mean?!" I said. "He's not innocent. He rammed me with his car and then he shot me!" I went to the party distraught, but trying to suppress my feelings.

At the party, I started drinking. Rich came up to me and said, "You've had too much to drink. You shouldn't have any more."

"But they said he was innocent!" I blurted out as I chugged more beer.

"Denise, please. You're embarrassing me," he pleaded.

"I'm embarrassing you! I don't care. I don't care about anything!" I bawled.

"Fine," he said angrily, and he got up and walked out of the room.

When no one was looking, I slipped out the back door. A layer of snow covered the ground. All I had on was a party dress and high heels, but I had to get away from it all. I started to run . . . and I ran and ran. I slipped in the snow a few times, but just kept running. I didn't know where I was. Somewhere along the way, I lost a shoe, but I kept on going. Finally, realizing that I was lost, I sat down on the snow-covered curb underneath a streetlight and sobbed.

A police car pulled up alongside me. The officer rolled down the window and asked if I was all right.

"No, I'm not all right!" I wailed. "The jury didn't believe me, and the guy who shot me got off. I've had a fight with my boyfriend, I'm drunk, I've lost a shoe, I'm cold, and I'm lost."

"Hey! Don't worry. Get in!" said the other policeman. "Everything is going to be okay."

I knew that everything was *not* going to be okay. The man whom I'd identified as the gunman was free, and he swore that if he was released, he was coming after me for testifying against him. Would he try to kill me again? No, everything was *not* okay.

But the warmth of the police car felt good. One officer put his jacket around me, while the other poured me some coffee from his Thermos. As they helped me find my way back to the party, neither one of them scolded me for overdrinking.

When I returned to Rich's sister's house, I was miserable. I saw the sad, distant look in Rich's eyes and realized that we would probably never get married and have our baseball team. We were too different. I would never fit into that community, no matter how hard I tried. I would always be the "girl who got shot." I had thought that it could work, but I realized that it was just a dream. However, I never stopped being grateful for having had Rich in my life.

I REALLY WANTED TO GO TO COLLEGE, but because of the time it took me to completely recover from my injuries, I hadn't taken an after-school job, so I was unable to apply to schools, let alone find a way to afford it. So I decided to work until I could save enough money to go.

I moved out of Nordon without any fanfare. Heather was sad to see me go, but Mother seemed indifferent and even glad when I left. I moved into another town in the next county, where I wasn't known, and rented a tiny trailer in a dusty trailer court situated on a dirt lot next to the freeway. The rumbling trucks on the freeway shook the thin walls of my metal home, and the constant din of the cars became the backdrop to my life there.

Although I occasionally got a call from Heather, it was as if a heavy black curtain had dropped over my old life. I was isolated and alone. I knew it was crazy, but I fantasized that my mother and father would swoop down and save me, and we'd become a real "Beaver Cleaver" family. But deep down inside, I knew that this would never happen. I was on my own.

Many of the people who lived in the trailer court were also down on their luck—road-weary truck drivers, people avoiding the law, mothers on welfare, and so on—yet I began to feel comfortable and safe there. These were people to whom I could relate; they had also seen hard times. I didn't feel as lonely as I had in the manicured lifestyle of Nordon.

When I thought about work, I decided that I'd go for my dream job. Although I'd only eaten in a few restaurants in my life, on those few occasions I was very impressed by the waitresses. I loved how they glided effortlessly between the tables. I envied their poise as they leaned over the table to ask, "Can I help you?" Every word sounded cherry-soft and sweet. I admired the way a waitress would slide her pad and pencil out of her pocket and take our orders as she beamed at us. Minutes later, with our meals hoisted high over her head on a tray, she seemed like some kind of priestess bringing offerings. I thought it would be wonderful if I could become a waitress.

The only position available was in a café frequented by truckers. The tightness in my stomach grew as I stood at the counter waiting for the manager. Striding like a bantam chicken, he strutted toward me. He was whip-skinny, missing his two front teeth, and his weasel-shaped face was smattered with pimples. His apron had dried, crusted food on it that looked several weeks old, reminding me of the wall in our home during my parents' food-fighting days. A cigarette dangled out of the side of his mouth.

"Yeah. Whadda ya want?" he asked. The cigarette bounced up and down as he talked.

"I wanted to see if your waitress job was still available," I nervously replied.

"Hmm," he said, as looked me up and down. With a tooth-less smile he said, "The job's been taken, but you can work as a dishwasher until there's another opening for a waitress."

"You mean I have a job?"

"Yup! You can start now," he said as he yanked off his apron and thrust it into my hands.

I looked down at the stained apron and gingerly wrapped it around my waist and tied it in back. I was so exhilarated by the possibility of becoming a waitress someday that nothing else seemed to matter.

The manager ushered me into the small kitchen. It was a dingy, windowless space, lit by a bare lightbulb. A deep-fat fryer was bubbling away, and French fries bounced around in the dark-colored lard. The floor was slick with oil that had splashed from the fryer. A thick layer of black dust clung to the oil-covered walls.

Two men stood over the sink. Their hands were deep in dirty water that had bits of food floating in it. The manager introduced me to the two other dishwashers, Juan and Carlos, who spoke very little English.

A little later, I was standing with my hands in scalding, dirty water, scrubbing pans and handing them to Juan to rinse.

I used my forearm to wipe the sweat from my brow. I kept shaking my head to discourage the flies from landing on my face.

When I returned to my trailer that evening, I flopped across the bed, exhausted and discouraged. Grease coated my face, body, and clothes. (In the entire time I worked there, I don't ever remember the fat-fryer oil being changed. In the morning, it was a hardened and congealed, grimy yellow that melted into a liquid-brown color once the fryer was turned on. We used a strainer to lift out food particles from the day before.)

I was too tired to even shower. As I lay on the bed, tears of exhaustion rolled down my cheeks. I even had a "talk" with myself: "Denise, you need this job. Even if you're tired, you're not going to quit. If you're ever going to get to college, you're going to have to earn money to pay for it. Besides, if you work hard enough, you might be able to become a waitress."

College was the gold at the end of my rainbow. I dreamed that once I got there, my real life would start and everything would be better. I fell asleep on top of the covers. Somehow in the night, a resolution must have filled me, because the next morning I woke up determined to become a great dishwasher. I showered off the grease from the day before and arrived early for work. I worked with a fury, scrubbing, rinsing, stacking and more scrubbing, rinsing, stacking. Days turned into weeks of scrubbing, rinsing, and stacking. Night after night, my dreams were filled with miles of dirty dishes.

One afternoon when I was out running errands, I saw that the secondhand bookstore had a "free" box in front. On top of the pile was a book about meditation. Since my grandmother had mentioned the topic when I lived with her, I was interested in reading about it. It was a strange book to find in a small town at that time. This was long before yoga and meditation were widely known in America. These practices were thought to be mysterious things that only monks in mountain caves did.

I took the book back to my little trailer and carefully opened the yellowed pages. "Sit still and focus on your breath," it proclaimed. I sat on my single chair, a rusted metal kitchen chair, closed my eyes, and focused on my breathing. As I relaxed, I found myself lifting out of my body and traveling beyond my trailer and the endless trail of dirty dishes, to the golden realm I'd touched when I was shot.

Meditation helped me distance myself from my life, and it was a much-needed respite from greasy dishes, but I couldn't seem to maintain that peaceful feeling while I was at work. In fact, the only thing that kept me motivated while I washing dishes was the tiny window in the kitchen, through which I could peer into the dining area. With my hands in dirty, steaming water, I peeked out that hole to the seemingly pristine world of the waitresses. They smiled and chatted with the customers, who were mostly truckers, tattooed bikers, occasional families, and off-duty cops. I watched the way they subtly pocketed tips into their apron. I practiced doing it at home so when I became a waitress I wouldn't fumble.

One day I came to work and Juan wasn't there. It was just Carlos and me washing dishes.

"Where's Juan?" I asked.

"Oh, I had to let him go," the manager said, and abruptly turned and walked out.

We had to work harder, because now two were doing the job of three.

A few days later when I came to work, Carlos was gone.

"Where's Carlos?" I demanded.

"Oh, I had to let him go, too," said the manager.

Now I was doing the work of three people. I worked in a fury. The dishes were a blur as I frantically washed, rinsed, and stacked them. But I kept looking out the peephole into the dining room. *One day I will be a waitress! I will be a waitress! I will!* I said to myself as I gritted my teeth and worked even harder.

One morning I came to work and glanced into the dining room. *There was a new waitress!* When the manager came into the kitchen, I confronted him.

"You've hired a new waitress!" I said.

"Yup, we were short," he said nonchalantly.

"You said that the dishwashing was temporary until there was an opening for a waitress!" I gasped.

"But Denise, you have to understand. Good waitresses are easy to find. It's a lot harder to find a good dishwasher. You're really good at washing dishes, and I can't afford to lose you as a dishwasher. In fact, you're so good that I fired the other guys so you could do their work, too," he said defensively. "Besides, I thought you liked doing dishes."

"You what? You broke your promise! You fired Juan and Carlos because I was doing such a good job! I've only been working so hard so you'd know what a good waitress I'd be!" I said, as my eyes narrowed in anger.

"Okay! Okay! I'll see what I can do," he said, backing away from me.

A few weeks later, I finally became a waitress. I was so proud of my black polyester uniform and my white apron. The uniform was used and worn in a few places, and the apron was stained, but my dream had come true. I enjoyed the easier pace compared to dishwashing, and I loved chatting with the customers. Every few nights I'd count my tips to see how much more I needed to earn to pay for college. I was making much more money as a waitress than as a dishwasher.

However, one night I realized that, at the rate I was going, it would be years until I could earn enough to go. I decided that I was going to have to cut back on my expenses. To lessen my grocery costs, I began to bundle up the food that the customers didn't eat. I didn't really think of germs. I just looked at it as a way to save more money for college. One time I took home some old, dried catsup that was being thrown away. I added hot water to it to make tomato soup. It wasn't bad. I even tried eating canned cat food once. The ingredients might sound okay when you read the label, but it was terrible.

THE WINTER NIGHTS WERE ESPECIALLY HARD for me, despite my attempts at meditation to create "deep inner peace." The penetrating coldness and the constant noise of the freeway seeped in through the metal seams of my trailer. The harshness of my job and the despair about my life seemed overwhelming at times, and I'd often fall asleep sad and exhausted.

One chilling winter night at about three in the morning, I woke up gravely despondent. I'd had enough. I wanted out of my life. A dead calm came over me. I knew what I had to do. There was a large river in town. I decided to jump off the bridge and drown myself.

With grim determination, I walked out of my trailer, down the road, and eventually across a large park on my way to the bridge. The ground was covered with patches of dirty snow. As I walked through the park, I saw a young man about my age sitting on a park bench with his head hung low. Normally, I would have never approached a lone male in this situation, but I believed I was about to die, so I thought, *What does it matter if he tries to hurt me? I'm going to be dead in a few moments anyway.*

I walked up and asked if he was okay. He looked up at me and said, "No, I'm not," and then he proceeded to tell me about some troubles in his life and said that *he was on the way to the bridge to kill himself!* (At the time, I didn't realize what an amazing coincidence that was.)

I sat down next to him and said, "Hey, you're young. You're going through a rough time, but things will get better."

We chatted for a long time. He perked up, told me how much I'd helped him, and thanked me profusely. I felt so good that I forgot about drowning myself, and I turned around and went back home. As I walked back through the park, the sun was rising. The patches of snow that had previously looked dingy and sullied, now glowed pink and looked beautiful against the dark earth. As I stepped into my trailer, I knew that, although I was going through a rough period, things would get better . . . and they did.

Years later, I realized that my encounter wasn't by chance. I believe that on that frigid winter night, I met an angel . . . a real angel. Of course there's no way to know for sure, but that man will always be an angel to me.

CHAPTER SEVEN

Spreading My Wings
(1968–1969)

I was grateful for my encounter with the angel, for that memory kept me going when things got rough. It seemed that no matter where I turned, there was nothing. No hope. No future. No joy. I was filled with a deep longing and restlessness for something I couldn't quite name. Something in my bones was searching and listening—yearning to be whole. I'd lost the inner substance of my life. Yet at the edge of my dreams and in the silent places in my heart during meditations lingered memories of the realm of golden light that I'd visited when everyone thought I was dead. These memories beckoned to me. It seemed that I could only glimpse that heavenly place when I was in nature. But every day I came home from waiting tables so exhausted that I just fell into bed, only to roll out the next morning to start work again.

Without, friends, family, or my boyfriend, Rich . . . and without time in the woods, heartache tugged at me as I sat by myself in my little trailer. Yet I wasn't alone. I began to talk to God—not the God that resided in church—I had met his priestly representatives, and they were wanting. My God was of the sky, of my beloved trees, and of the stars. I talked to Him through those long, lonely nights. Finally, one morning I felt a reconnection to the power that links all things. There was a vibration surging through the air, a humming in the earth. It was time to take a step forward, even if I couldn't see where that step would lead me. It was time.

My journey took me to college, but not to the small school in Ohio I'd visited before I was shot; the memories were still too fresh, too raw. I wanted to lose myself in a large university, a place where no one would point at me and whisper to another, "There goes the girl who was shot," while casting furtive looks in my direction. I no longer wanted to study art, psychology, and science. During the trial, I realized how much I valued justice, fairness, and integrity above all else. Journalism seemed to be an arena in which I could give form to these moral imperatives.

Thanks to a student loan I managed to secure, and the money I saved from working, I was able to enroll at Michigan State University (MSU). After so many months of solitude, I wanted to experience everything that MSU had to offer— classes, dorms, roommates, parties, lectures, concerts—every-thing. I felt like a new life was just about to begin.

Almost as soon as I arrived, I applied for a job on the Michigan State newspaper. The editor was a big, bulky Viet-nam vet who fancied himself a hard-hitting journalist. When he interviewed me for the position, he asked about my work experience. I was pleased to tell him that I *had* written for a newspaper.

"Well, do you have any copies of your work with you?" he barked.

"I don't have any with me, but I can send for some!" I said with enthusiasm.

I didn't realize that writing for my high school paper wasn't the kind of experience he meant. However, something I said must have penetrated his gruff exterior, because he hired me on the spot and told me to provide copies of my articles as soon as I could get them. By the time they arrived, I'd already written a number of articles, including interviews with various guest lecturers, including Dr. Spock, the baby doctor; and Ralph Nader, the safety advocate. With pride, I took my high school articles and placed them in the editor's in-box. I was excited to hear what he'd say about them. Later that afternoon, the editor came storming over to my desk. He slapped down the packet of my articles and loomed over me.

"This . . . this . . ." he sputtered as his face turned red. "This is your past experience? These are just articles for a puny high school paper!" he said. He was so mad that every word was punctuated with spittle.

"But . . . but you asked me if I had any writing experience," I said, "and I did."

"Well, I never would have hired anyone who'd just written for their cowtown high school newsletter!" he bellowed.

"Are you going to fire me?" I said quietly.

"Well, no," he managed to say ruefully. "You're doing good work, so you can keep your job."

I tried to look dutifully remorseful, but inside I was too exuberant to feel bad.

I LOVED WORKING FOR THE NEWSPAPER. It had a big office and a readership of 50,000. At the time, anti-war sentiments were running strong, and rallies and marches were common on campuses across America. The editor asked me if I'd like to cover the anti-war movement for the paper. That became my "beat," and eventually I even had my own column. In addition to keeping up with my university classes, I also attended local events, where I interviewed student radicals, "outside agitators," and disillusioned Vietnam vets who'd already fulfilled their tour of duty. It was difficult to maintain my objectivity in the wake of their impassioned views.

Images of war atrocities were splashed across the nation's media. There was a horrifying photo in one publication of a young naked Vietnamese girl with her face contorted in pain as napalm clung to her skin. That photo seemed to capture the anguish that was tearing our country apart. The war had cost more than three million Vietnamese lives and over 40,000 U.S. soldiers' lives. It was a turbulent time both in America and on our campus. As I walked to class, it wasn't uncommon to see student activists carrying anti-war placards as they marched past university administration buildings, or a cluster of students on the quad listening to a speaker with a bullhorn blasting the government.

The newspaper had a generous budget, so they began to fund my trips to big cities to cover riots. I worked out a way that I could keep up with my classes and still report on the anti-war movement. I never thought about the danger, even when Samuel, a fellow reporter and friend, was beaten while covering race riots in Detroit.

In June 1969, I was on a plane headed to Chicago to report on the Students for a Democratic Society (SDS) convention. The SDS was the largest and most militant group opposing the war. At the time, they boasted 100,000 members with chapters on 350 campuses across America. Their convention took place in Chicago, which was under the reins of Mayor Daley, a very tough politician. He wasn't going to let anything disrupt his city. The situation had the potential to be a powder keg that could blow up at any minute.

There were very vocal student gatherings on the street, and government agents were everywhere taking photos, documenting the growing SDS movement. They were easy to spot. Although they wore old jeans and beads to try to fit in, they just couldn't quite pull it off. Their shoes were always shined, and they wore sunglasses. Everyone believed that they were photographing protestors for later retribution.

I stepped into a smoke-filled café where a number of the leaders of the SDS were gathered for a meeting. Sunlight streamed through the window into the smoky room, and the silhouettes of the leaders against the window created the potential for a great photo to accompany my story. My camera was under my poncho, so I quietly positioned it so the lens peered out of a sleeve hole, and I carefully took the shot. Although the café was noisy, the instant the shutter clicked . . . everything stopped.

Springing like a leopard out of his chair, a man flung himself across the room, grabbed me by both shoulders, and pinned me against the wall. He was Mark Rudd, a well-known leader of the SDS.

"What are you doing?!" he hissed. "Who do you work for?"

"I'm a reporter for the Michigan State News. I'm on your side. I'm letting people know the truth about what's . . . what's . . . going on here," I stuttered as I tried to wrench myself out of his iron grip, but he pinned me even harder to the wall.

"Yeah, right," he said threateningly.

An antagonistic crowd gathered around us. An image of Samuel being beaten in Detroit during the race riots flashed before my eyes. I had to think of something quickly.

"My shoes! Look at my shoes! Would someone from the FBI be wearing these shoes?" They were scuffed and dirty. They definitely didn't look like the polished shine of those of the FBI. A sigh filled the room. (Finally, not polishing my shoes paid off!)

"Let her go. She's okay," someone laughed.

Mark was reluctant to release his grip. Finally, he said, "Okay, but I'm keeping her film." He didn't take his eyes off me as he pulled the film out of my camera and unrolled it.

Then, abruptly dismissing me, he turned to continue his meeting.

In November of that year, I was assigned to cover the Peace March in Washington, D.C. Reports at the time estimated that more than a million people demonstrated in the streets. Even if there were less, as I suspect, it was indeed the largest anti-war protest in U.S. history. Throughout the United States, in other cities, between 20 and 30 million people marched in protest that day.

In the march there were many different groups—student activists, Vets for Peace, feminists, civil rights activists, Black Power members, flower children, and more—but at the front of the march were the anarchists. Their chants were angry and loud.

"Peace now!" was shouted over and over in fierce, outraged voices, as though shouting loud enough would somehow create the desired end.

I couldn't take notes because it was too crowded at the front of the march, so I just tried to remember everything in as much detail as I could. The police who lined the streets were armed with riot clubs and guns. I tried to look into the eyes of a young cop who didn't look much older than I was. His face was stern, almost emotionless, as he held a big riot shield in front of his body. What was he feeling? Could he see me, or was I just a blur in the crowd? With men in riot gear on either side of him, he stood at rigid attention like a tin soldier in formation. Suddenly, in robotlike unison, he and the other police officers donned their gas masks and began to march toward us, clubs in hand.

People around me panicked, dropped their signs, and tried to run, but the crowd was so thick that there was nowhere to go. The chant "Peace now!" was still echoing from the stalwart voices of marchers behind us, unaware of what was happening ahead. I heard a sizzling sound as something flew through the air and hit the ground near my feet with a dull thud. I looked down.

A canister spewing sickly yellow gas danced at my toes. I tried to cover my nose and eyes, but when I couldn't hold my breath any longer and had to take a breath, it felt like scalding, melted iron was being poured on my eyes, nose, and lungs. I was desperate for air, but every breath was searing and painful. I began to choke and cough.

Another canister landed. And then another hissed past my head. What sounded like gunshots reverberated through the streets, as a dense cloud of yellow fog saturated the crowd. Hysterical screams spewed from the woman next to me as the gas began to envelop her.

Someone shouted, "They're going to murder us!"

Partially blinded by the gas, the demonstrators ran in circles, pushing and shoving, trying to get away from the canisters that were exploding everywhere. To my right, the crowd knocked over a woman as they ran like an angry frenzy of bees. She gagged as a canister near her head emitted volumes of gas. I reached for her limp arm and wrenched her up, but somehow she slipped from my grip and disappeared into the crowd that swarmed around us.

My arms, face, eyes, and lungs—anything that was exposed to the gas—burned as though my skin was peeling right off my body. More canisters of pepper gas and tear gas exploded around me. I wondered if I was going to die. I was caught up in the ebb and flow of the crowd until I finally crashed into the side of a building. I flattened myself against its cool stone surface to avoid being crushed. My breathing became more and more labored and frantic as I gasped for air. Suddenly, a door next to me opened a crack. A hand reached out, grabbed me, and pulled me inside.

I fell forward, bracing my hands on my thighs, and began

to dry-heave and cough, as the person who had pulled me inside kept me from toppling. My eyes were so irritated that I could only see blurry colors, but I heard a calm male voice say, "Here, put this over your nose, and your lungs won't hurt so much." He then handed me a soft cloth to breathe into. He explained that in sufficient quantities, pepper gas could cause respiratory failure, and in rare cases could be fatal, but he assured me that I'd be okay.

As my eyes gradually cleared, I saw a gray-haired man with a bandana wrapped around his head. He took my hand and escorted me to another entrance, opened the door out, and said, "Go that way and you'll be safe." I thanked him and turned and ran. Years later I wondered if, in fact, he was also a kind of angelic, guardian protector. Or perhaps he was a regular guy who happened to be at the right place at the right time. I'll never know. But I wonder how he just happened to be inside that building when all the others had been locked against the march that day? How did he just happen to reach out and grab me? How did he know so much about pepper gas? But I didn't think about any of that at the time, I was just so happy to be away from the crowd and the gas.

AFTER BEING PEPPER-GASSED, I was glad to return to Michigan and get away from the anti-war marches for a while. But things at MSU weren't unaffected by the changing times. The flower-child, make-love-not-war movement was starting to take root. It seemed as if everyone was wearing bell-bottoms, getting stoned, and protesting the war. The feminist movement was growing. Women were encouraged to burn their bras, throw off the shackles of male oppression, and take charge of their lives.

Even though I'd been in love with Rich Betts, we never did anything more serious than necking. Compared to most of my college friends, I felt like an old maid at age 19. I was still a virgin, despite what the Nordon press had said about me. It seemed like everyone but me was having sex. One night I was talking late into the night with several girls from my dorm. Eventually, as usual, the conversation turned to sex. At one point in the lively discussion, I casually mentioned that I'd never had sex. Everyone stopped and stared at me. Then their questions tumbled over each other like stormy waves tossing a piece of driftwood back and forth.

"You're still a virgin?"

"You're kidding! You've never had sex?"

"Well, I just haven't found the right man," I murmured.

"Honey, this isn't about love. This is about sex," Rachel said smoothly. Everyone nodded in agreement.

"Denise, we aren't stuck in the male chauvinistic times anymore. A woman has to liberate herself. Sex isn't just for men's pleasure. It's not just a woman's duty. It's for *our* fun and pleasure, too."

The next morning I decided to take action. I wouldn't stay a virgin one more day! Grabbing my books, I rushed to my first class, which had about 200 students in it. I couldn't concentrate, as the professor droned on vaguely about the Roman governmental system. I looked around the class to pick out a likely candidate. One good-looking guy caught my eye as he came in late and set his books on his desk. He was tall, and his hair was a coppery color. I liked the easy way he carried himself, and although he had a loose shirt on, his broad shoulders tugged at its seams. He had a mischievous smile that made him look innocent and devilish at the same time.

He's the one! I thought. (It never occurred to me at the time that I was acting exactly as my mother had 20 years before when she'd picked out my father.) After class, I sauntered over to him and managed to get asked out for a date that night. (I maneuvered until *he* asked me out. The mores of the '50s died hard.)

I was nervous while I waited for him to pick me up. The other girls in my dormitory, who'd been appalled by my lack of sexual experience, waited excitedly with me. As he escorted me out the door, my roommates waved me off with surreptitious winks.

We drove to a local drive-in theater, and shortly after the movie started, I explained my mission to him. He was at first amazed, then completely elated by my suggestion, and we drove back to his apartment. (Only freshmen were required to stay in dormitories.)

"Really! I mean really? You want to lose your virginity, tonight? I mean, really? Oh wow!"

My resolve wavered for a moment amidst his boyish exuberance, but I convinced myself that I was ready to be "liberated." As we flailed about—we fell out of the bed twice—I remember thinking, *This is all there is? What's the big deal? This is completely overrated.*

My first foray into sexuality was uninspiring, and it was a number of years until I truly began to understand the power, mystery, and majesty of a woman's sexual energy—and to comprehend what I'd lost that night.

LATER THAT YEAR, I MET RON COLLINS, who taught in the sociology department at the university. He was nine years older than I was and liked my carefree spirit. I liked his judicious academic approach to life. My discussions with him ranged from the worldly to the everyday. He gave as much careful deliberation to what kind of soup we should make for dinner as to who should be the next President of the country.

He had wisdom and compassion that had been honed in his years in the Peace Corps. He was a self-sufficient man who loved gardening and working for peace. Eventually, we moved into a rambling country house together, with plenty of room for a garden. I was happy with him. . . not in a giddy way, but in a comfortable, easy way. He stepped carefully into our relationship, whereas I embraced it with passion. In my life, I tended to jump into everything with gusto, which wasn't always wise, whereas Ron was, by nature, more thoughtful and even at times reserved.

Late one evening, Ron and I sat on old wicker chairs on our porch. Suddenly an immense storm erupted in the north. The rain fell in great floods, and bright flashes of lightning illuminated the black sky. Exhilarated by the power of the storm, I yanked off my clothes and raced into the open field behind the house and jumped and leapt through the air in a frenzied kind of dance. It was too dark for Ron to see me, but every time lightning struck, he had an instant, frozen image of me in a different place in the field. My body, he said, looked white and translucent silhouetted against the night.

I'd always loved dancing in storms (albeit, usually with my clothes on), especially while great peals of thunder boomed. Once, when I was ten years old, my uncle found me dancing in a thunderstorm on a knoll at my grandparents' ranch, not far from the house. He was so angry that I would do something so stupid and, fearing that I'd be struck by lightning, took a cattle prod and jolted me with electric shocks all the way home to make sure that I'd never dance in a storm again.

It didn't work. Well, in a way it worked, because I made sure that he never *caught* me dancing in a storm again. I don't know if Ron thought I was crazy for storm dancing, but he accepted me anyway, and I always felt safe with him.

ONE NIGHT I WAS ESPECIALLY GRATEFUL for Ron's comforting presence. I'd been working at the university library on a paper for my English class, and the hours got away from me. It was late by the time I left the cozy confines of the stacks. I could have called Ron and asked him to pick me up, but it was a nice night and I was glad to be out in the fresh air.

As I walked down a deserted part of the road, I heard footsteps behind me. Instead of turning to see who was there, I increased my pace. The sound increased. I went a bit faster, and the person behind me walked faster, much faster. I panicked and started to run, but he was gaining on me. Suddenly he thrust his burly, tattooed arm around my throat and forced a large hunting knife against my neck. Images of the man who'd shot me filled my mind. *No . . . it can't be happening again!*

I was just about to try fighting him off when a calm inner voice said: *Don't struggle, Denise. Everything will be okay. You're not stronger than he is, but you're smarter. Use your head.* Although I was taking karate classes (probably in a reaction to having been shot), I realized that if I tried any of my moves on him, I'd get hurt. A feeling of composure descended over me; it was almost as if I became the observer as well as the participant.

The blade of the knife felt like freezing ice as it pushed into my neck, making it hard to breathe. The inner voice spoke again: *Don't struggle. You'll be all right.* He was breathing heavily as he dragged me off the sidewalk and started to pull me into the bushes. Part of me was near panic as images of the gunman surged through my mind.

Again the voice spoke: *Talk to him.*

Suddenly my head became very clear, and in a calm voice I said, "It's nice to meet you. Would you like to go out for some coffee?" He didn't seem to hear me. While holding the knife to my throat, he started pulling on my blouse.

Talk to him! The voice was more insistent. In a calm, level tone, I managed to say, "I'd love to get to know you better, but my mother's waiting for me." (Of course, my mother was 400 miles away and was certainly not waiting for me.) "She doesn't live far from here. Let me go tell her that I'll be out late, but I'll come back here so we can spend some time together."

With an explosion of breath, he grunted, "Get the hell out of here. Just get the hell out of here!"

Men who victimize women are looking for just that . . . a victim. When I took control of the situation, I wasn't acting like a victim, and this must have rattled him.

I picked up my schoolbooks and walked the first few steps with dignity, and then darted away as fast as I could. I ran until I got home, banged open the door, and locked it behind me, heaving in exhaustion.

"What's wrong?" Ron said, looking alarmed. When I told him what had happened, he held me and rocked me. The soft, rhythmic sound of his breath on my cheek was comforting as he gently smoothed my brow until I fell asleep.

In later days when I thought about the incident, I felt ashamed that once again I'd found myself in a dangerous situation. Why had it happened to me again? Maybe I deserved to be harmed. Perhaps what happened to me was another kind of punishment because I wasn't a worthy person. But, even as these questions persisted, I marveled at the guidance from the inner voice. An unseen guardian had been at my side, watching over me and keeping me from harm. Could it be that there was a reason for these experiences in my life? I didn't know the answers to my questions, but I was glad that I hadn't been hurt.

DURING THIS TIME, a remarkable opportunity arose for me to attend an international journalism conference in Yugoslavia during summer vacation. I was especially excited because I'd never been out of the country before. I received a grant for part of my trip, which was an honor for someone of my age, and with the money from my job on the newspaper, I had enough to pay for the venture. (The newspaper said they'd hold my job over the summer.) Journalists and editors from major publications such as *Time* magazine were going to attend. It would be a great chance to learn from some excellent international reporters. I was hesitant to leave Ron, but we agreed to write often and swore our love to each other.

The conference was held in Omis, a small, picturesque seaside town. When not attending lectures on subjects such as journalistic ethics and the hazards of overseas reporting, I loved strolling along the pebbly pathway to the beach. I was very impressed with the Eastern European women who paraded up and down the beach in their bathing suits, with hair visible from every follicle on their legs and underarms. I thought that they were truly liberated, much more so than the girls in my dorm who touted the sexual revolution, bra-burning, and free love, yet would have died before a boy saw them with hairy legs.

The conference was held over a number of weeks, so there were often breaks of several days. During one of them, I spontaneously decided to visit Dubrovnik, a large city on the ocean to the south of Omis. The bus had been delayed en route, so by the time I arrived, it was getting dark and I had trouble getting my bearings. I went from hotel to inn to pension looking for a place to spend the night. There didn't seem to be a room available in the entire city. I hadn't booked ahead because it had never occurred to me that there would be a problem finding a place to spend the night. It was late, and I was exhausted, so I decided to find a park bench where I could sleep for a while.

When I was in New York City reporting on a peace march there, I'd seen a number of people sleeping on benches in Central Park. This was not a common sight in Nordon, or in any of the small towns in which I'd lived with my family, so I'd paid careful attention to what these people had done to keep themselves warm throughout the chill of the night.

Remembering what I'd learned in New York, I found a

faded wooden bench under a tree in a small park by the sea. I rummaged through a trash can until I found some newspapers. First, I layered a few of them underneath my body so the cold wouldn't seep up from below. Then I lay down on top of those papers and carefully overlapped more newspapers on top of me, from feet to head. I was quite proud of myself. I stuffed my purse under my head and tried to sleep. The bench was hard, and the breeze from the ocean was brisk and chilling. The newspapers kept flapping in the wind, so I had to position my arms in such a way as to hold them down. Occasionally someone would walk by, and I'd become alert. However, in the early-morning hours, I finally fell asleep.

I was soundly asleep when there was a sharp tap on my foot. Startled, I opened my eyes. A policeman, holding a night-stick, stood sternly at the foot of my bench. I jumped up with a start.

Two more policemen quickly arrived. They talked briskly back and forth to each other, and then gravely looked at me. My mind was scrambling. Was it a crime to sleep on a bench?

"Oh, I'm so sorry," I said, overly cheerful. "You see, I couldn't find anywhere to sleep last night. You're so kind for waking me, but I'll be on my way now." However, as I turned to hurry away, the nightstick brusquely stopped me. I looked at the cold black baton and up at the men's faces. "Oh shit," I said to myself.

The policemen indicated that I was to follow them. No one spoke English, or even understood my smattering of high school French, as I desperately tried to explain that I hadn't meant any harm. I gave up trying to communicate and dog-gedly resigned myself to going with them. Shock set in when I saw where they were taking me.

As I stepped in out of the light, my eyes took a while to adjust to the darkness of the police station. The room reeked of stale cigarette smoke and acrid cleaning agents. One of the policemen indicated that I was to follow him. As I walked down the worn linoleum hallway, the sound of his sharp footsteps echoed on the smooth, water-stained walls.

I was taken to a small containment room where the policeman pointed to a wooden chair that was in the center of the room, then he abruptly turned and walked out. I had a momentary fear that I was going to be interrogated or punished. My years with my mother prepared me to expect the worst. I wanted to get up and try to find someone who spoke English, but the policeman had very clearly specified that I was to sit.

Finally, a large muscular man in uniform came in and asked me a question that I couldn't understand. He repeated the question again—slower and louder—and seemed to get angry that I couldn't comprehend what he was saying. He eventually gave up and motioned for me to step into the jail cell, which was next to the room. I looked through the bars into the tiny room. It was only large enough for a small bed. A sinking feeling filled me as I stepped inside. He pointed to the bed in the cell. I slowly sat down on the side of it. He gave me a small, tight smile and walked away. I noticed that he left the cell door open.

I waited and waited. It didn't occur to me that I might be able to just get up and walk out. I was in a Communist country and felt I had to do what I was told. Memories of what I'd overheard about Communists as a child kept coming to mind. I knew that it was American propaganda, but I couldn't stop thinking about it. I also thought how ironic it was that I'd been accused of being a Communist, and here I was sitting in a Communist jail.

I watched the stream of sunlight coming through a high window. It created shadows that slowly traveled across the cell floor as the sun moved across the sky. Finally, exhausted from fear and from very few hours of rest on the bench, I stretched out on the bed and fell asleep. After a number of hours, they found someone who spoke English to translate for me. A young, thin man with pale skin and John Lennon glasses stepped into my cell and sat down next to me on the bed. I told him that I was really sorry that I'd slept on the bench.

"You not trouble," he said. "Police worry for you. They no want nothing happen to you. You safe in jail, no safe on streets."

An enormous wave of relief rolled over me. I hadn't realized how tense I was until my body relaxed after hearing his words. As I left the station, I shook hands with the policemen, relieved to say good-bye. Even though it was getting late, I caught a bus back to Omis. I wasn't going to attempt to find another hotel in Dubrovnik again.

The next morning a letter arrived from Ron. After my harrowing day, it was wonderful to receive it. His letter was my safety line, and I snatched it and sprinted to the sea. If he'd known what had happened to me, he would have held me and told me that it was all right. I wanted to cherish his every word. I sat under the shade tree that grew next to the shore. As I dug my toes into the warm sand, I carefully opened my letter. I read it over and over, word by delicious word. Part of the letter said: "Honey, I miss you. No hand in mine walking down the street. No one looks up and smiles when I walk into the next room. The only thing worse than going to bed alone, is waking up alone." Ron's letters were long, and his expressive images of our house in Michigan made me homesick.

I had some extra time at the end of the conference before my flight back to the States, so I decided to take a spiritual retreat on my own. My grandmother had inspired me when she told me that great insights about one's life often occur as a result of being alone in nature. Perhaps I could better understand the events of my life by meditating alone for a week to find the tranquility of the land of golden light again. The book I'd read on meditation when I lived in the trailer said that fasting in the outdoors helped one's meditation practice. The fact that I'd never done anything like that didn't deter me.

I thought that the beautiful islands in the Adriatic Sea would be the perfect location for my first spiritual retreat and settled on an island I'd noticed on a previous day trip. It had looked like a tiny gem floating on a sparkling sea, beckoning to me. There was no transportation to the island, so I went to the fishing dock hoping to find someone willing to take me.

The docks were empty except for one fisherman fixing nets on his boat. His skin had the leathery look of someone who'd spent much of his life outside, and his teeth were yellow against his bronzed skin. He didn't speak English, but I kept pointing to the island and gesturing that I wanted to hire him to take me there. He kept shaking his head no. It was such a small island that I doubted that it was inhabited. I knew that it would be perfect for my retreat. He kept shaking his head and pointing his weather-worn hand to other islands for my consideration. They were farther away and bigger. But I kept insisting that I wanted to go to the tiny one. There was only about an hour until sunset, and I was getting anxious to get to the island before dark.

"Please take me there!" I said emphatically as I pointed to the island and pulled money out of my purse. He violently shook his head and let forth a barrage of expletives. Although I was extremely careful with the very small amount of money I had, I reached into my purse and pulled out more money. The fisherman took a deep breath, looked at the money, and then peered deeply into my expectant eyes with his hard, stormy ones. Shrugging his shoulders and shaking his head, he started up his boat to take me to the island.

I stood on the bow of his boat, saltwater spraying in my face. As it was near sunset, the island seemed to glisten in the warm amber light. I was excited to begin my retreat. I only had my purse, a journal, a sleeping bag (which I'd borrowed from someone at the conference), and a gallon of water with notches on the container so I could mete out my daily allotment. I had no idea that a gallon wasn't enough water for a week.

There was no place to dock the boat, so holding my sleeping bag, purse, and water bottle high over my head, I jumped out into a shallow place in the water. My hands were full, but I turned to nod good-bye to the fisherman. As he looked at me, a cloud of concern reflected in his eyes. I smiled at him and turned to wade toward the rocky shore.

It was starting to get dark, but in the dusky light I had time to quickly explore "my" deserted island. I walked from one end to the other in about 15 minutes. It was rocky, but there were lots of trees and bushes. In the center of the island, I found a flat, open space surrounded by trees. It was an ideal location to camp out. Night descended quickly. Leaving my clothes on, I nestled into my sleeping bag, again using my purse for a pillow. I looked up into the night sky; the stars ignited the heavens. God seemed so close. I could almost touch the golden realm.

Just before I fell asleep, I realized that I hadn't made any plans for getting off the island. *But I have a week to figure that out*, I thought drowsily as I slipped into a deep slumber.

The next morning I lay in my sleeping bag looking at the birds hopping from branch to branch of a small, leafy tree. My back was sore from the hard ground, but my spirit was breathing in the fresh morning air and enjoying the wonderful feeling of knowing I had a week ahead of me to fast, write in my journal, and meditate.

Without warning, my sun-dappled solitude was invaded by the sound of a plane flying low overhead. I watched curiously as it approached. It came closer and closer. Too close! It was flying much too low.

Oh my God! It's going to crash! I thought as I panicked.

I jumped out of my sleeping bag and ran toward some bushes. Suddenly the ground around me exploded. Bullets were hitting everywhere, ricocheting off the dirt and the trees!

No! It can't be! The plane is shooting at me! I thought with horror. A momentary image of the man who shot me flashed through my head and I panicked. *Why?! Why is this happening to me?* Then I glanced down at my clothes. *Oh no! My pink top! They'll be able to see me easily with it on!*

As I ran, I yanked off my bright pink shirt and threw it down as I dove for cover under the bushes. On my knees, I frantically scrambled under the thick branches to hide. The brush tore at my hands, breasts, and knees, but I kept forcing my way through to escape the bullets.

Why are they shooting at me?! My mind screamed as another shower of bullets peppered the bushes near me.

And then, just as suddenly as it began, the shooting stopped and the sound of the plane dissolved into the distance. I waited until I couldn't hear it anymore. It was so quiet. Eerily quiet. I waited for a very long time. Finally, I crept out from beneath the jagged bushes, snatched my possessions, grabbed my top, and raced to the shore. I wanted to get as far away as I could from that island. There was a large rock in the water 20 feet from shore. I waded to it and climbed on top of it. In my hurry to get off the island, I hadn't put my shirt back on, so I stood in my bra on the rock and waved my pink top over my head as a flag. It wasn't very long until I was able to alert a passing fisherman.

I imagine that a young woman standing in her bra, waving a hot pink shirt over her head, and hollering at the top of her lungs was hard to ignore. The boat pulled up, and the man on board asked in halting English, "You need help?"

"Yes! Thank you for stopping!" I said breathlessly, hurriedly putting on my top.

As I climbed into the boat, my words jumbled together, trying to explain what had happened. The fisherman's eyes widened.

"No one should take you to island!" he said angrily in broken English. "Everyone know is used for aerial target practice by military. If someone on island, men in the planes feel they can shoot them. You lucky to be alive."

The saltwater splashed over the fishing boat as we headed to shore. I watched the island become smaller in the distance. My decision to reach the land of golden light by fasting and meditating had almost ended in disaster. It seemed that it was a dangerous, slippery journey beyond this world into the next. Whenever I attempted to find the portal to the light, it seemed that forces of the dark were drawn as well.

I sometimes felt that I had one foot in the fire of the living and the other in boundless space. I didn't know where my home was . . . in the world of spirit or in the world of form? I often felt caught in the shadowland between humans and wilderness— a place where the outermost boundary of spirit touched the innermost realm of man. However, as I tasted the saltwater on my lips and held on to the side of the boat, one thing I knew for sure was that I was glad to be returning to the safety of Ron and our farmhouse.

CHAPTER EIGHT

Adrift
(1969–1970)

W e are born of sky, stars, and spirit, yet when we meld into a physical form, we forget the far-reaching mystery that dwells in our depths. As with an underground river that we only see where it surfaces, I'd have glimpses and memories of the infinite golden land, but then it would disappear, buried deep in the aquifer of my being. These glimpses became my sacred pact with myself to always remember the truths that I realized in my short time there. But it was so easy to forget.

AS SOON AS I SAW RON AT THE AIRPORT, I threw myself into his supple arms. I was so glad to be back. When we arrived home, it smelled good and wholesome. Ron had picked wildflowers and had filled our farmhouse with canning jars full of them. He went into the kitchen to make a late lunch, and I went into the bedroom to begin to unpack.

A cold shudder suddenly ripped through my body. Lying haphazardly on the dresser was a photo of a smiling, naked women posed on Ron's bed . . . on our bed!

My face grew hot, and my fingers tingled as I held the photo in my hand. I turned it over. On the back she'd written,

"I thought you'd like this reminder of our time together." I sank onto the bed.

"Denise, what do you think about having potatoes with . . ." Ron stopped in mid-sentence as he stepped into the bedroom and saw me holding the photo.

"Oh, don't pay any attention to that," he spoke quickly. "We're old friends, and she was just joking around."

"But Ron . . . ," I said in shock. I couldn't take my eyes off the photo. "She's lying on our bed!"

"Oh, she must have done this as a joke when she was visiting. It's nothing," he replied jauntily.

I desperately wanted to believe him. He had told me he loved me and that I was the most important woman in his life. I needed to believe him. So I did. I was so used to suppressing my feelings while living with my mother and father that I just suppressed my disappointment and sadness in all aspects of my life.

Life continued much as before. I kept up my journalism studies and still worked on the newspaper, and Ron and I went on living together. We had so much in common—we were both passionate about peace, creativity, and good music—but somehow something had changed. I never mentioned the photo again, but it weighed on me like a heavy stone sinking to the bottom of the sea.

I DECIDED TO GO TO HAWAII for a semester to do a research project for my journalism major, but it really was an escape, a way to sort out my feelings about Ron. Also, Heather, who was 17 now, had run away to live in Hawaii, and I wanted to see her again. I was 19 at the time. I once again pooled together all the money I'd made at the paper and found a cheap student flight. I'd become good at living simply and saving money. I must have done this so that I always had a way out of any situation.

As my plane flew over the Pacific Ocean, I thought about all that I'd experienced since I was shot. The world was so much bigger than I could have possibly imagined while living in the limiting confines of Nordon. As my plane flew into Honolulu, I was astonished. Skyscrapers, huge hotels, condominiums, and automobiles were everywhere. I had naïvely expected more of an idyllic paradise. I imagined that I'd see people living in grass huts and hula girls on the beach, not so much "civilization."

I moved in with Heather, who was living in a studio apartment not far from Waikiki. She was living on her own and attending high school there. After I'd left home, all the rage that my mother had directed toward me was then directed at my sister. Our father was out of our lives at that point, and Heather had nowhere else to turn, so like me, she meticulously began saving her babysitting money, and after a year had enough to leave home.

One morning at 3 A.M., Heather left a good-bye note for my mother, hopped on a bus, and headed west. She wanted to get as far away from Nordon as she could, and Hawaii was that place. She successfully enrolled in school, got a job, and was living on her own. All this she did without the help of any family or friends. I was so proud of her for what she'd accomplished.

It was wonderful to have the time together. Although we'd both gotten out from under the fury of Mother, we feared for Gordon and Brand. But they somehow managed to survive her onslaughts until they left home, too. Brand often locked himself in the bathroom at night and slept in the bathtub—as I'd done when I lived at home—to avoid being beaten in the middle of the night.

IN HONOLULU, I STARTED DOING MY RESEARCH for MSU journalism credits about how living on an island affected the local media's perception of world events. I used the library at the University of Hawaii and scoured local newspapers and mainland periodicals for comparisons. However, my money was running low, so I needed to get a job. The next day I found an ad for an "escort service." Now, looking back, I can't help thinking, *What were you doing, Denise?! You can't have been that naïve.* But I guess I was.

I actually thought an escort service was just that . . . an escort service. When I called, I asked what the job entailed. I was told that sometimes tourists, or soldiers on leave, wanted someone to show them around or go out to eat with them so they wouldn't have to dine alone.

As I'd just arrived myself, I got a guidebook and studied all the attractions on the island of Oahu. Then I applied for the job. I was told I would be paid $10 for day escorts, and $15 for evening escorts. If I worked a long day, that meant $25. I thought that sounded pretty good.

My first companion was a young man on R&R from Vietnam. Although we were the same age, he seemed young and very scared. As we walked out of the escort-service office into the morning light, he jumped at the slightest sound. When a car backfired, he instantly flew to the ground. He was deeply embarrassed and apologetic as he got up and dusted himself off.

We went to a matinee and then had a late lunch. I asked him about his home, and he described his life on a farm in Iowa before he enlisted in the military. As he talked, one tear rolled down his cheek and then another. He kept trying to squeeze them back, but they kept flowing. When we parted, he told me that he was so happy to have had the time with me. He said I reminded him of the girls back home.

Most of my dates were boys on leave from Vietnam. I learned not to ask them about the war, so I just asked them about their life back in the States. They seemed to be so happy to have someone to talk to, and I was good at listening. It didn't occur to me at the time, but once again there was a parallel in my life with my mother, as she'd also served as a confidant to servicemen when she was in Hawaii before World War II.

One evening, a tourist I was escorting said something that unnerved me as I was shaking his hand to say good night. (I shook hands to say good-bye to my dates. I thought it was more professional than hugging them.)

"What about the rest?" he asked.

"What are you talking about?" I responded.

"You know. You're an escort, aren't you?"

"Yes. I escort people who don't know their way around the island," I replied.

"Aw, come on. Everyone knows what escort services are. How much money do you want for the 'extras'?" he leered.

I was horrified at his insinuation. "You should be ashamed of yourself for suggesting such a thing!" I said indignantly, as I spun on my heel and marched to the escort-service office to report him.

"What did my date mean when he said that 'everyone knows what escort services are'?" I demanded. I was shocked by the tourist's assumptions.

The manager looked at me slyly and winked as he said, "Well, what you do after the date is your business. We don't want to know about it."

My face flushed and my chest tightened. How could I have been so gullible?! I moaned with shame at what he implied. Then Sally, who was one of the friends I'd made at the service, walked in the door. I pulled her aside.

"Do you know what some of the girls here do? I think some of them are having sex with their dates!" I said, shocked.

Sally looked at me and carefully said, "Denise, we all are. Aren't you?"

I was completely aghast.

"You're wrong," I said. "I happen to know that Bobbi doesn't have sex with her dates. We double-date sometimes, and she shakes hands at the end of the evening like I do."

Sally leveled her eyes at me and said, "I think Bobbi has something she needs to tell you."

I was scheduled to have brunch with Bobbi the next morning at her apartment. Over the steaming eggs Benedict that was her specialty, I told her what Sally had said.

"Well, Denise, there is something that I've been meaning to tell you," she said quietly.

I waited expectantly.

"Umm. I don't know how to say this but . . . I'm not a girl."

I started laughing, "Yeah, right. And I'm an alien!"

"No, really, Denise, I'm a man. That's why I double-date with you. I know that your dates always end with a handshake, so I don't have to worry about my companion finding out about me."

"I don't believe you! You're not a boy! You can't be. You're my *girl*friend!"

"I'm a *boy*, and I can prove it," she said as she stood up and lifted up her skirt.

"Oh my God!" I said, looking down in disbelief. "You really *are* a boy."

I couldn't believe that I'd been so naïve. This was very different from what I'd encountered living in the Midwest. When I told Heather, she just shook her head as if to say, "Yup, you're stupid."

SOMETIMES, I WASN'T STUPID; I was just at the wrong place at the wrong time. One afternoon my friend Barb and I decided to go on a picnic. Barb said, "I know a great beach to go to. It's so remote that no one ever goes there."

We jumped into her battered yellow VW bug and drove

several hours over treacherous red dust roads to a truly isolated location. It took a long time because we had to slowly maneuver over deep potholes. "This land is owned by the military," she offered, "but in all the years I've been coming here, I've never seen anyone."

"Cool! Then that means we can go swimming naked!" I said.

"Great idea! But let's leave our clothes and towels in the car so we don't get them dirty scrambling down the cliff to the sea," Barb said as she parked near the edge of a cliff that dropped perilously to a small beach below.

Leaving only our sneakers on, we made our way down the cliff and had a delicious morning swimming in tropical waters and sunbathing on the soft white sand on our own private beach.

Climbing back up the cliff, I popped my head over the edge, then quickly popped it back down again. Only a few feet away was a military family having a picnic. The father was in full uniform, and the mother was serving sandwiches to three well-dressed young boys.

"Damn!" I whispered ducking my head back down. "We can't go now!"

"What do you mean?"

"There's a family up there having a picnic. We're trespassing . . . and we're naked!" I whispered.

"What are we going to do? I'm really cold. Do you think they'll leave soon?" Barb asked.

I peeked over the edge again.

"Nope. It looks like they're going to be here for a long time."

"What are we going to do?" she moaned.

"Did you ever hear of *The Emperor's New Clothes?* Well, we're going to climb over the edge, stand up tall, throw our shoulders back, and walk right by them as if we were fully clothed . . . and then get the hell out of here!"

"You're kidding!" Barb whispered. "We can't do that! We'll get caught for trespassing . . . and for indecent exposure. And we'll probably traumatize those boys."

"If we act like everything is perfectly normal, they'll hardly notice us. Trust me, the boys won't be traumatized. It will probably be a highlight of their life."

I imagined that Barb and I would look like goddesses rising out of the sea, but the reality was that the un-chic look of sneakers on our feet and our salt-crusted hair probably made us look more like renegade streakers than goddesses. In any event, I persuaded Barb to do it.

"Now, remember," I said, "stand up straight and tall. Act as if you're fully clothed and have every right to be here. Here we go!"

We heaved ourselves up over the edge, stood up, squared our shoulders, and sauntered past the family.

The father looked up and his jaw dropped. Then the mother and the boys all looked up, and their eyes opened as wide as golf balls.

"Have a pleasant day!" I said in my best English accent (at that age I thought sounding English would legitimize anything). Barb looked at me sharply, surprised at my assumed accent, and then slowly turned to the family and said in her best English accent, "Good day!"

With as much regal grace as we could muster, we got into the car and drove off, leaving a haze of red dust in our wake. As I turned and glanced through the back window, the entire family seemed frozen as they watched our retreating vehicle in stunned silence.

After leaving the escort service, my so-called English accent came in handy when I landed a new job as a waitress at a restaurant that was modeled after a London pub. We all dressed like English barmaids and tried to speak in English accents as we served businessmen lunch. It was a huge notch up from my last waitressing job.

IT WASN'T EASY FINDING ENOUGH TIME to work as well as do research, but I managed to do it. Finally my project was complete, and I flew back to Michigan and to Ron. Our time apart had been good. My time in Hawaii had put my life with him in perspective, and I realized how fortunate I was to have him in my life. I easily slipped back into my routine at the university and at home in our farmhouse.

After I'd been home for a few months, Ron mentioned that he was going to an educational conference for the weekend. I helped him pack. The next day I got a call from one of his friends who wanted to give him some information to give Jennifer.

"Oh, you must be mistaken. He's at a conference for the weekend," I said.

"No, he's not. He's camping with Jennifer and her parents," she said.

"What do you mean?" I said. Jennifer was one of my friends. She hadn't mentioned going camping with Ron.

"I thought you knew they were seeing each other. Everybody knows. I thought you were just staying at the farmhouse until you could find somewhere else to live. Maybe Ron didn't want to hurt you, so . . . so . . . he didn't tell you," she stammered.

"But we're living together. I'm sharing his bed! And Jennifer is my friend," I started to cry.

"Oh," she said quietly. "Well, I'm really sorry. Good-bye."

"Good-bye," I said and just stared at the phone in my hand.

Heather was right, I thought. *I am gullible and naïve. How could I have been so stupid to believe that someone could really love me? I'm not worthy of love and never will be. My mother was right when she said that if someone liked me it was only because I temporarily fooled them. She said that eventually they would find out what kind of person I was. Ron must have found out. I must disgust him. That's why he lied to me about the weekend. He must have lied about the naked woman on his bed, too.*

In the cupboard Ron had a bottle of Scotch, and in the medicine cabinet I found sleeping pills. I downed the pills and began chugging the Scotch. It burned my throat, and I hated the taste of it, but I just kept drinking. I knew that it wouldn't be long before I passed out. As I began to get sleepy, I decided to write about the physical effects of an overdose of sleeping pills and Scotch. In my stupor, my parents' belief in science above all else must have emerged, because I wanted my death to have some kind of value for medical researchers. It never occurred to me to write a good-bye note. I sat at Ron's typewriter and began listing my symptoms in detail. But it was getting harder and harder to type and hit the right keys. I finally fell asleep with my head on the desk.

Bang! Bang! Bang!

I heard someone pounding on the door. The sound seemed to be a very long way away.

Bang! Bang! Bang!

I slowly pushed myself up from the typewriter and stumbled toward the door. When I finally opened the door, my friend Sherrie was standing there. She'd forgotten something at the house that she needed, and the door was locked.

"Oh my God!" she exclaimed when she saw my face.

Incoherently, I tried to talk to her about the scientific information I was recording about the effects of Scotch and sleeping pills.

"Oh shit! We have to get you to the hospital right away!" She grabbed my arm; her hand felt cold and clammy as she dragged me into her car. I kept falling asleep as she raced to the emergency room.

"Denise, stay awake!" Sherrie screamed as she careened her car down narrow roads.

At the hospital, they gave me something to make me throw up. I vomited until I felt like my insides were coming out. I felt miserable, but I was alive.

My life was in a shambles. I was a mess. The only solution seemed to be to leave Ron and Michigan forever. I quit school, packed my bags, and returned to Hawaii.

YEARS LATER, I LEARNED THAT RON had been shaken to his core by my suicide attempt. He didn't think that I'd cared that much about him. He wrote me a letter saying that Jennifer represented the country club and the "good" life that he thought he needed at the time. He said: "You seemed brave and liberating . . . sometimes to the edge of dangerous, in your pursuit for life's meaning." He said that this, at times, scared him and made him uncomfortable.

He wrote: "Denise, for you to understand that you were brave would be like getting a fish to understand water. Being brave was just a part of your being. You were always questioning your direction in life and saying to yourself, 'Do I believe this?' You never necessarily went along with the crowd."

The ironic thing was that I didn't feel brave at all. I was scared. Losing Ron was like having my roots ripped out of the earth. I felt adrift, without direction or meaning. When I lost my connection with Ron, everything else disappeared—angels, the golden land, God, nature, trees. All of it was gone. I was floating in a black, empty void.

AS THE PLANE TOOK OFF, taking me away me away from Michigan, I looked out the window down at the patches of dirty, snow-covered land around the airport. It all looked so dismal and bleak. Suddenly, the smoke-gray sky dropped away, and the plane burst into sun above the clouds, reminding me of the first time I'd flown far above the clouds on my way to a better life in Los Angeles with my grandparents.

When I arrived in Hawaii, even though the sky was blue and the air was filled with the sweet scent of plumeria flowers, I felt like I was in a fog. When I told Heather that I'd tried to kill myself, she was sympathetic and took me for walks on the beach and into the rainforests, where we swam in spring-fed pools. However, I was brimming with guilt about doing these things; I didn't deserve to enjoy myself because I wasn't a worthy person. I was haunted by everything that my mother had said about me and by the feeling that I must have deserved what happened with Ron. I felt guilty just to be alive.

EVEN THOUGH I WAS SLOWLY STARTING to heal, I sometimes had horrifying nightmares in which someone was trying to kill me. These dreams were less terrifying than the ones I'd had in the hospital after I was shot, but in these new nocturnal onslaughts, I believed that I deserved to be killed. I continued to think that I wasn't worthy and eventually sought the help of a psychologist who asked, "Isn't there even one thing you like about yourself?"

"I can't think of anything," I replied glumly.

"You have one week to think of something," she insisted.

The next day, as hard as I tried, I couldn't think of something I liked about myself. For every noble quality I thought of, I found a reason why I was deficient. I tried to think of something I liked about my body, but all I could think about were the things that I didn't like. My hands were too big, my scars were too puckered, my nose was crooked. Finally, five days later, when I was brushing my teeth in front of the mirror, I looked closely at my eyes and got excited!

I like my irises! I thought joyfully. *I do have something that I like about myself!*

I was elated. My eyes were a pretty, golden-green color. I was relieved. I had something to tell the psychologist. The day before my appointment, I attended a festival at Diamond Head Crater, where there was a booth offering free iridology sessions (a health system that examines the structure and color of the eye). I was excited to have my revelation validated. Instead of complimenting my eyes, however, the iridologist looked at me gravely.

"You are toxic," he said with somber authority.

"I'm toxic?" I responded, crushed.

"Yes. That muddy-yellow color in your eyes means that you're polluted and toxic."

I was devastated. The only thing that I liked about myself meant that I was polluted.

EVERY DAY I PLUNGED DEEPER into despair. All the events of my past—my mother's outbursts, my father's abuse, getting shot, the trial, Ron's betrayal—weighed on me like old bones strapped around my neck. At night I would slip into the oblivion of sleep and wish that I would never have to wake up again. And every morning when I opened my eyes, my chest felt like it was being crushed by the despair of having to live another day.

No longer under the jurisdiction of my mother, I was free to communicate with my grandmother. However, although Grandma remained important in my life and we wrote to each other, I didn't want to burden her, so my letters were usually filled with pleasantries. And perhaps I was so set on distancing myself from my past that I didn't seek her advice often.

I knew that some kinds of mental illness were inherited,

so I feared that I was going crazy like my mother. I was terrified of becoming like her, and I kept thinking about taking my life. I believed that the only thing that could save me from my downward spiral was to commit myself to a mental hospital. Even though I was dubious of psychiatry because I'd seen how little it seemed to have helped my mother, I didn't know what else to do.

When I arrived at the Hawaii State Mental Hospital, which was near downtown Honolulu, I was escorted to the office of the head psychiatrist. As I looked at him across his oversized desk, I was impressed with the profound kindness in his eyes. When I explained that I was suicidal and I was there to commit myself, he looked at me carefully for a moment and then said, "Let's see what the tarot cards say about that."

My grandmother had talked about the tarot, but I was stunned that this spiritual tool was being put to use at a state mental hospital! *He's a psychiatrist, and he's going to ask the tarot whether to admit me or not? This is unbelievable. It can't be happening!* I thought, as I outwardly just nodded in agreement.

He pulled out a well-worn deck of tarot cards and began to shuffle them. After they were all arranged, he studied them carefully. "The tarot tells me not to admit you."

"It does?" I said, a bit in shock.

"Yes. If we admit you, we'll pump you full of drugs. You won't be able to experience what you're going through. What you need to do is go to the top of a mountain and scream for a few days, and you'll feel much better."

I left his office as hollow as when I first arrived in Hawaii but determined to take his advice, even if it did come from tarot cards. Early the next morning I drove up to Mt. Tantalus, hiked through the forest until I found a completely secluded area, and then started screaming. I shrieked and wailed and shouted while violently kicking a dead tree stump over and over again. I screamed at my father and my mother. I yelled at Ron for betraying me and at the guy who shot me. I hollered at the town of Nordon, at the lawyers for spreading false rumors, and at the newspapers for printing lies.

My screaming must have caught the attention of two big Samoan guys, presumably out for a hike on the mountain. They looked menacing as they pushed their way through the ferns toward me. Without a thought, I started screaming at them like a wild, crazy woman.

"Get the hell out of here! This is my place! Find your own place!"

I screamed irrationally, screeching almost like my mother did, but it felt good. It felt great!

They looked at each other, backed away, and hurriedly turned and left. I heard one say, "That haole lady—she loco!" In pidgin English, this means "the white woman is crazy."

The psychiatrist was right; after I'd screamed for a few days, I felt much better. I always meant to thank him, but I never got the opportunity . . . until we had an unexpected meeting.

I'd received an invitation from a journalist friend to attend an art opening. It was a fund-raiser, and many well-known people from Hawaii were in attendance. As I admired the paintings in the gallery, my friend, who seemed to know everyone in town, came up to me and pointed out various people including *the head psychiatrist from the mental hospital*. He was standing off by himself looking at a painting.

I was so excited that he was there. I could now thank him for his excellent advice. As I approached him, he turned and looked at me. I almost gasped.

Although his face and body were exactly the same, he seemed different, especially in his eyes. The eyes of the psychiatrist at the hospital had been kind and compassionate, but by comparison, this man's were dull and guarded, and he didn't seem to recognize me at all.

After a few pleasantries, I admitted that we'd met at the mental hospital when I attempted to commit myself. Mentioning that I was extremely grateful for the tarot reading that convinced him not to commit me, I thanked him for his great advice about "scream therapy."

As I spoke, he took a step back, his mouth pursed until it became a thin hard line, and his eyes narrowed. He said that not only had he never met me before, but he'd never seen a deck of tarot cards, let alone used them. He thought they were just superstitious nonsense.

As I watched him walk away, a tremble rumbled through me. Although his body was exactly the same, he *wasn't* the same man I'd met at the hospital. Once again, some kind of divine intervention had prevented me from being committed to that institution. As strange as this may sound, I believe that an angel masqueraded as the head psychiatrist on the day I tried to admit myself. I can't think of any other explanation. I often think of how different my life would have been if I'd been admitted.

I felt especially fortunate when, a few years later, I visited a friend who was committed to that very same mental-health facility in Honolulu. I hardly recognized the thoughtful, curious woman I knew. When I walked into her room with a big armful of flowers, I was devastated to see that the interns had put her in a straitjacket and tied her to the bed. She was lying in her own urine, and was so drugged that she didn't even know it. She was later released, and subsequently committed suicide.

CHAPTER NINE

The Crater

Every life has turning points. Even if we're not aware of them at the time, these pivotal moments change the direction of a life . . . sometimes forever. Landing in the hospital in Michigan for the suicide attempt was one of these times; however, a far greater one occurred for me in the depths of a crater.

Although my screamfest on the mountain had released some of my depression, an inner battle was waging between my light and dark sides. I fluctuated back and forth. Sometimes I believed that I was a worthless person who deserved to be mistreated; other times I caught glimpses of myself surrounded by the light of the golden land. During those times, I remembered the words of my grandmother telling me that every experience was part of my soul's journey and would make me stronger.

Would I surrender to the evolution of my soul as it moved toward the light? Or would I steadfastly embrace the view that I was worthless and become even more self-destructive? This ongoing struggle was perhaps never as difficult as one terrifying night alone inside Haleakala Crater.

At the advice of a friend, I decided to fly from Oahu to visit Maui, one of the other Hawaiian Islands. The defining landscape monument on that island is Haleakala Crater, which is the largest dormant volcano on Earth. The summit of Haleakala Crater is 10,000 feet high, and if over two-thirds of its height weren't underwater, it would be higher than Mt. Everest.

When I first saw Haleakala, it looked like a holy relic silhouetted against the purple evening sky. It seemed to ripple with life-force, and I felt its monumental power cry out to me, like a mother calling her lost child. So strong was the "call" that I knew I was meant to journey to her heights as soon as possible. Very early the next morning, I caught a ride up the mountain in the open back of an old pickup truck. It was freezing in the darkness of the morning hours at the higher elevation, so I curled up tightly with my knees to my chest to try to stay warm on that long drive. Somehow, I never expected to experience such chilling temperatures in Hawaii. As I bounced around on the bed of the truck, I gazed to the stars lingering above. Cold weather always seems to make stars appear more vibrant.

It was still dark when we arrived, but the faint traces of morning light were seeping over the horizon's edges. We stood near the crater's rim, and to keep warm I huddled with the people who had given me a ride. Only a thin red line to the east heralded the arrival of the sun. The rest of the sky was black. Someone began to chant "Om," as if that would hurry the sun. I joined in wholeheartedly, hoping that my volume would keep the cold at bay.

Suddenly, long shafts of sunlight streamed in all directions from the eastern horizon. One long lance of light seemed to hurdle straight toward my chest. I'd never seen anything as sublime as the sun rising over the crater's rim that morning. As golden colors filtered onto the crater floor, the panorama below looked otherworldly, like a vast, barren landscape of some distant planet.

I don't know what happened to the others. They must have

left, but I had no awareness of anything but the crater. I was so transfixed that I could barely breathe. Nothing else seemed to exist except for that immense, stark landscape. Perhaps the altitude was affecting my brain. In the years since, I've come to know that I have exceptional difficulty with high altitudes. But at the time it felt like my spirit was awakening and the crater was beckoning me to enter its sacred core.

I hadn't planned to hike, but only to watch the sunrise and then return. However, even though I was only wearing a short dress and chunky, high-heeled shoes, I knew that I was being summoned to enter the crater. I started down a path, appropriately named Sliding Sands Trail, because it was a scant excuse for a trail. Basically, I slid over pumice, gravel, and other volcanic debris, down 2,000 feet to the crater floor. By the time I reached the bottom, the heel on my left shoe had been wrenched off. Since I couldn't walk with one high heel and one useless one, I shoved both of them into my purse and continued to walk barefooted toward the center of the crater, as if drawn by some magnetic force. The sharp pumice cut into my feet, and they started to bleed, but I just kept walking.

As the sun rose higher, I observed my surroundings. Huge boulders as big as houses and enormous cinder cones, rising 600 feet high, dotted the landscape. There was almost no vegetation. There were no animals, plants, or birds. The air was silent. All I could hear was the sound of my labored breath. The throbbing pain in my bleeding feet punctuated everything, but I still continued forward. Sometimes I would stop for periods of time just to absorb the stillness, but then it felt as if an invisible force was propelling me forward.

I was beginning to doubt that I could continue on bare feet when I came upon a pair of shoes lying next to the path. I looked in amazement at the shoes and then looked around. As far as I could see in every direction, there was no sign of anyone.

Feeling that they'd been left for me, I slipped into them. They were a bit bigger than my normal size, but were ideal for my swollen feet. Tentatively, I tried walking in them. They were perfect. I had no water or food with me, but the shoes seemed to be an affirmation to keep going. I felt as though I was being drawn somewhere for a reason. Occasionally I stopped for long periods of time, waiting until I felt the pull of that invisible force, before continuing on.

As the night drew near, a thick fog rolled into the crater. As I looked at the approaching solid wall of fog—it was 30 feet high—I was filled with an irrational fear that something sinister and dark was hidden within it. It traveled rapidly toward me with the menace of an advancing army. Fingers of mists curled out and then retracted. It seemed alive and aware of me, even searching for me.

Although I knew it was irrational to think that there was something threatening in the mist, I was still terrified. Perhaps walking all day in the sun at high altitude, the lack of food and water, the pain in my feet, and having had very little sleep the previous night meant that my faculties weren't as clear as normal, but my fear was real.

Not far ahead, between the cloud bank and me, I could see a hikers' cabin. I judged the distance and thought that if I ran, I could beat the wall of fog to the cabin. As I broke into a run, the speed of the fog seemed to increase. The cuts on my feet burned, but I raced to the cabin anyway and pushed open the door just as the cloud bank encompassed the structure. Heaving from exhaustion and fear, I quickly looked around me; the cabin was sparsely furnished but clean. I imagine that it was usually locked, but for some reason it was open that night. Glancing out the window, I could see that the cabin was sheathed in thick fog. I couldn't see anything, but I could almost taste the dark force surrounding the cabin.

I groped in the dim light of the cabin until I found some candles and matches. Usually I felt comforted by candlelight, but the wavering shadows on the walls were ominous. I found some old blankets on a shelf, wrapped myself in them, and sat in the one dilapidated chair that was there, holding my arms around my middle. Some previous hiker had placed a skeleton head of some kind, perhaps from a deer or goat, on an open shelf in the cabin. The candlelight reflected through the eye-holes of the skeleton, making a ghoulish dancing shadow on the wall. It seemed to be balefully laughing at me. I knew that I should get up and move the skeleton, but I was too petrified to do so, so I just held my belly and rocked back and forth.

I'd spent time alone at night in remote areas, and I'd never been afraid of darkness or of being alone, especially in nature. But this was something different.

Then I began to hear noises outside the cabin. Lots of noises. The crater landscape was so barren, how could there be anything out there? I heard scuttling sounds, rasping coughlike noises, and at one point, the door even rattled. There was no phone. No one would hear me if I screamed.

I began to pray, hard and long. I prayed to God and to the angels and to my ancestors. I pleaded and bargained. I felt as if some demonic entity wanted in, and only the candlelight and my prayers kept it at bay.

The shuffling sounds heightened with the velocity of my prayers. I've never really believed in evil, but on that night I felt that a malevolent force was waiting outside to feed upon my soul.

There is no evil! I don't believe in it, I frantically tried to convince myself. But it seemed that whenever I attempted to find the gateway into the light, such as following a "holy summons" into the crater or deciding to meditate while on the small island in the Adriatic Sea, the darkness was attracted as well. Did my movement toward the light create a polarization of the dark? My mind scrambled as I tried to find answers.

I prayed almost throughout the entire night, but it seemed that my fear was giving strength to the dark force. The harder I prayed, the more ominous the malevolence became. Finally, in exhaustion, I just surrendered. I let go and quit fighting. *God, I can't do this on my own. I need help!*

In that moment of letting go, I had a glimpse of the land of golden light. For an enduring second, everything in the cabin was filled with the same glow that I'd experienced just after being shot . . . and I knew that nothing could hurt me. As the golden light flowed around me, I was aware that I was connected to a living, pulsating universe—one that sings with life and reverberates with the intensity of spirit. There were no "bad" and "good" parts of creation. Everything was relative to every other being; nothing existed in isolation. I knew that I had an intimate connection with it all.

The noises outside ceased and, like a great tide ebbing to the sea, the cloud bank rolled back. I opened the door, walked outside, and looked up to the heavens. Gazing at the stars, which were so bright and clear, I knew that I wasn't alone . . . and I would never be alone. There was a higher power watching over me—it was beyond the dualism of dark and light—and I wasn't separate from it or from the universe. It dwelled inside me, always and forever.

In the early-morning hours, exhausted, I fell asleep on the cot in the cabin. When I woke up, it was as if nothing had happened the night before. The sun poured through the windows; the day was clear. The fog was gone.

I knew that I'd gone through some kind of initiation . . . and passed. The experience was a turning point in my life. When I opened the door, I expected to find tracks around the cabin or some clue as to what had made all the noise. There wasn't anything unusual. My rational mind reasoned that it must have been a deer or raccoon looking for food in the night. But in a deeper place, I didn't actually believe that. I felt that I'd cast off some ancient, inner darkness that had manifested itself in a physical form.

Perhaps the malevolent force I experienced in the crater was a reflection of hidden fear and suppressed memories from my own life, and the churlish mists were a fitting metaphor for the concealed parts of my past. Whatever the truth, I was glad to have survived that experience. Something magnificent did happen that night, because although I hadn't had any water or food and my feet were bruised and swollen, I hiked out of the crater that day feeling lighter and clearer than I had in a long time.

CHAPTER TEN

The Quest
(1970–1974)

It wasn't long after my experience in the crater that I discovered that raking can be an art. This humble labor, when done with a focused heart, has a comforting rhythm and cadence. I found that the simple act of gathering debris and leaves had a calming effect on my soul.

I'd read an article about Zen Buddhism that said that simple, everyday acts, such as sweeping or raking, are considered a path to enlightenment. The article described enlightenment as a kind of surrendering during which practitioners realize that they're not separate from the world. They enter a realm of infinite light where there's no past or future—only an eternal "now." This sounded like my near-death experience and also like what had occurred in Haleakala Crater.

I was almost 21 years old, and I desperately wanted to enter the land of golden light again—it was only there that I truly felt at home—but I didn't want to have to almost die or be terrified to the depths of my soul to find it again. Maybe Zen Buddhism would be a pathway to return peacefully.

I'd heard about a Zen Buddhist monastery nestled in the tropical Manoa Valley on the island of Oahu and decided to visit. When I arrived, everything was so quiet that I didn't want to call out for someone, so I walked up to the door and slowly pushed it open. Inside was a simple, unadorned room. Small, round black cushions in a neat row lined the edge of the wall. Light filtered in the window through the large tropical leaves growing outside, giving the room a green cast. On an altar, a solitary stick of incense burned.

The serenity and stillness was a powerful contrast to the past events of my life. A ray of sunlight illuminated the thin line of smoke from the incense as it slightly swirled on its way upward. Everything seemed to slow down. In that simple room, I experienced the same deep serenity I'd felt during those moments near death at age 17. *This is my home*, I thought as I exhaled deeply. Something inside me unlocked, and tears rolled down my cheek. *This is where I belong.*

Even though I didn't really know anything about Zen Buddhism or what the requirements were to live in a monastery, I knew that I needed to move in. I found my way to someone working in the gardens and eventually to the head monk.

"Women don't usually want to live here. Almost everyone here is a man," he said.

In those days, it was unusual for women to practice Zen meditation (called *zazen*). It was a difficult practice usually only undertaken by men. To sit absolutely still with your legs tucked into very painful positions while your limbs cramped and your back ached, and to try to think about "nothing" for hours at a time was an arduous practice. Maybe it appealed more to men than women because it was so hard. Perhaps women realized that there were other ways to become enlightened without so much pain and suffering. But none of that mattered to me. I knew I was home.

"We only have space for two women to live in the *zendo* (monastery), and it is highly unusual for a place to be available. However, for the first time in three years, a space *is* available. One of the women moved out yesterday," he said.

"Do you have any experience with *zazen* or know anything about Buddhism?"

I'd read about various meditation techniques, but I didn't know anything about Zen Buddhist meditation. "I don't," I said. "But I know that it is my path. I know that I am meant to live here," I said with absolute certainty.

My sincerity must have been convincing, because I moved in immediately and prepared for my life in the monastery. There were very few expenses in the *zendo*, and I had a small amount of money saved from my waitress days, so I knew I'd be fine. Little did I realize on that first day that I would live there for more than two years.

Heather, of course, thought it was another one of my crazy ideas. She shrugged when I told her, assuming that it would be only a passing fancy and that I'd move out once I tried to sit still for a long period of time. To this day, I'm amazed I stayed as long as I did, considering the difficulty of that kind of meditation.

The first week I thought I was going to die from the pain and discomfort. I'd always been active, starting from the young age when I'd kept my mother busy climbing up the 12-foot ladder and toddling away into the neighborhood church. Before I moved to the *zendo*, I could hardly even sit still for a minute. So when I was required to "sit" on a hard cushion, with my legs crossed in the lotus or half-lotus position for at least four hours a day without moving at all, I thought I would implode. It was excruciatingly painful, my knees ached, my back hurt, and my mind ranted at me for doing something so ludicrous as sitting in pain all day.

Denise, are you crazy?! my mind would yell at me. *You could be at the beach, swimming in the sea, sunbathing, going to parties, dancing, and having fun. What the hell are you doing just sitting here?!*

I'm meant to be here, my spirit answered.

If you want to sit all day, then go sit at the beach! At least then you won't be in such pain! my mind spewed.

Go away, my spirit gently replied.

What about guys? Do you know how many cute guys there are on the beaches?

Get lost! I roared.

It was constant agony to try to still my mind and quiet my thoughts. The kind of meditation that the monks taught was very different from the book I'd read on meditation while I lived in the trailer in Ohio. I was instructed to focus on a spot below my navel while counting each inhalation until I reached ten, and then begin again *without having any other thoughts*. It was impossible not to think of anything! My thoughts crowded each other and completely occupied my mind. However, I was so sure that Zen meditation would take me to the land of golden light that I was determined to do it, no matter how painful.

I believed that the heavenly place that I'd entered after I was shot wasn't up in the sky somewhere. It was a dimension that I could reach while I was alive—I'd touched it for a few seconds in the crater. I intuitively felt that there were myriad co-existing dimensions here on Earth that could be likened to the stations on a radio. For me, meditation was like plugging into the universe of energy. Then, by correctly tuning an "inner dial" while I was meditating, I was certain I could reach the golden land.

But Zen meditation wasn't easy! I was exuberant the day I finally counted five breaths without thinking of anything else. *I did it! I'm not thinking of anything! I don't have any thoughts. I can do this!* I thought.

Damn! I am thinking! I'm thinking about "not" thinking! I said to myself in despair.

Even though I wasn't in seclusion in the zendo except during *sesshins* (intensive meditative retreats), my years in the Zen Buddhist monastery were austere. Sometimes we sat for up to 16 hours a day. During meditation, we faced a bare wall, with our backs ramrod straight. When I got distracted by pain or fatigue and forgot to count my breaths, the Zen master or monk would strike my shoulder with lightning accuracy with the long, hard *kyôsaku* stick to ensure my attentiveness. However, if the master deemed that I was doing well, he'd smack me just as hard to encourage me! So either way, I got hit a lot. We all did. It seemed strange that a peaceful practice of meditation included being struck, but that's the way Rinzai Zen Buddhism had been practiced for centuries.

After being hit, it was customary to *gasshô* (bow) to say, "Thank you." Usually I was grateful and bowed in sincerity, but some monks were better than others at using the *kyôsaku* stick. Whenever someone missed the fleshy part of my shoulder and bruised my shoulder bone, I wasn't grateful. In fact, I'd get mad, which is not a good Zen-like quality. But I'd still bow as I sat on my cushion and thank him anyway.

One day I put extra padding underneath my clothing, in the form of folded washcloths. No one could see the padding, but when the kyôsaku stick slammed down on my shoulder, it softened the blow. This time, when I bowed, it was in true gratitude (for the padding).

Although the meditation was very difficult, I gained an enormous amount through my Zen practice as well as from the chores that I did around the zendo, especially raking and working in the garden. I found the rhythm of the rake over the gravel to be immensely soothing. Slowly, the creases in my soul began to ease. My life was simple but very fulfilling.

ONE SUNNY AFTERNOON WHILE I WAS in my sleeping quarters, which was a plain, unadorned room with a solitary futon on the floor, I heard a small crackling sound. I turned and was shocked to see what looked like a three-dimensional square picture frame floating in the air about five feet in front of me. It was approximately two feet wide and long, and four inches deep. Inside the frame there was a moving scene of brightly colored geometric patterns overlaid with red and orange flickering flames. Tiny, ferocious humanoid creatures with sharp teeth shifted and moved around the flames.

I was bewildered and frightened, but also curious. It was real. It wasn't my imagination. It just floated in front of me. I watched the tiny creatures as they swayed and danced in the fires. It was one of the most incredible things I'd ever seen.

I felt drawn to it . . . almost mesmerized. I wanted to look at it more closely, but as I stepped forward and reached my hand out to touch it, it instantly disappeared.

Incredible! I was wide-awake—it was the middle of a sunny day! I immediately went to the Zen master to ask him about what I'd seen. He just nodded and said, "It is just *makyo*. Ignore it." (*Makyo* refers to the visions that appear to some Zen students as a result of their intense meditative practice.) Zen masters always instruct their students to ignore these visions because they can distract from one's practice. However, I just couldn't forget what I'd seen, so I went to talk to one of the Zen students who had trained as a Jungian analyst before he entered the zendo. He said quite simply, "Oh, what you saw was a mandala. Other people have had the same experience."

"So I'm not crazy. I really did see it," I said, relieved. I'd never heard of mandalas before.

"You're certainly not crazy, Denise. What you've had is a very special occurrence. Carl Jung considered the spontaneous appearance of a mandala to be a healing symbol of integration and wholeness." He explained that the creatures represented sacred deities, but they looked like little demons to me.

He explained that a mandala (which means "circle" in Sanskrit) usually contains geometric forms surrounding a central point. He said that it represents the whole self and the entire universe, and that it can spontaneously appear to someone in a time of transformation. In India and Tibet, monks create mandalas out of colored sand, or they paint them on canvas or paper. They feel that meditation upon a mandala can clear the mind and allow a person to peer into inner realms.

As hard as I tried during my time in the zendo, I never had what I considered to be a true enlightenment experience. We were told that the way to *satori* (enlightenment) is by not trying to achieve it. So I worked hard at "not trying," yet nothing happened. The Zen master said that enlightenment wasn't the point of Zen meditation, but secretly everyone at the zendo still wanted it. Although I'd gained a depth of inner peace during my time there, after two years, I still hadn't found the way to the land of golden light. I knew that it was time to leave.

REMEMBERING HOW DETERMINED I'D BEEN to get a higher education while I was working at the truck-stop café, I decided to go back to college. I received a generous grant, which allowed me to attend the University of Hawaii and pay for a rented room in a small cottage with beautiful gardens within walking distance of the campus. I also received an additional stipend for living expenses. Heather was attending the same university studying botany and biology and doing research on native tropical plants. She had also gotten her pilot's license and worked with search-and-rescue missions on the islands. It was wonderful to take hikes through the Hawaiian rain forests together while she described various medicinal plants growing on the forest floor.

While living in the zendo, my interest in journalism had waned, and I'd become interested in spirituality. In a special experimental program through the university, called New College, I was able to create my own major. I incorporated my experiences at the monastery into my research, as well as my interest in spiritually altered states of consciousness.

For my year-end project, I didn't just want to write about altered states, I wanted my college instructors to actually experience them. It was a highly unorthodox project that I had in mind. However, my teachers agreed because it was an experimental program. They were open to exploring different educational modalities.

After the spontaneous appearance of the mandala in the zendo, I'd developed a fascination with them, so I decided to use them as the focus of my project. The most intricate and beautiful ones I found came from Tibet, so I took slides of various Tibetan mandalas. Then I obtained a recording of Tibetan monks chanting. For my presentation, I ushered my instructors and a number of university students into a darkened room where they sat quietly in anticipation.

First, the sound of quiet chanting filled the space. I then spoke in a low voice. "You are about to enter the *bardo* states." I explained that the bardo states are the layers of consciousness that Tibetans believe you advance through as you die. (In retrospect, I think I chose this theme because of my several brushes with death and the subsequent journey that each of those experiences had initiated within me.)

I then projected the first photo of a mandala onto the screen. I chose one that looked very similar to the fiery red and orange one that had appeared to me. As I talked about each *bardo* state, I projected another mandala image.

My understanding of Tibetan Buddhism was relatively shallow, but as I continued to talk about letting go of normal consciousness and entering into other realms, teachers and students alike began to have profound, spontaneous spiritual experiences. They reported that floating lights, sounds, and images involuntarily occurred for them during my presentation. It was my very first foray into what later became my profession . . . creating sacred environments within which people could have spontaneous spiritual awakenings.

AT THE SAME TIME THAT I ATTENDED classes at the University of Hawaii, I also developed an interest in nontraditional healing. Because of the severity of my injuries stemming from the shooting, numerous doctors had told me that I would have physical problems throughout my entire life, including not being able to have children. One doctor even told me not to expect to live very long. I know that doctors say these kinds of things so their patients can face life realistically; however, in many ways, telling someone that they'll always be unhealthy, or that they don't have long to live, can become a self-fulfilling prophecy.

I instinctively knew that if I was going to live a long, healthy life, I needed to turn my back on allopathic medicine and embrace alternative healing. (Now, however, I embrace both traditional and alternative medicine, and use the best from each one.) My spiritual journey toward health and healing led me to a Hawaiian *kahuna* (a shaman).

I'd heard about the health benefits of massage, so I decided to experience it. I opened the yellow pages in the Honolulu phone book to find page after page of masseuses. I was uncertain whom to call, but one ad seemed to glow, so I looked at it more carefully. The Royal Hawaiian, a stately old hotel in Waikiki, listed a massage center, so I called and booked an appointment for later that day. Arriving at the clinic, which was in the hotel basement, I sat in the waiting room thumbing through a magazine. Suddenly I "felt" someone enter the room.

As I looked up, I saw a beautiful, middle-aged Hawaiian woman with incredibly kind eyes looking at me. Slowly, a warm, salty tear rolled down my cheek, and before I knew it, I was weeping. My tears turned to sobs, and my shoulders began to shake. I was utterly confused. Here I was sitting in a hotel waiting room crying uncontrollably for no apparent reason.

When I could speak, I looked up and asked her, "What's wrong with me? Why am I crying?"

Gently she said, "It's just a release. Don't be concerned. Come with me. I'm your massage therapist, Morna Simeona."

Because of the reaction I had to her presence, I knew that I'd met someone very special. In the massage room, Morna instructed me to lie down. As she put her hands on me, I felt an electric pulse surge through my body, and instantly I fell into a deep sleep. When I awoke from the massage, I felt refreshed and cleansed. I also knew that I wanted to learn from this remarkable woman.

In later meetings, I found out that Morna was a revered healer to the native Hawaiians. She came from a long line of healing kahunas; her mother, her grandmother, her great grandmother, and so on, had all been shamans. She worked at the massage studio because she believed that the healing that she gave tourists would travel back home with them to touch others. It was her way of helping the planet. (Eventually, she came to be considered by many to be a living treasure of Hawaii.) After my first massage, I immediately booked a second one with the sole purpose of asking Morna to teach me about healing. I felt that I'd discovered what I wanted to do with my life—I wanted to become a healer.

"Morna, please train me," I begged her.

"No, Denise. You're not ready," she said kindly.

"I am ready! I'll do whatever you say. Please train me to be a healer," I implored. She just smiled and shook her head back and forth. I continued to book massages with her, and each time I was there, I begged her to teach me, but she always told me that I wasn't ready.

One day I mentioned in passing that my mother's family was Cherokee.

"Oh, then you'll understand the old ways. It's in your blood. I will train you," she said. (I don't believe that you need to have native blood to understand the ancient wisdom of earth-based cultures. I believe the ability to understand comes from your heart rather than from your blood, but Morna thought that my heritage would be helpful to me.)

After just a few lessons, Morna asked me to work with her at the Royal Hawaiian Hotel doing massage. Although I didn't know very much, the practice came naturally to me, and I also appreciated the extra money to help with my college expenses.

Thus began my initiation into the healing field. Morna taught me the old Hawaiian ways to allow healing energy to flow through my hands into someone else. She also taught me about the use of herbs, how to banish ghosts, and how to talk to beings in the invisible realm.

Sometimes I went with Morna into the tropical forests to give gifts and fruit to the *menehunes* (Hawaiian elves and fairies). She could see them clearly and would have long, animated conversations with them while I stood on the edge of the clearing observing her. I couldn't see anything solidly visible, but the air around Morna seemed to shimmer in the same way that heat wavers above the desert on a hot day. She told me that I was beginning to see the *menehunes*, and the glistening air that I saw around her was my first step to being able to see these spirits of the forest.

Morna was often called upon to exorcise spirits from individuals and buildings. Through her I learned how to cleanse energy from houses and how to release earthbound spirits and ghosts. She used techniques that were directly descended from ancient rituals that she'd learned as a child. (Later in my life, I shared methods for cleansing and blessings homes that I'd learned from her and from a number of other shamans in three of my books: *Sacred Space, Space Clearing,* and *Space Clearing A–Z.*)

IN MY QUEST TO LEARN all I could about natural healing methods, I sought out the wisdom of a Japanese healer named Hawayo

Takata, who lived in one of the high-rise apartments near Waikiki. As I took the elevator up to meet her, I thought, *What a strange place for a healer to live.* Somehow I thought that healers would live in a temple or in a retreat in the woods, but not near Waikiki. Living in the rarefied environment of the zendo had unrealistically colored my perception about how "spiritual" people should live.

I knocked on the door, and a diminutive, spitfire-filled Japanese woman swung open the door.

"What took you so long?!" she demanded.

"Well, uh, I thought I was on time," I sputtered.

"You are on time for our appointment, but you are almost a year late for our meeting!" she said, as her eyes blazed.

"I am? But I didn't know about you a year ago," I said, genuinely surprised.

"I've known that you were coming for a long time. I've been waiting for you. You are the person who is going to organize my first Reiki courses for Westerners. I have been teaching Japanese students, but now I am ready to teach others," she said.

"Um, okay," I said.

She was charismatic, focused, and dynamic. There was never a thought of not doing what she requested.

"Now let me see your hands." She looked at them and said, "You are an excellent healer. Good."

She said everything with such authority that it never occurred to me to doubt her. Her words brought back the words of my grandmother, who had also told me I was a healer.

"Now just lie down here," she said.

I stretched out on the table she'd set up in her living room. I could see out the window to the Waikiki condos. When she put her hands on me, I felt a bolt of heat surge through me. The heat intensified, and I had the image of a burning inferno flashing through the space between my atoms. She had the ability to allow energy to flow through her hands that was similar to the method Morna had been teaching me.

However, Takata Sensei seemed so matter-of-fact about it all. (I called her Takata Sensei because *sensei* is a Japanese term of respect that means "teacher" or "master.") I was having a major experience, but to her it was quite ordinary. During my first treatment, she stopped twice to answer the phone and chat. Once she even left to go into the kitchen to stir her soup.

At the end of the session, I wanted to talk about what I'd gone through, but she just took it for granted that everyone who went to her would have a profound experience. She was, after all, the Reiki Grand Master, and the individual who introduced this type of healing to the West.

Even though I was still attending school, I also took the time to organize her classes. The transmission of healing ability through touch is an ancient tradition, and in her classes, she didn't just teach us techniques; she also transmitted to us the ability to heal. To instill the Reiki healing ability into me, she told me to put my hands in the prayer position and close my eyes. She then stood before me and transferred a fluid flow of energy into me through her touch. After that I could feel that my ability to heal was magnified.

SINCE HAWAII IS A MELTING POT of cultures, it was a great place to embark on my quest to learn about natural healing. Many healers from around the world, especially from the Orient, made their homes on the Island. I eventually trained with healers from the Philippines, Indonesia, China, Korea, India, and Japan. Although I was immensely happy for my years of college, I found that my real education came from this hands-on training. After I left the university, I also trained with an eccentric shiatsu master. Through him, I learned to balance the body by putting pressure on various spots, which are similar to the points used in acupuncture. Each teacher helped me apply a different piece of my life's puzzle.

During my questing period, I also attended one of the first "est" courses, and I eventually worked with this organization. The name stood for Erhard Seminar Training after the man who started it. (Est was a kind of motivational course, which was later called the Forum and Landmark.) There were about 200 people in these courses. When we had to go to the bathroom, we were told to hold it. Whenever someone peed in their pants because they couldn't hold it any longer, they stood up and "shared" about it, and then we all cheered for them. If someone confessed that they picked their nose or masturbated, we applauded them. It was actually great fun and liberating, but then again, I wasn't one of the people who peed in her pants!

I don't think I'd be inclined to attend such a course now, but at the time I gained a lot of value from it. It was the first place that I heard about not being a victim and taking responsibility for the events of one's life.

I also sought out numerous gurus and spiritual teachers, including Muktananda from India. I danced with the Rasneesh devotees, studied with the Theosophists, and chanted with the Hare Krishnas. I took yoga classes, and I explored every healing modality I could find. Ever since I'd been shot, I could sense and see energy fields, but I wanted to learn more about what that energy was and how to use it to help others.

THE MORE I EXPANDED MY ABILITY to understand and use energy, the more synchronicity I experienced. A remarkable coincidence transpired after I moved into another small cottage in the Manoa Valley. After I'd set up, a friendly neighbor brought by some freshly baked bread to welcome me to the area. There was something familiar about her that I just couldn't quite place.

Over tea, as we shared our backgrounds, we both discovered

that we'd gone to Michigan State University and that we'd been there over the same time period. It even turned out that we knew some of the same people. I told her that I'd been a journalism major taking courses in the communication department. Then I mentioned the sociology department, and she perked up.

"It's funny that you mention the sociology department, because I had an affair with a man who worked there," she said smiling. "We had to keep it quiet because he was living with someone else."

As she chatted merrily about her relationship, I looked warily at her. An image of a photo of a naked woman lying on our bed popped into my mind.

It's her! It's the woman in the photo! I thought. My next-door neighbor in Hawaii was the woman with whom Ron had had an affair! Luckily, the situation was far enough behind us that we had a laugh about it all and eventually became friends.

ALTHOUGH THE EARLY '70s was a period of change and upheaval for me, it was quite an exhilarating time in my life. In addition to exploring New Age beliefs, alternative healing, yoga, and acupuncture, I also joined a women's circle. It represented a different kind of feminism than I'd encountered at Michigan State University, where we would rant at the injustice that women had suffered through the ages and read feminist manifestos. With these women in Hawaii, instead of raging at the male-dominated society, we bared our souls and encouraged each other to integrate our emerging new sense of feminist freedom into our lives.

Women's circles were also a way to begin to move beyond shame about our bodies. As unbelievable as it may sound now, at that time, it was fashionable for women's groups to use a speculum and a mirror to help each other examine her own genitals. When looking inside her own vagina, usually for the first time, the responses ranged from "I had no idea that what it looked like" to "Wow, it's beautiful!" to "Yuck—I wish I'd never looked!" No matter what the response, the exercise and the subsequent discussions brought us together in our exploration of our womanhood.

What courage we had to share such an intimate act together! It was the first time I'd ever really seen what I looked like inside. How odd that there was a part of my anatomy that I hadn't seen and was even ashamed of. It was a part of me—and a very important part of all women—that I learned deserves to be cherished.

In the group, the other women kept telling me what a good teacher I could be because of the way that I shared my experiences with them. Morna had also told me that when she looked into my soul, she saw that my destiny was to be a teacher. I was very depressed when she said this, because I immediately thought of the uninspired teachers of my childhood. Teaching would have been one of my last choices for a career. However, she was right. I became a teacher sooner that I would have ever imagined.

A FRIEND OF MINE WHO WORKED in the University of Hawaii Continuing Education Department asked if I would be willing to teach a course on massage through their program. Even though I only knew the small amount of massage that Morna had taught me, and I'd never formally taught anyone anything, I agreed. As always, I jumped first and asked questions later. Sixty people showed up at that first class. In spite of my lack of experience, the class was a huge success. By studying a book on massage every day before class, I somehow managed to make it through every session.

My classes became Continuing Education's most popular courses. As I taught massage, I became fascinated by the way the energy fields of the body responded to touch. My ability to see and sense the energy flows of the body increased. Sometimes I'd see wavy lines coming up off the body that looked like waves rising off a hot highway, similar to what I'd seen in the forest with Morna. Other times I would see colors around different parts of the body. I was fascinated by the energy that flowed in and around it, and after a rather harrowing direct experience of it, learned to respect this potent force.

During this time, I was on my way back to Honolulu after visiting a friend in Big Sur on the coast of California. Out the window of the plane, the Pacific Ocean seemed to stretch forever, and the cumulus cloud formations were so brilliantly white that they almost hurt my eyes. Suddenly, like a bolt of lightning, I felt myself catapult out of the plane and into the clouds. I didn't physically eject out of the plane, but I found myself looking at the plane from about 100 feet above it.

My pulse was racing. Even though I'd experienced this phenomenon before when I was meditating in the zendo and also when astral-traveling at night, it was still frightening. It was in the middle of the day, and I was on a plane. Then, just as suddenly, I was jolted back into my body, but something was wrong. My spine felt like hot lava was surging up it and exploding out the top of my head. The experience was so intense that I couldn't speak. The flight attendant asked me a question, and I could only just shake my head, hardly able to breathe. It felt as though flames were surging through my body.

By the time my friend met me at the airport in Honolulu, I was having trouble walking. When I got home, I immediately went to bed. All night long my spine burned. The next day, a friend dropped by and was concerned when I could barely talk or move. I whispered to him about the intense heat raging up my spine. Fortunately, he'd heard of these symptoms before and instead of calling a doctor, he arranged for a man who'd trained as a Tibetan lama (monk) to come to my home and examine me. When the lama arrived, he looked intently at me and then focused on the area above my head. He stepped forward and put his hand a few feet over me.

"Feel this. You can sense the outpouring of heat," he said to my concerned friend.

"Oh my God! It feels like a furnace over her head!" exclaimed my friend.

"Denise, I don't know exactly how it happened, but you've had your 'kundalini' rise," he explained. "In India, the symbol of this force is the coiled serpent. It's a vast store of energy that lies coiled and dormant at the base of everyone's spine but rarely ever awakens. Usually this doesn't occur without many years of spiritual preparation. Disciples train their bodies for years for the rigors of a kundalini rising. In very rare cases, it happens spontaneously, which can cause great difficulties if you're not prepared for it. A person who's not ready for a kundalini experience can become violently sick, mentally ill, or even die."

Although I should have been frightened hearing his words, I felt confident in his presence.

"Right now, life-force energy is moving up your 'chakras,' which are the subtle energy centers of your body. You're going through a spiritual purification, which is why there's so much heat coming out of your head," said the lama.

"Come here. I want to show you something," he continued. "Do you have a scale?"

I could barely talk, but my friend told the lama that there was one in the bathroom. They helped me up, and I stood on the scale. It said I weighed just over 50 pounds! At that time I weighed about 150 pounds, so how could the scale register that weight?!

"Sometimes when the kundalini rises, it has a temporary

effect on one's physical structure, and a person will be much lighter for a while, as in your case," he said as he lifted me up. "See how light she is?"

My friend came over and picked me up.

"It's unbelievable!" he said as he put me down. "She hardly weighs anything."

I started to get very tired, and I just wanted to sleep. Friends came over, and I became a bit of an attraction as they took turns lifting me up, while feeling the heat emanating from my head.

When I finally fell asleep, I slept for three days. After about a week, the fire was gone . . . and I weighed 150 pounds again. However, there was still a subtle buzz at the top of my head that took about a year to completely subside.

I didn't find that my kundalini experience was a particularly valuable one except that I noticed that I became a better healer after that. Perhaps if I'd prepared my body for such an experience, it would have been more beneficial. But having my kundalini rise did give me insight about how powerful the body's energy field is and how even just a tiny bit of its life-force could be helpful when it's directed toward healing.

AT THE SAME TIME THAT I WAS EXPLORING many different kinds of healing methods, I was also exploring the dating scene in Hawaii. However, after my difficult relationship with Ron, I was wary of getting too involved with anyone . . . until I met Robin Lee.

Robin was an instructor at the photo lab at the University of Hawaii where I was taking some photography courses to help me prepare the Tibetan mandala slide show. He was extraordinarily tall for a man of Korean descent, and I was instantly attracted to him. His eyes twinkled, and his long black hair hung straight down his back. His quiet inner strength reminded me of the monks at the zendo.

Even though he wasn't of Native American heritage, his strong connection to nature helped me reconnect with my Cherokee roots. We spent time hiking on mountain trails and resting quietly in the rain forest together. When I was with him, I could "see" and "hear" the spirits and voices of the trees, birds, and clouds much more intimately than before. It wasn't anything that he said, for there were times when he didn't say much. It was deeper, and more profound. It happened just by being in his presence.

His lovemaking was both strong and tender. Nestled in his arms afterward, everything seemed liquid and flowing. After the closeness of making love, I could see energy fields even more clearly. It seemed as if his connection to nature seeped into me and altered my ability to view reality. We'd been together for over a year, and I thought we might always be, but fate had other plans for us.

I loved being with Robin, but there was some kind of barrier in our relationship. Maybe it was because he wasn't totally comfortable with the world I lived in, which was filled with healers and New Age adherents. I was his first introduction to that world. He came from a conservative Asian background, and I wanted him to jump right into my world, but he was hesitant.

I knew that things weren't working between us, so I decided to spend some time thinking about exactly what I desired in a long-term relationship. I made a list of every quality that my ideal man would have, including characteristics such as being loving, strong, kind, generous, loyal, self-sufficient, and being able to fix things and having a sense of humor. I put my list on the wall so that the reality of my potential future relationship could begin to sink into my subconscious mind every time I walked past it. I was astonished at how quickly this simple technique worked.

Two weeks after I made my list, I attended a weekend

self-growth communication course. It was very expensive—I worked it out—it was 62 cents a minute. I justified the cost of the course because I felt that if I improved my communication skills, I could improve everything in my life, maybe even my relationship with Robin. Every time I went to the bathroom, I figured that it cost me $3 to $5, depending on how fast I was. I'd taken out a loan to attend the course, but unfortunately, it seemed that the teacher only talked about his real estate investments. As the course drew to an end, I became angry. I raised my hand, and the teacher called upon me.

"I paid a lot to come to this course, and I don't feel like I've gotten anything out of it!" I said. "It's going to take me a year to pay back the loan I took out to pay for this."

Looking at me carefully, he was quiet for a moment. He then gazed at the man who happened to be sitting next to me. Rather than deal with my concern, his solemn response was, "So why don't you marry that guy sitting next to you?"

"What?!"

"You heard me," he said, almost under his breath. "Ask the guy next to you to marry you."

Although I knew that this teacher used very unorthodox teaching methods in his classes, his question shocked me. Nevertheless, for some reason, I slowly turned to the man next to me, who wasn't exactly a complete stranger; we were friends. His name was David, and I'd met him at a garage sale. Later he'd attended one of my lectures sponsored by the Continuing Education Department of the University of Hawaii. He was tall and serene, and his long blond hair and beard gave him a look reminiscent of the way Western artists portrayed Jesus. There was also something very accepting about his manner, yet he seemed strong and solid.

Then the words just slipped out of my mouth. "Will you marry me?"

I couldn't believe what I had just said. Yet somehow the words felt right.

David looked into my eyes for a moment. It seemed like such a long time, yet probably less than five seconds passed. And to my shock and utter amazement, he said simply, "Yes."

Oh God, what have I done? I thought. My momentary feeling of certainty was suddenly swallowed up in a tangle of doubt and fear, as I realized I'd just asked David to marry me.

David later told me that he looked into my hazel-green eyes and thought, *Could I spend the rest of my life with this woman?* In that moment, his soul opened, and he heard a resounding *Yes!* rumble from deep within him. There was no hesitation. No second thoughts. No wondering if it was the right thing to do. In that moment, he knew with absolute certainty that this was exactly what he wanted to do with the rest of his life.

But I didn't know. I was scared and confused.

The instructor scrutinized me closely and asked, "When are you going to get married?"

"Hmm, maybe next year," I said hesitantly, as fear climbed into my throat.

"Denise, are you a person of your word?" the instructor asked carefully.

My word has always been important to me. I always kept my word. This quality is inherent in my definition of myself. I felt that it was inherited from my Cherokee ancestors, who were known for their integrity.

"Yes, I am," I said with confidence.

"Well, you have just given your word to this man that you will marry him. Are you going back on your word?" he asked smoothly.

He was right. I had just asked David to marry me. I wasn't a person to go back on my word. Finally, I declared impulsively, "Okay, we'll get married tomorrow."

My logical, conscious mind thought, *This is completely absurd.* But a gentle tugging welled up from deep within my subconscious. It was a tender remembering of something that I couldn't quite touch, but I could feel, and it was comforting.

The next day was a blur. I called a friend who was a judge. He lived on the Big Island, the largest of the Hawaiian Islands, and he agreed to marry us there. Everything was happening so fast that I was more concerned about what I was going to wear than taking time to wonder if I was doing the right thing. I didn't have anything that looked even remotely like a wedding dress, but I'd recently purchased a peach-colored polyester outfit for a TV interview about massage, which I decided to wear.

I was in such a whirl that I didn't call anyone to say I was getting married. I knew I couldn't reach Heather because she was on an extended hiking trip with the search-and-rescue team she often led. And I made a feeble attempt to try to reach Robin, but failed. As much as we cared for each other, we both knew that ultimately it would have never worked out. Somehow it seemed easier to cut off the relationship cleanly and swiftly, rather than allowing it to slowly fester and die.

David and I found an inexpensive flight to the Big Island for the next day. As we flew out of Honolulu, in a small plane that held ten people, I looked at the water near the beach. It was so clear and deep. I could see shadows of a school of fish in the coral beds that flashed silver and then dark again as they twisted and turned. Farther out to sea, various shades of turquoise and lapis-blue water merged together and then drifted apart, until far away from shore, the entire sea became a dark, rich blue. As we flew close to the surface, I tried to see into the depths, but the ocean seemed to stretch out forever. Looking out the window, too shy and confused to say much, David's hand softly slipped into mine. "Don't worry. Everything will be all right," he said.

When David told the pilot and the other people on board that we were getting married, the pilot responded, "I've got a special wedding gift for you then."

He sharply banked the plane and headed for the island of Maui. As we flew over the island, tropical forests, tin-roofed shacks, meandering streams, red dirt roads, and pineapple fields stretched below us. Looking ahead, I glimpsed Haleakala, and I held my breath for a moment. She seemed almost alive. All my memories of the night I'd spent there clamored to the surface. In a swift ascent that threw my stomach to my feet, we seemed to barely clear the lip of the crater and then immediately dropped down inside. Below us was the moonscape terrain. Even though the plane's engines were loud, I could sense a profound stillness below, and could even see the tiny cabin where I'd spent the night.

Months before, on that terrifying night in the crater, as I looked into the stars, I would have been amazed had I known that only a short time later I'd be flying overhead on the way to my wedding. Looking across the landscape, tears rolled down my cheeks as I sensed the spirit of Haleakala blessing my union with David. After leaving the crater, we followed the coast of Maui, entranced by the tall waterfalls that gushed down the sheer sides of high cliffs to the beach below.

When we arrived on the Big Island, the judge's wife picked us up. She drove us to Waimea-Kamuela, an area where the grass-swept foothills of the Kohala Mountains form the backdrop to a small stream. A low-lying mist, cascading from the mountains, lent a mysterious aura to the place. She instructed us to slowly follow the water to its source, while she hurried ahead.

The mist was so thick that we could only see a few feet in front of us. *Trust.* I heard the word as clearly as if someone had spoken it out loud. I knew I was being asked to trust that I was doing the right thing, but I was afraid. The low-lying fog shrouded our entire journey as we made our way along the stream.

Even though you can't see where you are going in the mists, trust that you are going in the right direction. Have faith that this marriage is right for you, said a silent inner voice.

Trust? I was so used to protecting myself that having faith was a new concept for me. Yet with every step I took, I remembered the words of my grandmother and tried to believe that my life would turn out all right.

The rippling water sounded like the ebullient laughter of children as it widened into a clear, deep pool surrounded by tall ferns. A single ray of sunlight burned though the mists, illuminating a waterfall that tumbled over a wall of rocks into the pool. Growing on either side of the waterfall, bright orange nasturtiums and wildflowers glowed in the light.

An intimate group gathered around the pool for our wedding ceremony: the judge, his wife, her sister, a friend who lived on the Big Island, and David and me. The judge had stayed up most of the night making all the arrangements. His wife's sister played the guitar as we arrived. After she finished singing, David and I sat next to each other in the tall grasses and listened to our celebrant as he talked about the joys and responsibilities of being married. I hadn't had time to talk to him about what we wanted him to say, but I do remember that he never said anything about "richer or poorer," "sickness and health," or "till death do us part." Instead he said, "May you be married as long as it is good." I knew that this was a commitment I could keep—"As long as it is good!"

The judge stopped talking, solemnly looked at both of us, and said softly, "Walk over to the waterfall." We were surprised, but did as he said.

Calling across the pool, the judge told us to stand naked under the waterfall.

What? Take my clothes off? Take off everything? Stand naked under the waterfall? Suddenly I reverted back to the shy girl from Ohio, rather than the woman who danced naked in rainstorms.

His words put me into a kind of shock, then a calm filled me. A forgotten memory of sacred waters in an ancient time nudged at the edge of my mind. In my depths, I knew that what I was being asked to do was profound and holy. The request to stand nude with David under the flowing waters no longer seemed strange or wrong.

David seemed to take everything in stride. We both dropped our clothes on the moss, climbed over the rocks until we stood on a rock ledge, and let the cool water shower over our bodies. The judge then pulled off his clothes, dove into the pool, and swam over to the waterfall. I watched in amazement as he climbed up on the rocks to stand next to us, while water cascaded over us. He held our hands and said, "Water is the source of life. It is purifying and renewing. You are now reborn into a new life. I pronounce you husband and wife."

I looked at the judge and then looked at David, both completely drenched under the waterfall, and then laughed in release and exuberant joy, letting my peals of laughter tumble over the rocks, fill the pool, spill down the stream, and flow into the sea. I was married . . . naked . . . under a waterfall! And I was happy.

Now, 30 years later, I'm still married to that remarkable man (whose last name, *Linn*, is a Celtic word meaning "waterfall" or "flowing waters").

We vowed to stay married as long as it was "good." And it has been good for all this time . . . and just gets better every year!

CHAPTER ELEVEN

Wizards, Mystics, and Meadow

(1974–1985)

When I was a child, I used to hide under the bed or behind the clothes in the closet when my parents fought. Covering my ears to drown out my mother's harsh shrieks, I swore over and over to myself that I'd never get married. Never. Never. Never. Yet I was now a married woman at age 24.

Mrs. Linn—my new name—sounded so strange. Robin was hurt that I'd gotten married, but it also seemed to me that he was subconsciously relieved. My friends were shocked, and I couldn't blame them. *I* was in shock. Sometimes when I questioned what I'd done, my thoughts scattered around me like foam on the rocks at the shore. Would my marriage be like that of my parents? Would I repeat their patterns? However, there were times when my hopes swelled with the power of big waves, and I knew that, in spite of my fear and doubts, my marriage was right.

Heather concluded that David was a good choice for me. After Robin got over his astonishment, he eventually agreed. My connection with him proved strong, and he and David became good friends. Robin even blessed our union with the ultimate gift three years later when he became our daughter's godfather.

Immediately after our wedding, David asked me to move to California with him. He said he was feeling cramped on the islands and was yearning for wide-open spaces. I loved Hawaii—the beaches, the mountains, the sun, my great circle of friends, and my burgeoning career—how could I leave all that to be with someone I didn't know very well? However, I trusted that my marriage was right, even if it meant following David, so I agreed to move to the West Coast.

The first year of our marriage was hard. Neither one of us wanted to live in the city, so we moved to a little bungalow on the coast of Northern California, miles from any town and hours from San Francisco. At first it seemed like a great adventure, but then my spirit began to plummet. The weather was cold and overcast, I didn't have any friends, and we were broke. Trying to make ends meet, David would sometimes be gone for days at a time, taking carpentry jobs in San Francisco. While he was there, he slept on a pad on the floor amidst sawdust, cans of paint, and bags of plaster in the empty apartments that he was remodeling. I didn't have a car, and there weren't any towns nearby in which to find work, so I was alone for days, sometimes a week or more, at a time. Once in a while when I was especially lonely, I went with David into San Francisco and made picnics for him on the floor and slept on the pad with him, but mostly I got in the way of the other workers, so I didn't go often.

I knew that "trust" was important, but I'd thought that when you surrendered to it, miracles happened. I *had* surrendered in the crater, and it did seem like a miracle followed. However, I "trusted" when I got married and when I followed David to California, yet now I was miserable. Every day I sank deeper into depression.

Our tiny cottage was on a cliff, about ten feet from the edge, overlooking the sea. On one of the gray mornings when David was gone, I sat staring out the window at the ocean as I cradled my mug of tea in my hands to keep warm. A storm had hit during the night, and murky waves thrashed and pounded the shore below. To stave off the chill from the wind, and the cold dampness that seeped in through the thin walls, I wore a thick wool hat and draped myself in blankets.

I must have sat for a very long time because my tea became cold. However, something was brewing within my subconscious mind; suddenly I had a realization. True trust meant letting go of control and accepting that I was on the right path *even if it didn't seem like it at the time.*

As I gazed at the waves crashing onto the black rocks of the shore, I realized that even though I'd been happy in Hawaii, I'd also been living life at a frantic pace. I raced from class to class—the ones I was teaching and those I was taking—and from activity to activity, making up for lost time. I tried catching up on all the joy that I'd missed out on as a child, but I subconsciously worried that all my happiness would be yanked out from under me, so I packed it in as fast as I could.

Tightly wrapping the blanket around my shoulders, I walked outside into the wind. My senses were heightened, and for the first time since I'd moved there, I really tasted the salt in the air. I could hear delicate rhythms woven within the stormy cadence of the sea. I'd been so busy being miserable that I hadn't experienced the immense beauty of the area around our home. My solitude by the sea had a deeper purpose.

All I need to do is have faith that I am exactly where I need to be . . . and my world will be filled with beauty. As soon as I had that thought, the world around me changed. Just as a great symphony begins at the tap of the conductor's wand, with the next crash of a wave the universe became a fluid and vastly interconnected harmony that ebbed and flowed as surely as the sea. I realized that the realm of spirit was only a thought away. All I needed to do was sink into the divine "now" rather than reliving the past or worrying about the future. I once again found myself at the shore of the land of golden light and knew my place in the cosmos . . . and my love for my life and for the man I married grew.

OUR CONSTANT SEPARATIONS GREW TOO GREAT, so David and I decided to move to San Francisco. By the time we left, I was sorry to say good-bye to our sweet cottage by the sea. We were fortunate to find a reasonably priced flat in the Marina district with a big deck that overlooked the bay and the Golden Gate Bridge. The city was exhilarating. Over steaming cappuccinos, we'd listen to opera music Sunday mornings in North Beach coffee shops. We snuggled in red naugahyde-covered booths in restaurants in Chinatown while devouring lemon chicken.

I worked on Union Street at a clinic doing shiatsu massage, and David became a general contractor, while he followed his dream of studying jazz piano.

After I was married and living in the city, Grandma and Grandpa came up to meet my new husband. When David asked them if they'd like to do some sightseeing, my grandma's eyes lit up. She asked if we could visit the cemeteries in the area, so we spent a pleasant weekend exploring gravesites. I'd told David that I had an unusual family, so he took it all in stride.

My healing practice at the clinic expanded so rapidly that I was often booked many months in advance. I discovered that I could take away pain and sometimes even serious diseases by simply laying my hands on my clients and waiting until I felt their pain transfer to my body. I didn't learn this from any of my teachers. It was simply an innate ability that came to me naturally. I was certain that those months of solitude by the sea had enhanced my gift. I felt the sensation of a client's discomfort for a quick moment, but it seemed a small price to pay for the rewarding results this method produced.

As soon as I felt their pain, the client almost always reported an instantaneous release. Even people with incurable diseases healed instantly. They'd call later to say that when they went in for medical tests there was no sign of their disease. The patients I worked with called me a "miracle worker."

The number of people coming to me for treatment often overwhelmed me, yet I was unable to turn anyone away. I wanted to help as many people as possible, so I often started work at 6 A.M. and didn't finish until 9 P.M. Still, there were more and more people who wanted to be healed. It felt like a huge responsibility, and I often got tired, but I was compelled to help all those I could.

What I didn't fully realize at the time was that when someone gets sick, there are often unresolved issues in their life that contributed to the illness. In a sense, I wasn't doing anyone any favors when I took away their disease *without creating the opportunity for them to release the underlying source of that disease.* It took a dramatic experience to fully understand this truth.

ONE MORNING I AWOKE WITH A DULL PAIN just below my heart. I used my intuition to "look" inside my body and realized that the six-inch plastic tube that replaced part of my aorta had begun to separate from it. I could "see" hundreds of tiny blood clots surging through me. When I got out of bed and looked at my body, I saw long thin lines of bruises down both my arms and legs caused by the blood clots stuck in my veins.

"David!" I cried from the bedroom. "I need help!"

When he came in, I explained what I thought was happening and showed him the long pencil lines of bruises on my arms and legs. The rosy hue of his cheeks quickly turned ashen.

"Call Jack," I said firmly.

Dr. Jack Mantos lived in the flat above us. He was a respected medical doctor and one of my shiatsu students. (He later became president of one of the est organizations.) Jack would know what to do. David didn't want to leave my side, so he telephoned Jack, who immediately rushed downstairs in his pajamas and began taking my vital signs.

"Denise, I know how you feel about hospitals," he said. Previously I'd told him that I was wary of them. "But we're going to have to get you to one immediately. I think you're right about the blood clots. Even one clot can be a problem, and it looks like you have hundreds."

I begged for another alternative, but Jack was insistent. I could see the fear in his eyes as he warned me that there was a very real possibility that I would die without hospital treatment. Jack rushed out the door to change his clothes and grab his medical bag, calling over his shoulder that as soon as he returned, the three of us would go directly to the hospital.

I began to have trouble breathing and started to get very cold. David kept piling blankets on me, but I continued to shiver, and my eyesight began to blur. David wanted desperately to call 911, but I pleaded with him to hold off.

Just then, we were both startled to hear a knock at the front door. Jack always came to the back door. We weren't expecting anyone, but I assured David that I'd be all right if he left to answer the door.

When David opened the door, a stocky man with a full beard pushed past him and said with authority, "I'm here to see Denise. It's urgent."

In shock, my husband followed the man as he walked with certainty to our bedroom.

"Hi, Denise. You don't know me, but I know that you're in trouble. I came as soon as I could."

Although it was startling to have a stranger barge into our bedroom, at the same time there was something about his presence that was reassuring and comforting. I was too ill to question why he was there, who he was, or how he'd found out about me. All I knew was that I felt safe.

"Let's see what we've got here," he said as he looked at me carefully.

"Well, you won't die," he told me. "Aha! I see what's happening. I can see a plastic tube inside of you that's started to separate from the aorta. You'll need to go to the hospital."

He quickly went through my body, giving me a detailed account of what was occurring.

"But I don't want to go to the hospital!" I cried out adamantly. Images of the troll-like creatures I'd encountered when I was 17 enveloped me.

"I'll see what I can do," he said as he closed his eyes and focused his attention on me. I began to feel energy flow into my body. My breath deepened, warmth poured into me, and my eyesight improved.

"It's incredible. I feel so much better!" I declared.

The "wizard," as I later came to think of him, smiled and said, "I have to go now, but you don't have to go to the hospital. You're going to be okay."

"Please, can you tell me who you are?" I said.

"First, let's just say that I'm a friend who knew that you were in trouble. I have some special abilities, and one is to know when someone could use my help. I knew I had to get here immediately," he said simply as he started to leave.

"I'm so very grateful to you! Thank you so much for coming. Before you leave, can you explain why this happened?" I asked. It seemed very important to know why.

"In your job as a healer, you help people by removing their

diseases and their pain, but in a deeper sense, you don't really help them. And you're harming yourself in the process.

"By taking their illness into your body, it damages you. Every disease has a cause or a source. It might be unresolved anger or unexpressed grief or resentment. When you take away the symptoms without addressing the cause, you only delay the time when they'll have to confront the deeper problem. Work with people by helping them find the source, and then they become their own healer. And you will be strengthened as well," he said.

He then turned and walked swiftly out the front door, just as Jack was letting himself in the back.

As David stared in disbelief at the retreating figure, he said, "Who was that masked man?" for the "wizard" was indeed like the Lone Ranger who shows up to help people in need and then disappears.

I didn't care who he was, I just knew that I felt so much better. Jack flew into the bedroom in a flurry, keys in one hand and his medical bag in the other.

"Did you see him?" I said.

"See who?"

"The 'wizard' who came here and healed me. Jack, it was absolutely amazing! I've never seen him before, but he just walked in the house and channeled energy into me. I feel so much better."

"What are you talking about? I was only gone a few minutes."

"I know, but it's true. It happened. Ask David."

David was dumbfounded but nodded in agreement. Jack looked dubious. He took my vital signs again. He said that although he'd prefer that I went to the hospital, I didn't have to since I'd improved so rapidly. As he monitored my health over the next few days, he was astounded by my quick recovery.

Although it took two weeks for all the clots to dissolve, I didn't go to the hospital, and in two days I was out of bed. I found out later that this man, who stepped into my life at such a crucial time, was a trance medium. I'm not exactly sure how he knew to come to me at that moment, but his intuition was so strong that he was able to almost magically appear to help people in need.

I was so impressed by my first meeting with the "wizard" that when he came to check on my progress, I asked to train with him. Studying with trance mediums later became quite fashionable, and many well-known personalities consulted their "channel" for advice. At that time, however, channeling seemed really weird to me, but this man had saved my life. And the information he imparted during his trance sessions was valuable and practical.

To enter into a trance, he would sit quietly in a chair until he slumped over abruptly. When he sat up, his gestures and voice were those of an old Chinese man who gave insights using parables, presumably from ancient China. The "wizard" could do many things that didn't seem physically possible, for he was truly a magician in the mystical sense of the word. It was a secret training. He never advertised, and never lived in one place for long periods of time. The expression, "When the student is ready, the teacher appears," was true. I was ready, and my teacher had appeared.

As a result of my training with him, I changed the way that I approached my patients. The results weren't always as dramatic, but they were much more profound. For example, I realized that if I took away a woman's breast cancer without creating the opportunity for the resolution of an inner resentment (or other suppressed emotions) that may have contributed to it, eventually the resentment would fester, and some other illness or problem would emerge. Through my new approach,

I healed and addressed the *source* of the disease, rather than its manifestations.

For example, a surgeon came to me with serious back problems. She wasn't able to work, but this meant that she had time at home with her three-year-old son. As long as her back was a problem, she was able to do what her heart yearned for and spend time with the boy. In her case, I just talked about ways she could attain the same results without having to experience so much pain.

Another woman had severe migraines. When we got to the core, she realized that she was suppressing anger at her mother-in-law, who had moved in with her and her husband and was dominating her husband's time. As soon as she realized what the source of the extreme headaches was, we were able to design strategies to deal with the problem. If I'd just taken away her migraines, the true issue would have still existed, and she probably would have developed some other physical ailment.

Thanks to the wizard, my healing work brought me greater satisfaction and didn't damage my own health. Although I had remarkable intuition regarding my clients, I was so much more insightful with them than I was with my own family and close friends.

EARLY ONE EVENING AS I STOOD on our deck hugging my sweater close to my body, I watched the San Francisco fog settle over the bay for the night. The foghorns were wailing in the background. Usually I liked listening to them, but now they sounded sad and mournful. The phone rang, and I hurriedly stepped into the warmth of our home. When I picked up the phone, I heard a woman crying on the other end. It was a co-worker from the same clinic where I did my healing work.

"David's dead," she sobbed.

"David's dead?" my whole body went cold. "What do you

mean 'David's dead'? He was here just a few minutes ago," my voice trembled.

"Oh my God! Denise, I forgot that your husband's name is David. I'm so sorry. Please forgive me. David Roberts is dead. He committed suicide. He jumped off the Golden Gate Bridge."

"No! Not David!"

David Roberts was a medical doctor and one of the other practitioners who worked with me at the clinic. He was my good friend, and we were scheduled to have lunch together the next day. He had a youthful exuberance and passion for life that uplifted everyone around him.

Why would he kill himself? He had so much to live for. His practice was thriving, he and his wife had just purchased a beautiful home in Mill Valley, and they were anticipating the birth of a child. I eventually found out that David had been in a bad argument with his wife and had driven away from home very upset. While driving over the Golden Gate Bridge, in a momentary surge of emotion, he skidded his car to a halt and threw himself over the edge.

I stumbled through the next few days. *Why didn't my intuition warn me so I could have helped avert his death?* It all seemed senseless. The numbness I experienced reminded me of the way I'd felt after my suicide attempt, when I staggered through the motions of life in a dense fog. Then something very strange began to occur. Whenever I walked into a room in our flat, the lights flickered on and off. Vaguely I thought about calling an electrician but never got around to it.

Just before Christmas, a group of my students gathered in my living room for a class. I had the room decorated for the holidays, and in one corner was a small Christmas tree with miniature lights. As the class began, the lights began to blink furiously. This was strange, as the lights *weren't* blinking lights. I simply explained to the group that we'd been having trouble with our electrical system and that we should ignore the disruption caused by the lights.

However, with great persistence, the lights continued to blink feverishly. Turning our attention once again to the tree, an individual in the class asked, almost as a joke, "Are you trying to tell us something?" Immediately the lights went out, then methodically blinked twice, and went out again. Suddenly, an image of David Roberts came into my head.

"Is that you, David?" I asked.

The tree blinked twice again. I couldn't believe what was happening, so I asked again, "Is that really you, David?" Again the tree blinked twice.

It occurred to me that the flickering lights in the house were David's way of trying to communicate with me. "Have you been trying to contact me by turning lights on and off in the house?" The lights blinked twice. It *was* David. Normally I was alert to the presence of spirits because of the skill I'd acquired while training with Morna, but my grief had blocked my intuition.

Different people in the class continued to ask the "tree" questions, to which it responded with blinking lights in answer to yes and no inquiries. In this manner, we were able to garner information that David wished us to pass on to his wife, whom I called immediately.

I told her about the blinking lights and how I believed that David had indeed contacted me with some messages for her. He wanted her to know that he was okay and that he was very sorry for what had happened. I also passed on information from David about some papers that she was going to need to help put things in order and told her where they were. She put me on hold while she looked for them.

When she got back on the phone, she said, "You're right. I need these papers, and I wouldn't have known where to find them. Mostly, I'm relieved to know that David is all right. I'm mad at him, but I miss him so much. Thank you for calling me."

The lights in the house stopped flickering, and even though I used the same Christmas lights for years, they never blinked again.

DURING MY APPRENTICESHIP WITH THE WIZARD, these kinds of otherworldly experiences occurred more and more. Additionally, my intuitive and psychic abilities expanded. The wizard confirmed what my grandmother had told me—I had the "Sight." As a result of my training, I began to have spontaneous and vivid memories of past lives. Before I met the wizard, I had a vague awareness of other lives in which I might have lived. Now, however, I began to vividly remember my past incarnations.

Once, when I was studying with the wizard in Italy, I decided to visit Venice. (David had stayed home because of his expanding construction business.) While I was near that beautiful city, I had an experience that I believe originated from a past life.

I had hired a gondolier to do some sightseeing for the afternoon. The gondola gracefully glided through the soothing Adriatic waters, while the oarsman bellowed off-key arias as we moved smoothly past one island after another. One particular island seemed to draw my attention. I pointed out the island to my amiable singing host, and he gently nudged the gondola in that direction until we finally pulled up to the dock. With hand signals, I told the oarsman that I wanted to get out for a few moments to explore. He indicated he'd wait for me.

As I stepped onto the dock, a slightly balding, round Franciscan monk, who spoke English, came scurrying out to show me around the island. He explained that the entire island was a Franciscan monastery. I followed him and was overwhelmed with a feeling of déjà vu. Surprisingly, as we walked through the buildings, I knew exactly what was around each corner, even before we reached it. How could it be that I knew my way so clearly? I'd never even heard of this island.

Suddenly, as we rounded another corner, I was surprised. It wasn't what I'd expected. Without being able to help myself, I exclaimed, "Oh, this is new!" With an astonished look, the monk replied, "You're right. It's not the original structure . . . but it is hundreds of years old." As we strolled, detailed memories of having been a monk on that lovely island flooded my mind.

I remembered the beauty of the morning sun as it poured through my monastery cell window and how the floor stones felt smooth and comforting to my bare feet. I recalled how much I enjoyed working in the monastery garden. The richness of the soil in my hands in that life filled me with contentment. Perhaps my love of my dirt hole as a child was a result of my hours in the Franciscan garden. My life as a monk there was simple, yet filled me with a profound feeling. Perhaps I was attracted to life in a Zen monastery because of the peace I felt as a Franciscan monk.

I BECAME SO INTERESTED IN REINCARNATION that eventually I began to use past-life regression to help my clients in my healing practice. When I "guided" people back to their past lives, often the true root of their problem was exposed. I remembered what the wizard had said about the importance of going to the source. I found that many present-day difficulties had their source in the distant past. By simply regressing my clients into a previous life, they were often able to overcome obstacles in the present day.

My passion for reincarnation expanded, and I began to do group regressions all over the world. I eventually did past-life seminars in 19 countries, sometimes teaching groups as large as 1,000 at a time. The results achieved in my seminars were astounding. Simply by regressing participants into past lives associated with their current difficulties, we could find the true source of the challenge and achieve so-called miracles.

In England, a woman attended because she had a large and painful tumor on her uterus that kept her from having children. The week following the course, she went in for a checkup. There was no tumor. Three months later, she wrote to tell me how happy she was to finally be pregnant.

In Norway, a woman enrolled who'd had a damaged voice box for over 30 years. Remarkably, during the seminar her voice returned. She was thrilled because this meant that she could finally talk to her grandchildren.

In South Africa, a woman had a brain tumor so severe that it put intense pressure on her optic nerve so she had a hard time seeing. During the weekend course, she got her sight back. When she went in later for a test, she was told that the tumor was gone.

A couple from India asked me if their brain-damaged young son could come to the seminar. I explained that he was too young, but told them they could take what they gained back home to him. At the conclusion of the weekend course, I suggested that they go home and hold their son, unconditionally accepting him exactly as he was. The parents were then astounded when the next time they took their son in for tests, they were told that he no longer showed any signs of brain damage.

A woman from Spain had used a hearing aid for 52 years. During the course, sounds kept getting louder and louder until she pulled out the device and found that her hearing had improved so much that she could hear without it . . . and she continues to do so.

These results weren't unusual. They happened in every course I taught. I eventually discovered that it wasn't just my past-life regressions that produced this type of healing. *Any* guided visualization I led created remarkable results. *The key was the meditation!* When I led a guided visualization, a deep feeling of relaxation filled me. It was almost like I entered into a kind of light trance state. I never knew quite what I was going to say, but somehow the words always seemed to flow. Sometimes the meditation would go in a completely different direction than I'd planned, but it always seemed to be right for the people who attended.

A very strange phenomenon began to occur for many of my seminar participants. I'm not sure why it happened, but it was not uncommon for people to have an effect on electrical systems for three or so days after the meditations. Their TV set would come on spontaneously, car alarms would activate as they strolled by, and streetlights would go off when they walked beneath them at nighttime. Sometimes lightbulbs would blow out when they turned the lights on. One woman had 12 lights burn out in her home within one hour, the evening after the meditation. Additionally, the magnetic strip on the participants' credit cards often become demagnetized during the meditations. This occurred so often that I had people take their credit cards out of their pockets or put them under their chairs while they took part in my guided visualizations, to avoid the inconvenience of replacing their cards.

These unusual occurrences didn't happen for everyone, and there was no evidence that those who *did* experience these strange happenings benefited more than those who didn't.

I wasn't sure why these events transpired, but I hypothesized that the meditations subtly contributed to healing shifts in a person's bio-electrical system. Some people, however, found this phenomenon disconcerting, especially when their TV continued to come on spontaneously. So I developed meditation techniques to "ground" people, which minimized their disturbance of electrical fields and yet still allowed them to reap remarkable benefits from the meditations.

Also during meditations, sometimes seminar participants would smell fragrant flowers, feel a light touch of an unseen being, or hear celestial music. I never understood exactly why this happened, but I assumed it was a sign that spirit helpers were near.

I don't know why these things happened, but maybe when I was 17, an inner door was opened within me—a portal to the land of golden light, healing, and angels. Perhaps my guided meditations and visualizations allowed seminar participants to pass through that gateway as well . . . to access healing energy, touch angelic realms, and even contact loved ones who had passed on.

In Finland, a man who had murdered his mother attended my course. After the workshop, he spoke to me through a translator. He told me that even though he'd gone to prison for ten years and had been forgiven by society, never for a moment had he forgiven himself for what he'd done. He'd led a deeply tortured existence since the death of his mother. During the guided meditation, his mother spontaneously appeared to him and said, "Son, you are absolutely and totally forgiven." He was a big man, yet he was sobbing in relief as he told me. He looked completely different from the downtrodden man who had entered the room only a few hours before.

The requests for my guided visualizations became so great that I eventually made meditation tapes and CDs that have become available worldwide. (There's a list of my products on the second page of this book.)

The subjects I've taught have changed throughout my 35 years of leading seminars. I've given workshops on dreams, vision quests, medicine-wheel philosophy, women's issues, reincarnation, angels, space clearing, feng shui, and various kinds of massage . . . and now, what I call Soul Coaching. However, the vehicle is the same: I guide seminar participants on mystical inner journeys, and the results are profound and lasting.

My own inner journeys and meditations explained so many things in my life, but they didn't explain my most unusual experience— one that, I must confess, David didn't think I should include in this memoir.

"Whatever you do, don't tell them the you-know-what story," he pleaded with me. "Can't you write the book and just leave it out? Nobody will believe that this happened to us. And they won't believe *you*. Either that, or they'll think that we're nutcases."

"That's a chance that I'm going to have to take," I told him. "Besides, why would angels, wizards, and reincarnation be acceptable, but not this topic? I *am* going to write about it."

"Suit yourself, but I'm still not sure that it's a good idea," he replied.

To write this memoir and leave out this experience would mean omitting one of the major events in my life, especially in light of what happened as a result. So, after much deliberation, I decided to include it. It *is* a true story, and I'm telling it exactly as we experienced it:

It was early January 1977. David and I had driven up the Northern California coast along the steep and dramatic Jenner Cliffs to the tidal area where Alder Creek flows into the sea. He wanted to go fishing for steelhead, and the river mouth provided an ideal spot. Like two kids, we scrambled down the cliff to the long, sandy beach that ran along the river. It was a perfect day. The sun sparkled on the water as wisps of mist floated in the distance over white-capped waves.

By the time we were ready to head home, it was dark, and there was only a tinge of red lingering on the western sky over the ocean. As David drove our old blue pickup truck along the coastal cliffs, I rolled down the window and looked up at the stars. The night felt holy. Every star was bright and clear.

"Hey, there's a really big satellite up there," I said.

"Uh-huh," David said distractedly.

"I mean it's a *big* satellite."

"Uh-huh." His mind was on fishing.

Suddenly the "satellite" just stopped. It then made a 90-degree turn and sped high over the truck.

Satellites didn't do that, as far as I knew. Then it happened again. The "satellite" paralleled our vehicle on my side, then suddenly stopped and made a 90-degree turn and sped back behind us. Again and again this happened. Somehow it seemed like it wanted us to turn around. From David's position, he couldn't see any of this.

"David, there's something up there that wants us to turn around," I said quietly.

"What?!" He abruptly came out of his fishing reverie. "What are you talking about? Are you telling me that a satellite wants us to turn around?"

"Yes, I am. I don't really think it's a satellite, but whatever it is, it wants us to turn the truck around," I said.

"No way! I'm tired, and it's late! We have a long drive ahead of us. I'm not turning around for any reason! Have you gone crazy?"

"David . . . turn . . . around . . . please," I said in a low, restrained voice.

David glanced at me and looked back at the road. Sighing, he pulled over, turned around, and began driving back north.

I exhaled with relief. We drove in silence for quite a few miles. We didn't see any other cars on the road as I continued to look out my window to the sky. The "satellite" was now on my side of the car. Once again it stopped and made a 90-degree turn, but this time heading inland.

"It wants us to go east. Look, there's a road. Go up there," I said.

David gritted his teeth and turned up the small country road.

"Thank you," I whispered.

As we drove down the road, I continued to watch the "satellite" as it stayed just ahead and above the truck on my side. From where David sat he couldn't see it. Abruptly David pulled the truck off onto the embankment.

"What are you doing?!" I asked. "It wants us to go on."

"Denise, I love you and I trust you, but so far I haven't seen this 'satellite' that you're talking about." (It wasn't visible from the driver's side of the truck.) "It's late. I want to go home."

"David, please, please go on."

"No! I'm not doing it," he said. When he spoke in that tone, I knew he meant it.

"Well, at least come outside and look at it," I said.

Reluctantly, he set the gear and got out of the truck. High overhead was a very bright light. At first it was stationary, then it zigzagged rapidly and was still again.

"Wow!" he said, suddenly not tired anymore. "Cool! What is it? I haven't heard of any airplane or satellite that can do that, and it's completely silent. It must be some kind of new defense aircraft that the military has cooked up."

"David, it's not military. It's a UFO!" I said emphatically. "We're having an encounter with a UFO!"

David ducked back into the truck.

"Where are you going?" I asked.

"I'm getting my peanuts."

"What?! We're about to have an encounter with a UFO and you're eating peanuts?!"

"Yup!" he said, as he leaned up against the truck and began to shell them.

I looked at him in disgust and walked onto the field. I knew that this was a special encounter. I wasn't sure how best to approach these beings, but it sure as hell wasn't going to be while eating peanuts.

Maybe I'd watched too many B-grade science fiction films, but as I stood in the field, I put my arms up over my head and said, "Welcome!" I wasn't quite sure what else to do.

In a whoosh, a large round ship came down and floated just above the trees. It was totally quiet and immensely beautiful in its silence. It was about 30 feet across and smooth in appearance, with a row of glowing lights around its middle. I looked back at David. He had momentarily stopped eating peanuts, as he too stared in amazement.

I gazed back up at the ship, and I felt a tentative presence touch my mind. "Oh my God! Whatever is up there can hear my thoughts!"

If you can hear my thoughts, blink your lights. I silently projected my thoughts toward the ship, thinking back to David Roberts and the blinking Christmas-tree lights. Instantly, the lights blinked off and on again. *Could you do that again?* I silently asked. The lights blinked again.

Again, I felt a presence enter my mind . . . so soft, kind, and questioning. It was like the feeling you get when someone comes up behind you; where you can't see them, but you can feel them there. This was much more intimate, however. A wave of love, homesickness, compassion, and wonderment all tumbled together inside me.

Shouting in my mind, as loud as I could, I said, *Please help me be of service to others! Help me to help others!* Over and over again I mentally shouted this as tears streamed down my face.

More than anything in the world, I wanted to be able to help others. I had felt there was a reason that I'd been miraculously spared when I was shot, and I was sure that my purpose was to be of service to my fellow human beings. As I looked at the UFO, I believed that asking for assistance from whatever or whoever was floating above me might help me fulfill my purpose.

Suddenly, in the distance. I could hear the approach of a small plane. It sounded so loud in comparison to the silence of the ship above us. I turned to see it. At that moment, the ship above us doused its bright lights and then put on one green light and one red light, as if to mimic the lights of the airplane. Then rapidly, yet silently, it zipped away. After the small plane had passed, the UFO came back for a few moments, silently hovering over the trees before it hastily departed.

I walked back to David, who was still noisily chomping on peanuts, and hugged him.

"Wow! I don't know exactly what that was. It sure doesn't seem to be a military craft, but it was incredible!" David said.

We waited for the UFO to return. When it hadn't returned after 15 minutes, I said, "Let's go farther up the road. I know it wants us to go up there."

"I don't think that's a good idea," said David.

"You're afraid? They won't hurt us. Please, let's go. It'll be okay," I said.

"I'm not driving any farther up this road."

"Please, David, please. It'll be all right."

"I'm not going, and that's final!"

As we drove back down the coast to San Francisco, we had one of the worst arguments we've ever had. I was angry that we hadn't gone farther down the road, and David was mad that I'd accused him of being scared. We went to bed still raging at each other; however, in the light of morning, all was forgiven as we sweetly made love.

As I lay curled up in his arms afterward, I said, "I'm pregnant."

"How do you know?"

"I just know."

"You can't know something like that only a few minutes after making love."

"Okay, but I know I'm pregnant," I said serenely. Just as my mother had known the instant she became pregnant with me, I too was certain.

David looked at me with concern, worrying that the events from the previous night had unhinged his wife.

"Denise, you can't have a baby. Remember what the doctors told you. A pregnancy will kill you." Suddenly he was really alarmed.

"I won't die. I am meant to have this baby. I know that everything will turn out fine. Please don't worry," I said contentedly.

I've always believed in signs. I didn't believe that it was an accident that I got pregnant the morning after we saw the UFO. If it weren't for that experience, I would have never attempted to have a child. I was reconciled to being childless. However, it was such a powerful portent that I absolutely knew that I had nothing to be concerned about. But David was worried. Very worried.

I was so excited that I told the old Italian women who sat sunning themselves every morning on our front steps that I was pregnant. They all jumped up to pat me on the shoulder and give me lots of advice—much of it conflicting—on what to do to be healthy while I was pregnant. I was only a few hours pregnant, yet I was so certain of the positive outcome that I told everyone I was going to have a baby.

I immediately started taking vitamins, exercising, and watching my diet. I meditated daily and did affirmations for a great pregnancy. I put headphones on my belly and played hours of classical music to the baby growing in my womb.

I was so sure that I was going to have a baby that I never did get a pregnancy test, and after a few months there was no reason to do one. I was definitely pregnant.

I decided to have my baby at home. As a result of this decision and because of my many injuries from the shooting, I couldn't find a doctor or even a midwife who would agree to take me on as a patient. They thought I was too much of a medical risk for a home delivery. So I decided to have my baby on my own without any expert assistance.

"David, women have been doing this without doctors for thousands of years. It can't be that hard. You and I are going to do this together," I said. "I'll push and you'll catch."

David's face turned white, "You mean . . . it'll just be you and me?"

"Yup! We can do it. No problem," I said with extreme confidence.

"Well. Umm. I guess. I mean. Well, okay."

"Great! It's decided then."

When I was eight months pregnant, a friend took me aside to talk to me about my plan to deliver without any medical personnel in attendance.

"I know that you can do this, Denise, but do you think this is fair to David? This is going to be really hard on him," she said.

I'd never really thought of how stressful my plan might be on David, so I decided to find someone to help.

Eventually I found an alternative-medicine doctor who agreed to come to my home birth. I am so grateful to this dedicated man. When I finally went into labor, he was on a spiritual retreat in Northern California and had to drive five hours to get to me. I was very glad when he finally arrived since David had been in an extremely deep slumber from the moment I told him that I was in labor. He was seemingly unconscious, and no matter how hard I tried, I couldn't wake him up.

I shook him. I yelled. Nothing worked. "I'm in labor! Wake up!" I shouted. Nothing stirred him. I think he got scared and passed out, terrified that he would actually have to deliver the baby on his own. In any event, a splendid baby girl, Meadow Marie, was delivered at 10:06 P.M., October 15, 1977. I was 27 years old. She didn't cry—but just looked around in wonder and fell fast asleep in my arms, like her dad.

Even though the labor was extraordinarily painful, the doctor assured me that it was an easy birth. I remember thinking that if that was an easy birth, I had immense sympathy for any woman who had a difficult one. I had stupidly read a book called *Childbirth without Pain*, in which Dr. Grantly Dick-Read assured me that in the absence of fear, childbirth could, in fact, be pain free. As I remember, he said that native women had painless births as they squatted in the field, and then just continued to work minutes later with their new baby strapped on their back. I believed him.

I wasn't afraid of having a baby; I had meditated and done relaxation processes. I was sure that I'd feel no pain, just as the doctor said. As soon as the first strong contraction hit, though, I wanted to strangle Dr. Dick-Read. And with every contraction, my urge to do bodily harm to him increased.

I forgot about how angry I was at the doctor, however, as I gazed into the eyes of my new baby. She was so beautiful, and I was so happy. The next morning, the wizard showed up at my house. I was surprised, but also delighted, to see him.

Although he'd been living in Europe at the time, he'd sensed that I was about to go into labor and had flown in the day before to send energy to me. He'd always looked vibrant and healthy, but on that morning he looked haggard. I felt that he'd spent a lot of energy to make sure that there were no problems with my labor. I was very grateful for his assistance and sorry to see him go, as he planned on traveling back to Europe that day. He always came into my life at the most opportune moments.

David's parents, who lived in the Bay Area, visited immediately after the birth. They were thrilled to finally have their first grandchild, and my grandparents from Los Angeles were ebullient. They were getting older, so it was hard for them to travel, but Grandma sent a bright orange, brown, and yellow crocheted baby blanket. I didn't like the colors or the acrylic yarn, but I loved the fact that Grandma had made it.

I wrote to my mother to tell her of the birth, but she never replied. However, my father and his wife came down from Oregon to visit. (Several years after his divorce, my father had met and married a woman who had two children, and later they moved to Oregon.) Some of the sweetest memories of my father occurred during that visit to see our new baby. Since my father was a big man, Meadow Marie looked extra tiny in his arms. He cradled her preciously, as if he could protect her from the world. The day they arrived, we went to Chinatown for dinner; I remember how my father held Meadow high above the crowd to safeguard her—daring anyone to come close—as we made our way to the restaurant. Heather was still living in Hawaii so she couldn't visit, but she was excited to be an aunt.

ONE AFTERNOON WHILE I SAT holding my baby in my arms, I suddenly had a vision of her with a high lace collar around her neck. "Oh no, David! I think that she was royalty in a past life!" I said. "This is going to be interesting."

As far as I can remember in my past lives, I was never royalty. I was a nun, a monk, a renunciate, a laborer, oftentimes a healer, and several times a warrior, but never royalty.

My insight proved to be telling. As a two-year-old, Meadow Marie always wanted to sit at the table with a full set of silverware, while David and I wanted to sit and eat on the floor in front of the fire . . . vestiges of our years living a casual lifestyle.

When she was three, she said, "Could you please lay my clothes out for me on the bed. My servants used to do that for me."

Another time, as a three-year-old, she said, "I can't go outside and play."

"Why not?" I asked her.

She replied, "I'm not allowed to play with other children because I'm not allowed to get dirty." It was such a strange thing for her to say, since I never cared about her getting dirty. I figured that was every child's birthright. It's not unusual, however, for children to have spontaneous past-life memories and confuse them with their current life. However, by the time she was four, her memories had faded and she was just like any other normal child.

ALTHOUGH I KEPT DOING SOME TEACHING and counseling after Meadow was born, I turned my focus to being a full-time mother. When she was one, we decided to move. David and I both loved mountains and wilderness areas, so we decided that the Pacific Northwest would be a good place to raise a child. He could work in the city, yet at the same time, we would have access to vast expanses of nature.

So on October 15, 1979, Meadow's second birthday, we all squeezed together into our old Dodge pickup truck, with all our possessions piled in the back, and headed north. Our mattress, strapped on top of the load, flapped dangerously in the wind as we tottered down the highway.

It was a rainy, cold November day when we finally arrived in Seattle. We had very little money, so we immediately began looking for rental accommodations. Finally, David found a bungalow not far from Lake Washington. It was so tiny that what

I mistook for a closet was actually the bedroom. We moved in our household goods and were home. David found work as a carpenter, and I decided to stay home with Meadow. For a while, everything was exciting and new, but then the weather became gray and unbearable, and my mood began to mirror my dismal surroundings.

Every day was rainy, overcast, and cold. It reminded me of how depressed I felt after we'd moved into our first home in Northern California. I didn't have any friends in the area, and David was away all day. I felt so alone and miserable. Not only were the skies gray, but it seemed that my life was gray, too. I doubted myself; I doubted my mothering skills; I doubted everything about my life.

Finally one day I dragged in some branches, strung them with white Christmas lights, and made a kind of forest in the living room. The lights seemed to help perk up my spirits. As I began to add things from thrift stores and garage sales, my little home began to feel more like a haven. It was my first foray into the field of feng shui and sacred space which, a few years later, became my passion and my profession.

The early years in Washington State with Meadow always seemed centered around nature. I recently found a diary entry I wrote during that time:

> "Meadow and I went to pick blackberries. We left early, as the day promised to be very warm. The berries were fat, black, and sweet. I think more reached our mouths than ultimately reached the jam we were planning. However, there were also fat red ants there which ran up our legs, so we picked berries and then stomped to shake the ants off our legs . . . pick and stomp . . . pick and stomp."

Meadow loved to go fishing with David. When she was four years old, we went fishing in David's wooden rowboat on a small lake in the Cascade Mountains. It was one of those warm, sleepy summer days when you drift across the water and fishing is really just an excuse to sit back and watch the clouds. I heard Meadow, who was sitting in the back of the boat, talking to herself. I had to lean back to hear what she was saying.

"Fish are coming to me. I know I will catch a fish. A fish is now on my line," she said quietly under her breath.

She had her head cocked in a peculiar fashion as she spoke. (She told me later that her head position was absolutely essential for the affirmations to work.) Then her head popped up and she said brightly, "I got a fish!"

"In spite of what your mom might have told you about affirmations, they play *no* part in fishing," said David. "That's not the way you catch fish. I'm sure it's just weeds on your line."

According to David, experience and technique are the cornerstone of fishing. However, when he did pull in her line to "take off the weeds," she had a fish. Meadow just smiled smugly.

A little later we heard more incantations from the back of the boat. "I know a fish is coming to me. A fish is now on my line." And then a little later, "Papa, I have another fish." David pulled up her line and there was another fish. David didn't catch anything, but I wouldn't have been surprised if the next time he went fishing, under his breath he chanted, "A fish is coming to me."

WHEN MEADOW WAS SIX YEARS OLD, she complained that she had a stomachache. She had a low-grade temperature, and when I pushed on her belly, she had pain on the rebound. As a result of my many years of training in alternative medicine, I was averse to going to doctors unless absolutely necessary.

"David, I think Meadow has appendicitis, so I'm going to take her to the ocean to heal," I said.

When I look back now, I'm amazed by how incredibly naïve and irresponsible I was. Obviously, if a child has appendicitis, you take her to the doctor. I foolishly put Meadow in a potentially dangerous situation, but at the time, it felt like the right thing to do. I was fortunate that it had a positive outcome.

"Do you really think that's the best thing to do?" David asked. He was concerned, but he'd come to believe in my instincts.

"Yes, I do. I heard that in China they very rarely do surgery for appendicitis. The patient only takes fluids and herbal drinks, and the body heals itself," I said.

A friend and I packed Meadow into the car and drove four hours to the coast and rented a small cottage near the water. I told Meadow that she would only be having fluids, but that she'd be absorbing healing energy from the sea. Looking back now, it's remarkable that she didn't complain. I gave her lots of water and made herbal drinks for her, and for two days we gathered seashells and walked along the shore. At the end of the second day, I took her temperature and it was normal.

"Hey, this is great news, Meadow. You don't have a temperature, so tomorrow you can eat," I said.

"No, Mommy, I can't eat tomorrow. I have to go one more day without eating," she said in her very solemn, wise way.

"Are you sure?"

"Yes, I'm sure."

The next morning Meadow woke me up. "You know that red stuff that you and Papa put on your food?" she said.

"Yes. It's called cayenne," I said.

"I need you to get me some."

I knew that there was an innate wisdom in the body, especially during illness, so if Meadow wanted cayenne, I was going to get some for her. I quickly dressed, and we jumped in the car in search of cayenne.

"I need to eat some of it," she said.

I sprinkled a tiny bit in a glass of water.

"No, I need more," she said. I kept adding more until I said, "Meadow, that's too much. It'll be too hot. No one can drink that much cayenne."

"I can," she said, and she hastily emptied the entire glass.

"Now everything will be all right," she said as she bent over to organize her shell collection.

A little while later she said, "Mommy, there's something I want to show you." In the bathroom she pulled down her underwear and showed me a pile of greenish-yellow infected matter in her underwear.

"Tomorrow I can eat again," she said serenely.

Meadow has always had a gracious wisdom beyond her years, and there's a remarkable inner strength that radiates from her.

WHEN MEADOW WAS EIGHT, I began to travel, teaching healing classes and doing past-life group regressions. I also began to continue my studies of native cultures. Sometimes the whole family went, and David would help Meadow with her school-work as we traveled to countries such as Australia, New Zealand, or England. I never quite figured out how I happened to be blessed with such a remarkable daughter, but I sure was glad. I had an ongoing struggle with self-esteem, and I was delighted that she didn't seem to share that quality with me.

Meadow had a depth of optimism within her that I found inspiring. For example, she was on a soccer team that didn't score a point for three years. I would sit on the sidelines and cringe at one more devastating defeat after another. Yet when my daughter would come off the playing field, even though she really wanted her team to score, she'd say, "We sure are improving. Didn't we work together well as a team?" She valued the experience above the outcome. When the team finally scored, our shouting from the sidelines must have been heard on the moon, and the other team couldn't figure out why we were so jubilant—it was only a point, after all. They didn't realize what a big deal that point was after three years.

THERE WASN'T EVEN A SECOND when I regretted my decision to have a child. The events preceding Meadow's conception, and the magic surrounding her birth, were just the beginnings of a wondrous life together. When Meadow was a teenager, we wrote a book together called *Quest* about vision quests and solo retreats in nature. It was based on our experience of participating in and leading quests.

After getting a degree from Williams College in Massachusetts and receiving a master's degree in French cultural studies from Columbia University, Meadow taught at The Maine Coast Semester, a boarding school in Maine, which in many ways was a rite of passage for 16-year-olds. While taking rigorous academic courses, the students also learned to balance academics with practical experience. They chopped their own wood for the fire in their cabin, helped grow organic food, and raised livestock. Also, they embarked on solo retreats in nature, which Meadow organized.

Sometimes at night I look to the stars and think about the UFO that heralded Meadow's conception, and I wonder what her future will hold. For now, however, she is a gracious, kind, creative, 27-year-old woman who is the joy of her mother's life.

CHAPTER TWELVE

Spirit Voyages
(1985–1994)

I was out in the garden when the ringing phone interrupted the tranquility of the afternoon. Glancing at the dirt beneath my nails, I wiped my hands on my jeans. Too late I remembered the trick of putting soap under the nails. Conscious that I was going to have to clean a grimy phone later, I picked up the receiver.

"Hello. Is this Denise?" asked a deep male voice in an accent that made his words hard to understand.

"Yes," I said.

"My name is Tom. I am an Indian, and I live on the Taos Pueblo in New Mexico. I have been sending you prayers from the kiva for a year," he said hesitantly.

"You've been sending me prayers? Why? And how did you know about me?" I was so curious as to why he was sending me prayers.

"I read an article about you and wanted to contact you, but I wanted to wait a year," he said. "I know it's far to travel, but if you would be willing to come here, there are some things that I would like to teach you."

Surprising even myself, I agreed to fly to New Mexico to meet him. It was a decision that I never regretted. Tom was a humble man, yet he carried a deep wisdom that in part came from the respect his family enjoyed within the tribe. After our first meeting, I traveled to Taos a number of times, and he eventually became one of my most important teachers.

I loved listening to Tom. His wisdom was simple and direct, and it connected me with my own Native American heritage. One warm, late afternoon during one of my visits, we sat cross-legged together on the wild grasses of the sun-baked high mesa. A soft breeze rustled leaves dried by the August heat and scattered them to either side of us. He was dressed in a faded cowboy shirt and well-worn jeans.

His once jet-black hair was now a peppered gray and white, and his copper-colored face, etched with deep lines, reflected the glow of the setting sun. I strained to hear his gentle voice as he talked. Sometimes he'd stop and stare off into the distance, as if peering into some other world.

That was the day he told me that he was in the fox family and that he could turn himself into a fox . . . as could his father, his grandfather, and all his predecessors.

"You mean you imagine you're a fox?" I asked.

He looked at me with sadness in his eyes, surprised that I would ask such a question.

"No, Denise, we don't imagine we're foxes. We actually become them," he responded.

Even though I risked sensing his disappointment, I had to ask more. "I know it *seems* really real to you when you become a fox, but if I were looking at your body, would I see it become a real fox?" I asked, trying not to sound as skeptical as I felt.

"Denise, some things are true even if you can't understand or comprehend them. I know you have trouble believing this, but I become a fox—a real fox—not an imaginary one. I hunt. I eat. I run. I'm real," he said quietly.

I knew he was telling me what he believed to be the truth, I just had trouble accepting it at the time. Years later, after having witnessed many things that couldn't be explained logically, I knew that it was possible that he could actually turn himself into a fox.

During one visit, he seemed sad and distracted. He told me that he wasn't well and wasn't destined to live much longer. "The reason I contacted you originally was because I wanted someone to pass on what I have learned before I die. It took me a year to be sure that you were the right person, and once I talked to you, I knew you were the one.

"I have passed on what I know to you, and now my death is not far away," he said wistfully. I told him that surely he had many more years to live. However, when I looked into his eyes, I could see that he was resigned to his fate.

In a short time, Tom was diagnosed with a very aggressive cancer. I flew down to see him as he lay dying in the Santa Fe Indian Hospital. He looked very pale and shrunken. I sat next to his bed listening to his labored breathing. He said, "Before I die, I want to share with you my true name. My spirit name is my power, so only a few family members know it. In this way, my power is guarded. Whoever knows it is connected to my soul. Because of this, I want to tell you my name before I go."

He exhaled with exhaustion from speaking and was quiet for a long time. I knew that he didn't like to appear weak, so I turned my head away and looked out the window. A late summer storm was gathering, and dark black clouds threatened in the distance. He shifted his position in bed and spoke in a low voice: "My name is Dancing Feather."

I turned to look at him. Speaking softly, I said his name: "Dancing Feather." In my mind I saw an image of a feather falling from the sky. It turned around and around, dancing in the wind. Saying his name out loud seemed to cement the bond between us that had grown over time. As we gazed at each other, I realized what an immense gift it was for him to tell me his true name. To say thank you seemed too mundane an honor for his gift, so I said nothing.

Looking at his withered body, I realized how ill he was. We both knew that this would be the last time we'd see each other. I remembered ancient traditions in which the teacher passes on secret wisdom to the student just before death. I was sad to ask, but felt that what he might tell me would be important, so I said, "Dancing Feather, what is the most important thing for me to know?"

With a gnarled finger, he beckoned me to come closer. I leaned my ear close to him and waited. Finally, he whispered, "Keep it simple."

I kept my ear near his mouth and waited for him to say something else. There had to be more than that. He said nothing else but just smiled slyly.

Keep it simple? That was it? *That* was the great wisdom passed on from the teacher to the student in his dying moments? I expected a Native American secret word or sacred ceremony to perform or something profound. Then the truth of Dancing Feather's words sank in: *Keep it simple.*

It was the greatest gift he could give me. I've always had a habit of getting so busy that I fall out of tune with the yearnings of my soul, yet these words—*keep it simple*—brought me back to what was authentic and important in life.

As I stood up to leave his hospital room, Tom's very last words to me were: "Wherever you are, wherever you go, Denise . . . I will be there." I didn't want to cry in front of him, so I hurried out of the hospital and began to sob. Overhead, storm clouds were forming. It had been a very dry year, and crops were suffering because there hadn't been much rain, so it was unusual to see rain-heavy clouds. Suddenly, a cool wind blew as one huge raindrop after another bounced off the dusty red earth. Ragged shafts of lightning tore across the sky. I knew that the Spirit of the Sky was also grieving the loss of my teacher.

After his death, a peculiar thing began to happen. Feathers began to appear almost mystically at important junctures in my life. They'd drop out of the sky right in front of me, or appear in unlikely places such as my car seat, my purse, or in my bathtub.

A couple of times when I was onstage giving a lecture, a feather twirled in front of me. Feathers became a means for me to receive secret messages and signs from the spirit realm. Sometimes the message seemed to be "You're doing just fine. Keep going." Other times it seemed to indicate a new direction to head in.

I believe that the appearance of those feathers was a fulfillment of the covenant that Dancing Feather made with me on his deathbed when he said, "Wherever you go, I will be there." He was always a man of his word, and I believe that his word carried forth even from beyond this plane of existence.

IT'S A COMMON SHAMANISTIC TRADITION to have a spirit name, or a "true" name, as Tom did. Most often stems from nature and represents the individual's essence and power. During the years when I traveled and studied in native cultures, I was often gifted with a name. This was an honor, and connected me to the people of the tribe or culture. When I studied with Morna, I was given the Hawaiian name "Maileonahunalani." When I was "adopted" into a New Zealand Maori tribe, I was called "Whetu-Marama-Ote-Rangi." To the Zulu, my name is "Nogukini."

Curiously, almost all the names gifted to me in various cultures seemed to have a common similar theme meaning "the one who sees far" . . . into the heavens, into the stars, or beyond the mountains into the sky. Although I cherished these names, I had a desire to have one that came directly from my soul and the earth.

It was a hot summer afternoon in the Cascade Mountains. All day I'd been thinking about how to find my true spirit name. To escape the heat, I decided to take a walk into the coolness of the woods near our small mountain home. I stopped under a large old tree and closed my eyes. It was very still. There wasn't even the usual hum of insects or the chatter of birds. It reminded me of the mystical stillness that I'd experienced in the woods of Oklahoma, so many years before as a child.

When I finally opened my eyes, a great horned owl rested on a branch a few feet in front of me, so close that if I reached out I could touch him. He must have landed in the few moments that my eyes were closed. All I could see were his enormous eyes as he stared at me. It seemed an endless amount of time, but probably was less than a minute. Then, with a solemn blink, he lifted his massive wings and silently glided away into the forest. I looked at the branch where the owl had landed. Three small downy feathers were caught on the branch. I picked them up and held them in my hand. They were soft and white.

I heard an inner voice say: *Put the feathers in your medicine bag.* The words puzzled me. I had a beautiful medicine bag, but it wasn't with me. Again I heard the voice say: *You are your own medicine bag. Put the feathers in your medicine bag.*

Without further thought, I put the feathers into my mouth and swallowed them. (I don't recommend this. Feathers are *very* hard to swallow and not sanitary, but that didn't occur to me at the time.) The inner voice continued: *As you have taken owl feathers into your body, the spirit of owl has permeated your being and shall always be with you.*

Gradually, with a feeling of serenity and strength, I came back to the reality of the woods around me. This experience precipitated the awareness that my spirit name is "White Feather." (David can't believe that I actually ate feathers. He jokes that my true name is "Eating Feather.") I feel comforted by my spirit name. Every time I say to myself, "I am White Feather," a sense of peace washes over me.

As an experience at a seminar in Norway confirmed, I believe that my spirit name was White Feather long before my encounter in the woods. Partway through my lecture, a late arrival broke my concentration. Although there were several hundred people in the room, from where I was on the stage, I could see her clearly as she entered the back of the room. When she looked at me up on the stage, her face went white and she seemed distressed. Someone ran over to help her to her chair. Although I was concerned about this curious woman, after a few moments, she seemed to collect herself. During the break, she approached me.

"Do you know who I am?" she asked with intensity.

"I'm so sorry. I don't seem to recall you," I answered.

When I said this, she became visibly agitated. She grabbed my shoulders and asked again, "Don't you remember me?"

"Please forgive me, but I really don't remember you," I apologized.

Upon hearing my words, her body slumped and she started to cry softly.

"What's wrong?" I asked, concerned.

"You were responsible for changing my life, and you don't remember me? Many years ago I was going through a very rough time in my life. I was deeply depressed and suicidal. I decided to go camping, and as I went to sleep, I prayed for help—any kind of help. I was desperate.

"In the morning, I heard a noise outside my tent. When I stepped out, you were there. You look exactly the same as you do now, only a bit younger. You told me that your name was White Feather and that you'd come to help me. You said everything was going to be all right and to listen to the songs of the grasses, and then you disappeared. You just vanished into thin air.

"I never heard of you before I came to this lecture, and I hadn't seen your photos, so you can imagine how shocked I was when I saw you here," she explained.

To my knowledge, no one in Norway knew my spirit name, so I was surprised that someone who looked just like me and had that name had appeared to her.

She continued, "From that point onward, I was no longer suicidal, and I even began to see energy fields. I could see energy flowing out of everything—the trees, the grasses—everything. I felt so much better, thanks to you. How can it be that you don't remember me?" She started to cry again.

Over time, numerous people have shared similar stories with me, or told me that I appeared in a dream, stating that my name was White Feather, and gave a helpful message or a powerful healing. Every time I heard one of these stories, I felt really uncomfortable. I didn't want to take credit for something that I hadn't done. However, when I denied that it had anything to do with me, the person who shared the story with me would become deflated or upset. It was as if by denying my involvement, I was also denying them the value or healing they'd gained from the encounter. I didn't know what to do.

Then it occurred to me that perhaps finding my spirit name also helped deepen my connection to another part of myself—a divine part. I've come to believe that there's a magnificent part of each of us that exists, even if we're not consciously aware of it. So even if we're screwed up, unhappy, or dysfunctional, that's only one part of us. There's another part of our being that is divine and wondrous. So it may be that, on some level, I *was* helping people, unbeknownst to my conscious mind.

I DON'T KNOW WHY I had such a hard time believing that Dancing Feather turned himself into a fox or that I could be helping people in their dreams, because in my travels I've seen many things that defy explanation. In the three continents in which I've given seminars, and in the additional countries that I've visited, I've sought out local and native healers. I've always wanted to discover as much as I could about healing. Often the things I experienced pushed the limits of what seemed believable.

For example, I once met a man named Geoffrey Boltwood while I was in London giving lectures. He worked as a healer in a small clinic. I'd heard that he could produce fragrant healing oils out of his hands. When I was ushered into his office, he seemed ordinary and unassuming. He didn't wear a turban, nor did he have mystic symbols on the wall.

I told him that I was skeptical about his abilities. Geoffrey kindly laughed and said, "Here, let me show you something." He put out his hand, palm side up. His palm began to fill with oil until it flowed out of his cupped hands. The room filled with fragrant smells of flowers. I was astonished, yet my skepticism, probably born of living with scientific parents, continued.

"That's amazing, but would you be willing to take off your shirt so I can make sure that there isn't some kind of tube or something." I was a bit embarrassed to ask, but I wanted to be sure. Again Geoffrey laughed and took off his shirt. Once again, he put his hand out, and I watched as fragrant oils filled and overflowed from his hand. Dancing Feather was right: Some things are true even if you don't believe them.

WHEN I WAS GIVING SEMINARS in Hong Kong, I heard about a chi kung master with amazing abilities. His clinic was in Kowloon, just outside of Hong Kong, on a narrow street lined with vendors of all kinds. Barrels of dark swimming things, crates of chickens and other fowl, and piles of sea creatures that I couldn't identify filled the street. Aromas of food being cooked melded with the smell of human sewage and piles of old garbage.

In his clinic, I was witness to a miracle. The translator I brought into the clinic with me suddenly had a stroke. He collapsed to the floor, and the muscles on one side of his face went slack. Instantly the chi kung master pointed his finger at a pressure point on the man's fallen body and, with laserlike precision, channeled energy into him. In a matter of seconds, the translator sat up totally restored *and continued translating!* I was astonished, but to the master it wasn't a miracle, it was just an understanding of how to tap in to the natural flow of energy from the earth.

My experiences with Geoffrey and with the chi kung master and many others expanded my belief in alternative healing. Even though doctors had told me that I wouldn't live long and I'd be physically debilitated my entire life, the numerous healing miracles I witnessed made me believe in the power of the body to heal itself. This also helped my healing work, because I believed that no matter what the condition, there was always hope.

Every time I witnessed something beyond the bounds of normal reality, it served as a reminder of the mystical realm that I'd touched when I was 17. One such experience occurred in Bali, where I was leading a weeklong retreat for a hundred people. I called the retreat the White Owl Seminar, in honor of the experience I had in the woods with the owl.

The day that we were leaving Bali, and the seminar participants were loading their suitcases into the buses, I walked to a nearby beach, rolled up my pants, and stepped into the churning surf. I wanted a few minutes to talk to God alone before everyone left. I silently asked for a sign so I could know if there had been value for people during the seminar. Just as I thought those words, I felt something bump my leg. Reaching into the surf, I pulled out a small quartz carving *of a white owl!*

I just stared at it. How could it have gotten there? And how did it happen to bump into my leg at just that moment? I clasped it into my hand and smiled, realizing that my question had been answered.

IN MY LIFE THERE HAVE BEEN a number of times that objects have seemingly manifested out of thin air. Once I was standing alone in my kitchen when I heard something drop to the floor. I looked in the direction of the sound, and in the middle of the floor was a very old silver-and-rosewood crucifix. I had just swept the floor, and it hadn't been there. I don't know why it appeared or what it meant, but somehow it seemed special.

Another time, the three blue pearls that I kept in the center of my bedroom altar mysteriously disappeared. No one else besides David had been in the house. A week later the pearls spontaneously showed up on the altar again, but they looked to be about a thousand years old. They were tarnished and pitted and had lost their luster. I didn't know why they'd disappeared or why they returned. Yet, every such event seemed to be just one more reminder of Dancing Feather's words when he said, "Some things are true even if you don't believe them."

When I lived in the zendo, the zen monks said to ignore these kind of events, which they called *makyo*, so I tried not to pay too much attention, but I still found them valuable because they helped me remember that the universe is more mysterious than we know.

JUST AS OBJECTS WOULD OCCASIONALLY MANIFEST themselves at "the right time," people and experiences seemed to present themselves to help me step beyond the traumatic events of my past. Once when I was teaching in Sydney, my friend Lynora, who worked with Aboriginal women in the outback, invited me to take part in tribal dances in a remote part of Australia.

When my plane landed, Lynora was waiting to pick me up. As we bounced over bumpy dirt roads in her rugged Land Cruiser, the red dust stuck to the ends of my hair and gathered in my nostrils. There were places where the tracks were extremely faint, and there were no road signs. It was often hard to tell what was a road and what was just desert, but Lynora seemed to know where she was going. We were in one of the most desolate places on Earth, yet the seemingly barren landscape was rich with activity. We passed kangaroos, dingoes, and goanna lizards that swaggered across the dirt track.

When we finally arrived at the Aboriginal gathering, the women elders were already dancing and swaying to the rhythm of the digeridoo. For each dance, they painted their breasts in colorful patterns, which had been passed down for generations. Each design had a meaning appropriate for each dance.

The women urged us to join them. Following closely behind a gray-haired woman, we entered a lean-to made of tall sticks that served as a dressing room. I intently observed the women as they decorated each other's breasts for the next dance. A large woman with a round black face and gleaming white teeth instructed me to take off my shirt and bra. Catching a glimpse of the nonchalant expression I was struggling to make, her lips rose at the corners to form a huge smile, illuminating the whiteness of her teeth against her dark skin.

A woman next to me reached her thick fingers into a pot of paint and made dabs and strokes above and around my nipples. There was something almost primal about having my body so lovingly adorned. Her fingers felt rough and warm against my skin. It didn't feel sexual—it was soothing, almost holy. In the past, my breasts had been ogled, squeezed, caressed, and pinched, but never treated so reverently. This was a powerful first step in my journey to move beyond my past, to love and cherish my breasts.

On the other side of the wall, we could hear the Aboriginal male elders return to their drone-like song. The rhythm of the click sticks was hypnotic. It was an invitation for the women to come out to dance. As everyone piled out of the stick shelter, I held back. One of the younger women, sensing my hesitation to dance exposed in front of the men, gave me a playful shove.

My shyness disappeared into the cadence of the music, and I began to dance. At first I felt awkward, yet as I danced I could feel an energy surge upward from the earth and through my body . . . and I disappeared into the sound.

That night, Lynora and I slept in "swags" on a dry riverbed. A swag is a kind of instant bed—you roll it out, and it has sheets and a pillow all tucked inside. The stars seemed extremely bright that night. They reminded me of the ones I'd seen above Haleakala Crater many years before.

The next morning I awoke in time to see the final stars dissolve into the awakening sky and watch the darkness give birth to the day. There was, however, a moment when the world seemed to stop, an instant of stillness to mark the end of night and the beginning of day. Then slowly, a few insects began to hum, and then more until their sounds became a dull drone, like that of the didgeridoo the night before. Then the birds—green parrots, port lincolns, galahs, and crows—began to add their song to the symphony. I could feel the rhythm of nature in my bones. I inhaled it into my body. It was like an immense heartbeat surging inside me, around me. I knew that it would continue like this until slowly, one by one, the songs of the desert would fade away, until only the hum of a few insects remained. Then, once again, there would be silence to mark the arrival of the first star.

LATER I FOUND MYSELF IN PERTH, AUSTRALIA, teaching a seminar to a packed room of about 600 people about dreams and astral travel. Ever since having astral-travel experiences as a child, I'd maintained a lifelong fascination with this ability. I even developed methods to teach others how to do it.

After my talk, as everyone filed out of the room, a stately Aborigine man in traditional kangaroo-skin clothing ambled forward. He introduced himself as the senior elder of his people, which was one of the tribes in South Western Australia. He was very revered among his people. Part of his upper body was exposed, showing long, deep scars across his chest made during the ceremony that marked a young boy's transition to manhood. Ash had been rubbed in the scars as they were healing to make them more pronounced.

"I heard there was a white woman here from the States talking about dreams. I wanted to hear what she had to say," he said.

"Well, what did you think?" I asked, curious about his opinion.

"Everything you said was accurate, especially what you said about astral travel. All the old fellas astral travel; it's how we stay in touch with each other. In fact, we can tell who visited us in the night because we each leave a dusting of the earth from our area. Every area has a different type of soil, so it's easy to tell where the dust came from. But the young folks have forgotten the old ways," he said.

He went on to explain that as the senior elder of his tribe, he visited young aboriginal men in prison and taught them astral traveling. "I teach them how to travel, so even though their bodies are imprisoned, their spirits are free," he said.

"After hearing your talk tonight, there are some things that I would like to teach you, but I can't teach you unless we are of the same clan. To find out what clan you are in, we have to go to Aboriginal land."

I wasn't sure what to think, but I remembered that I'd never regretted responding to Dancing Feather's invitation. Perhaps this elder could teach me how to deepen my ability to sense energy flows in the earth. I had a few days free, so I accepted his offer.

When he arrived to pick me up the next morning, I was nervous but also excited. I didn't know what to expect. My clothes stuck to my body in the heat as I waited for him. He drove up in an old truck that noisily announced its arrival. I wrenched open the rusty door of the truck and climbed over kangaroo skins that were layered over the torn seat. Their odor was pungent in the morning heat as we bounced along the road.

We drove quite a distance to the tribal bushland. When we arrived, I jumped out of the truck onto the red earth. The air was stifling, and the sun-baked land radiated the climbing temperature.

"The spirits are very strong here. They will injure you if you proceed. Only Aborigines can be here without harm. But we have to come here to find your clan, so we are going to fool them into thinking that you are Aborigine.

"First, we have to disguise your odor. White fellas stink, and the spirits can smell 'em. The first time I smelled a white fella, I thought it was the worst thing I ever smelled," he confessed.

I thought of the ripe odors in the cab of his truck and smiled to myself. What smells good and bad to us is often culturally inspired. He then reached under his arms and cupped his sweat into his hands and then rubbed it over my clothes and on my face and hair. It was strong and musky.

As he rubbed more sweat on me, he talked of female initiations where long cuts were made on the woman's upper arms and then rubbed with ash to enlarge the subsequent scars. I started to worry that he would cut *my* arms. It's funny, but I didn't think about the pain, I only thought about how unsightly the scars would be. I don't have a spleen, which helps the immune system, and because of this I was afraid of getting an infection. When I've been in other cultures, I've tried to adapt to local customs. I wasn't sure if refusing to be cut would be a cultural insult.

My heartbeat quickened. *What am I doing here? Yesterday I was talking to 600 people in a hotel conference room, and today I'm trying to figure out how not to get infections in potentially deep slashes!* I had images of seeing my mother's wrist just after she slit it and the blood pouring out of it. I started to panic. Then a calm, inner voice said: *Don't be afraid. Everything is all right.* Hearing the voice, I relaxed, and accepted that I was exactly where I needed to be. I even accepted the possibility of being cut. Perhaps, not coincidentally, the instant that I accepted that possibility, the elder continued ". . . but I'm not going to cut you." I sighed in relief.

I didn't know anything about the Aboriginal culture at the time. I learned later that females *always* perform female initiations, so a man would have never done such a ceremony. I did know, however, that by actually surrendering to the potential of being cut, I'd overcome some kind of inner fear, and as a result, I felt stronger and clearer.

To further my disguise for the spirits, the elder told me to rub red and yellow ochre over my skin. He reached into the earth and gave me a handful of the red dust. Then he gave me yellow dust, and I completely covered myself with it. He looked at me. My hair, face, arms, feet, and my clothes were coated in yellow and red dust. He then sniffed all around me to make sure that I didn't smell "white," and announced that it was safe for me to venture farther into the land. The spirits wouldn't hurt me. I still didn't look Aboriginal, but somehow he seemed to think that my "disguise" was good enough.

"I'm going to hide behind that tree over there," he said as he pointed to a large eucalyptus. "And you go over to it. Sit with your back against it and wait to see what animal approaches you. The spirits will decide which clan you are and will send a representative to approach you."

With the heightened clarity gained from overcoming my fear of being cut, I felt comfortable as I leaned up against a eucalyptus tree and waited. I was aware of my own sweat rolling down over my ochre-covered body and making long thin streams on my skin. I hoped that I wouldn't sweat so much that the spirits would recognize that I wasn't an Aborigine. Feeling itchy as flies dive-bombed my head, I tried hard not to move, as I'd been told to be still.

The elder didn't tell me what his clan was, so I didn't even know what kind of animal or bird I was waiting for. Hours passed. Periodically his black face would appear from behind the tree, as he looked from side to side to see if any animals were approaching me. The sun was getting low on the horizon. I was tired, hot, and getting nervous that nothing would come, when a large raven-sized crow came hopping toward me. I sat still so as to not disturb him. He hopped closer and closer— seemingly unaware of me—until I could have reached out and touched him..

Suddenly the elder jumped up in delight and ran over to me as the bird noisily flapped away.

"That's it! You're crow clan! I'm also crow clan. I can now teach you."

The concepts I learned from him were an echo of the Native American beliefs that I gained from Dancing Feather and other native peoples. Basically, he taught me that there's a living spirit in the land, and it's important to live in harmony with it. The lessons I learned about the earth energies were helpful in the later work I did with feng shui.

ALTHOUGH IT WAS INTERESTING TO DISCOVER my Aboriginal clan, for me the greatest value of the experience came from pushing through my fear of being cut. Every time I overcame fear in any form, it was a badge of courage for me because I'd been afraid for so much of my life. As a child, I was frightened of my mother's violence and my father's simmering undercurrents. I was scared at every new school I attended. I was afraid that no one would like me and I wouldn't have friends. But I was also afraid that if I *did* make friends, I'd lose them when we had to move again. In many ways, my childhood was defined by my fears.

As I grew up, I suppressed fear and denied its existence, but it shaped my life in hundreds of ways. On my journey to wholeness, I recognized the importance of bringing hidden fears to light. One day I uncovered a fear that had been buried so deep for so many years that I didn't even know it existed.

After receiving an invitation to teach a large seminar in New York, a feeling of panic tore through me at the mention of the substantial publicity that would accompany the event. I didn't understand why I was so frightened. I had led large seminars all over the world and had been featured on magazine covers, in high-profile newspapers, and had appeared on numerous top-rated television and radio shows worldwide. Why would media in the States be so upsetting to me?

I almost never lectured or did media in the U.S. Even though every week I received invitations to teach in foreign countries, it never seemed curious to me that I was almost never invited to speak in my own country. I accepted the maxim "Never a prophet in your own land." However, because of my visceral reaction to the invitation, I wondered if, for some reason, I was afraid of being known in America. But why would I desire to remain obscure and unknown in my own country? I decided to meditate upon this to see if I could discover the reason. Closing my eyes, I took a few deep breaths to relax.

Suddenly the image of the face of the man who shot me burst into my consciousness. I was stunned, as I never consciously thought of him. Even when I mentioned my near-death experience, I never actually thought of his face. This event in my life had become almost like a story to me, which created a kind of distance from those terrifying events. In the image that appeared before me in my meditation, he looked threatening and hard. When I opened my eyes, I was shaking.

The answer came as piercingly loud as a police siren. *I was afraid of doing public lectures and media because I was subconsciously afraid that the man who shot me would find me again!*

I reasoned with myself that this was an illogical fear. My last name was now different, and certainly the man who shot me was still in prison. (Although he hadn't gone to jail for shooting me, he was later incarcerated for other offenses.) There probably wasn't anything to be afraid of.

After I calmed down, I decided to confirm that the shooter was still in prison. I picked up the phone and called directory information to get the number of the Nordon police. When I finally reached them, I was shocked, because the policeman who answered my call remembered all about the shooting, *even though it had been almost 30 years before!* I couldn't believe that something that happened so long ago was fresh in the officer's mind.

When I asked if the gunman was still in jail, he said, "Actually, he was let out recently."

I went cold. I could hardly breathe. When I was 17 I'd been told by a guard that the gunman said that when he got out of jail—after the trial—he was going to come after me. If the local police hadn't forgotten in 30 years, did the gunman sometimes dwell on those events? *Was there a chance that he was looking for me? Was my life in danger?* Maybe there was a very good reason that I didn't do any media in my own country. My mind started spinning all kinds of frightening scenarios. Then the policeman's words brought me back to the present.

"Denise, I've put away a lot of guys over the years. Quite a few of them said that when they got out of prison they would hunt me down. I've learned to live my life without fear. There's no way to predict the future. Learn to live without fear," he said simply.

"Live without fear." The words echoed inside me. I didn't think it was an accident that I just *happened* to decide to find out about the man who shot me—only to learn that he'd recently been let out of prison. I realized that I'd been presented with a remarkable opportunity to face a huge fear—one so alarming that I subconsciously shunned public recognition in my own country for fear of being found.

I thanked the policeman for his advice and hung up the phone. *He's out of jail!* Forgotten memories about the shooting and the trial filled my mind. Numb from the call, I stumbled outside, got in my car, and drove to a nearby candy store. I grabbed boxes of chocolate off the shelves. I didn't care what kind they were, just as long as there was a lot of it.

As soon as I jumped in my car, I ripped open one of the boxes and started shoving one chocolate after another into my mouth, as if it would ease the fear in my belly. Once I arrived home, I quickly ate another box. Then I got sick, really sick.

This is ridiculous! He victimized me once. I'll be damned if I'll let that happen again. I refuse to be afraid of him. I'm ready to release this fear of being publicly known in my own country! I thought as I ran back and forth to the bathroom.

Then I spoke to the Creator: *God, please help me overcome this fear of doing media here. I don't think I can release it on my own.*

Then one of the most incredible synchronicities in my life occurred. The phone rang, and when I picked it up I heard a confident, cheerful voice on the other end. "Hi! I'm calling from *The Oprah Winfrey Show.* We've come across some articles written about you in the London press. We're interested in having you on our show, but it means that you would have to fly here tomorrow."

It was as if God had heard my prayer—and answered immediately. But I didn't feel ready. It was too soon. Verbally declaring my intentions to the universe was a lot different from actually taking action. I got scared. Why couldn't it be a local radio show or newspaper? Why did it have to be such a big show? Then again, I reasoned with myself, what was the chance the gunman watched the Oprah show?

"Well, do you think you could come?" the producer asked, breaking into my train of thought.

"Um, yes, I think maybe I could," I said, "but I don't want to say anything about being shot." And I explained my reasons.

"No problem. We won't mention that," said the producer.

The next day I was on my way to Chicago. During the flight I fluctuated between determination and terror. It certainly wasn't my finest hour on television, but after the interview was over I felt exhilarated that I'd been willing to face my fear. Although I didn't completely shift my concern about the man who shot me, I told myself that the Creator was watching over me, and I had faith that I would always be at the right place at the right time.

CHAPTER THIRTEEN

Angels, Aliens,
and Great Mystery
(1994–1998)

*F*aith. It's such a simple word. I don't know why I had such a hard time with it.

I had touched a heavenly realm when I was 17, and had also experienced remarkable events beyond the parameter of normal life. However, even though one part of me understood that every moment was divinely woven into the greater texture of an individual's destiny, another part of me constantly questioned it all.

Were there really angels watching over us? Was it true that there were no accidents, and every experience was designed to allow us to grow spiritually? Could I always maintain my faith that I'd be at the right place at the right time?

After the Oprah show, I started to do a bit more in the States. Although I didn't feel that I'd completely broken through my fears about being known in my homeland, I made enough progress that I began to do a few events in America. Sometimes, however, my faith was tested when it came to believing that I was always at the right place and time.

I went to Las Vegas for the first time when I was asked to give a lecture about angels for a conference. A couple of hours before my event, I realized that I'd forgotten my music CDs for my guided meditation and I needed to purchase some more. Just out of town was a store that carried ambient music, so I quickly caught a cab to the shop. After making my purchases, I asked to use the phone to call for a taxi.

The store owner said that I'd have trouble getting a taxi because they liked to stay near the casinos. When I mentioned that I was running late and had to get back in time to give a talk, the woman in line behind me said, "I'll give you a ride."

I was so grateful that I immediately accepted. We stepped out of the air-conditioned store—into the bright sunlight and harsh desert heat—and into her red sports car. As we sped out of the parking lot, she started chatting at a frenzied pace. Looking out the window, I realized that we weren't heading toward town. In fact, we were speeding into the desert.

"Um, this doesn't seem to be the right direction to get back to the hotel," I said, concerned.

"It's not. Don't worry. I'm taking you to where I work. It's out of town. I'm a working girl, you know. I guess you could say I'm kind of a prostitute. But just don't worry. You're okay. I'm taking you there so you can be one, too. Just don't worry."

I was startled by her words . . . and I *was* worried. I'd been in such a hurry to get back in time for my talk that I hadn't really focused on this young woman. As I looked more closely, I realized that her eyes seemed overly bright and glazed over—the look of someone on drugs. Was it possible that she got a finder's fee for bringing in a new recruit and she was so doped up that she didn't realize what she was doing?

Diplomatically I said, "That's very kind of you, but I think that I'm a little old to be a prostitute." I was in my mid-40s at the time.

"Oh no," she answered. "There are prostitutes of all ages where I'm taking you. You'll be just fine."

She started to drive faster and more erratically. The road was fairly deserted, and I could only see one other car. I didn't quite know how I happened to be in this situation, but I reminded myself that I was at the right place at the right time, even if it didn't seem like it. I noticed that she was having difficulty managing the car. Almost in answer to my thoughts, she said, "Yeah, I'm having trouble driving, but after all, I've never really driven this car before cuz it's stolen."

Damn, I'm in a stolen car with a prostitute high on drugs . . . and I'm here to talk about angels! I thought. *Well, maybe it isn't an accident. Maybe I'm exactly where I need to be.* We were going so fast that I didn't want to alarm my host by doing or saying anything abrupt, so I continued our conversation, "Well, I'm not sure I have the skill to be a prostitute."

"It's easy. You won't have a problem," she responded. I knew I needed to be very careful to not startle her while she was driving fast, so I calmly asked her what it was like growing up and why she'd chosen to be a prostitute. As she began to talk about her life, she slowed down. I kept asking her questions about what gave her joy in life and what was really important to her.

I knew there was a reason that I was with this woman, albeit in somewhat unusual circumstances, so I really listened to her answers. I listened with my whole heart. As she expressed herself, I learned about her pain growing up and the yearning she had to create something more out of her life. Suddenly, without any explanation, she pulled over, turned around, and headed back to town. I didn't say anything about the fact that we were heading back, but just continued to ask her about her life.

As she pulled up in front of my hotel, she began to cry. "I'm really sorry for taking you. Thank you so much for all your advice. My time with you has been really special. I'm going to change my life and make something of myself."

A little in shock, I thanked her for the ride and wished her well in her life. As I stood in front of the hotel watching her car pull away, I realized that I hadn't given any advice or suggestions. I hadn't even hinted that she should change her life. All I'd done was listen to her and accept her as she was . . . and that had made all the difference.

I was exactly on time for my lecture on angels. As I spoke to the attendees about celestial beings, I couldn't help but wonder if there hadn't been an angel or two along for the ride in that red sports car.

SINCE MY FIRST ENCOUNTER, when they held my hand in the hospital, angels have played an important role in my life. They can come in many forms; however, most often they're unseen. Not only have I been blessed in my life with invisible angelic visitations, but numerous people in my seminars have also experienced the same thing.

I was teaching a course about angels in Ireland when something remarkable occurred. In one exercise I asked people to raise their right arm into the air. A man in the center of the room was in a wheelchair because he had a very serious, debilitating disease. He was dismayed that, because of his illness, he was unable to lift his arm, and he really wanted to follow the instructions. Suddenly he felt someone from behind lift his arm. When he turned to see who it was, there was no one there.

Nevertheless, he could still feel the fingers and hand of someone holding his arm up, *and there was an indentation in his arm where it was being held.* Five times I asked for participants to raise their arms, and five times the invisible hand lifted his arm. His wife, who sat next to him, also saw the indentations in his upper arm, as if an unseen hand held his arm high. At the completion of the course, the couple came to me, their eyes glistening with tears. They felt that they'd witnessed a miracle.

Although angels are usually unseen, they can also appear in human form, like the angel who appeared when I was having coffee with my friend Andrea in London. At the time, she was the editor-in-chief of one of the world's largest women's magazines.

We were sitting in a very small, deserted café, huddled around our small table, chatting about the events in our lives. We were concluding our conversation when a striking woman who looked to be in her 70s with white coiffed hair and wearing a pink suit came into the café. She ordered a cappuccino, walked directly to our table, and asked if she could join us.

Andrea and I were both startled by her request. All the other tables were empty, and ours barely had room for us. Yet we agreed that she could join us. She sat down, placed her coffee in front of her, turned to Andrea, and began to speak as if the words flowed straight from her soul into the heart of my friend.

The insight and guidance she offered about Andrea's life was remarkable. At one point Andrea and I looked at each other, as if to say, "Isn't this incredible!" and when we looked back, the woman was gone . . . completely gone! She wasn't in the café and she wasn't down the street. She had literally vanished. We stared in amazement at her full cappuccino and then back at each other. Andrea leaned forward and whispered, "That was an angel!"

I nodded in agreement. "That *was* an angel."

EVEN THOUGH I FELT that I'd been blessed with what I believe were angelic experiences, I still wanted to see one with wings. Almost every culture throughout the world has had adherents of winged angels. Native Americans called angels the Winged People or the Bird People, alluding to their winged appearance. In my travels, I heard quite a number of accounts from people who'd seen actual winged angels. Even Meadow said she'd seen one. I loved hearing these stories, but they instilled a yearning in me.

One day I was walking on a paved pathway around a lake near our home, and I kept repeating to myself: *I really want to see an angel with wings, I really want to see an angel with wings*, in rhythm with the cadence of my walk.

Suddenly, an older black man in colorful clothes and gliding along on roller skates, twirled in circles around me several times and then began skating backward in front of me. He kept laughing as he looked at me. Then he said these words: "The only thing important in life is love of self, love of others, and love of God." And then he laughed, turned around, and skated off. I remember thinking two things. First: *That was an angel!* And the second, almost instantaneous thought was: *I still want to see an angel with wings!*

I STILL DON'T FULLY UNDERSTAND what angels are or why they appear when they do. They'll always be one of my life's mysteries. When Native Americans refer to the Creator, they say, "Great Mystery." I like this term because there are so many inexplicable mysteries in life, and God seems beyond what we can conceive of with our limited human perceptions. However, often the closest we can get to the Divine is in moments of stillness—or in moments of intense stress.

David, Meadow, a friend, and I were on vacation in Madeira, a Portuguese island, off the coast of Africa, when an event occurred that brought me close to Great Mystery.

Madeira is called the island of eternal spring because the vegetation is so lush. Precipitous mountains thrust straight out of the water into the clouds, creating deep valleys for subtropical plants to thrive on the ancient volcanic ash. We spent our time hiking and enjoying the vast array of plants and flowers. One evening we decided to attend a festival in a remote fishing village. The town was strung with colored lights, musicians strolled on cobbled pathways, and the smell of outdoor cooking blended with the rich seaweed smell in the air.

As we sauntered along the eight-foot-tall stone seawall that separated the ocean from the town, far ahead we saw a small child, about three years old, running along the top of the wall. We gasped as we saw him stumble and fall headfirst onto the rocks below. We ran forward. A crowd gathered around the mother, who was rocking her limp child in her arms. Tears streamed down her face.

I whispered urgently to David, "He has to get to a doctor immediately." A local person next to me, who spoke English, said sadly, "The doctor is three hours away, but I think the child is already dead. Nothing can help him." What happened next continues to astound me.

Holding the boy in her arms, the mother stood up. Her face was white. She stumbled for a few steps with the child and then began to walk in our direction. The crowd was quiet as they parted for her to pass. She continued to walk until she stood before me. Suddenly, she thrust her son into my arms.

For a moment I panicked. *Oh my God! This child has to get to the hospital. Why did she put her child in my arms? What am I going to do?!*

The panic had gone out of her face, and the mother looked at me expectantly, with a deep look of hope. Her simple look of faith touched something inside of me. I thought, *I don't know why this child is in my arms, but since he is, this is no time for self-doubt. I'd better pray hard—now!*

I closed my eyes and prayed for angels, guides, God—anyone—to help the boy. I prayed harder than I could ever remember. Suddenly I found myself in the land of golden light. It was as if a portal had opened, and I swooshed through it into that realm. Surrounded by the light, I cried out, *Help! This boy needs help!*

I said it with all the intensity I could. Instantly, I found myself back by the beach with the boy in my arms. An image of a priest in old-fashioned black garb came into my mind and I "saw" the spirit-priest reach out and put his hands on the child. Warmth surged into the boy's body, and he wiggled in my arms. I opened my eyes to look down just as the boy took a breath, opened his eyes, and looked up at me. He was breathing . . . he was alive!

Handing the boy back to the mother, who was sobbing in relief, I gave thanks to God and to the spirit-priest. I was surprised that a priest had appeared. Perhaps Madeira's long Catholic tradition was part of the reason. I don't know why the woman handed her child to me, a stranger. I don't know if the boy was dead for a few moments or just unconscious and would have revived anyway. I do know, however, that in those few blessed moments, I was witness to the profound mystery of the Divine.

IT MUST BE VERY DIFFICULT to continue to hold fast to the belief in the Divine in places of political upheaval, war, and strife. The first time I arrived in South Africa was before the 1994 election in which Nelson Mandela was a candidate for President. It was a monumental time, and no one knew what was going to happen. Would civil war break out? Would there be massive slaughters?

In my seminars, I taught about creating inner peace and finding balance in life. It was therefore fascinating to teach in Cape Town and Johannesburg where many of the people showed up with guns and weapons. It was remarkable to be with people who were vegan, did yoga, meditated, and were against apartheid, and yet carried guns. If I lived there, however,

I might have considered carrying a gun, too, considering how dangerous it was.

There was extreme fear in the air about the future. The potential for violence was just a breath away. During carjackings, which were common at that time, the passengers would be pulled out and killed, leaving no one to witness the theft of the car. One night I was traveling in a car with a woman who had assisted at my seminar. On a lonely stretch of a country road, a number of black men were standing in our way. Instead of slowing down to avoid hitting them, she stomped on the gas and roared through them, as they jumped to the side. She barely missed injuring or killing someone!

"What are you doing? We could have killed those men!" I yelled out.

"Yes, or they could have killed us," she said, unflustered.

"But what if they were just walking down the road?"

"They might have been just walking home from work, but I can't take the chance that they might have planned on hijacking our car," she said in a matter-of-fact way that suggested that she often sped toward pedestrians at breakneck speeds.

I'd been invited to spend the night with her and her husband at their estate, which was in a remote place in the country. When we arrived, I felt like I was inside a prison compound because the fences around the home were so high. Evidently, during the transitional time in the government, a substantial amount of their land holdings had been seized and given to the native tribal groups.

The border of the appropriated land was about 30 feet away from their home. When the first native Africans arrived to claim it, the couple brought food and clothing to help them because the people arrived with no food and little possessions. But more and more settlers arrived until 10,000 people were crowded together, living 30 feet from their house, and they couldn't provide enough food and clothing for everyone.

The native Africans either lived in lean-tos made of corrugated metal or just slept in the dirt. There was no running water or sanitation, yet 30 feet away from their encampment lived a prosperous family with running water and plenty of food. Tempers rose, violence began to escalate, and eventually the couple had to put up a high fence around their home for protection. Every night around the evening fires, the settlers would chant and *toi toi*, which is a jumping-up-and-down kind of dance that's traditionally performed before battle.

The evening I was there, they got word that their neighbor's home had been broken into and the residents had been attacked. As I went to sleep that night, I could hear the sounds of the frogs croaking with the disconcerting, yet surprisingly comforting, sound of native chanting in the background.

In the middle of the night, the house siren went off. The walls seemed to vibrate with the sound. *Intruders must have activated the alarm!* I panicked, imagining 10,000 furious warriors swarming into the house armed with makeshift knives and clubs. I raced to the windows to escape, but they were securely barred. There was no way out. I dashed around the room trying to find someplace to hide, but there was nowhere to go. Finally, I jumped in an empty baby's crib in the corner and covered myself up with the baby blanket.

Lying under the blanket, listening to my pounding heart and the blaring siren, I suddenly felt stupid. *If I'm going to be attacked, I should find some weapon. It would be better to fight than to cower here*, I reasoned. The lessons I learned about fighting from Peggy in the schoolyard filled my mind.

Just as I was slipping out of the crib to find some kind of weapon, a huge spotlight shone in the window accompanied by the pounding sound of helicopter rotors. The security helicopter, which had been alerted by the alarm, was so close that the plants outside the window were flattened to the ground by the wind it created.

I was naked, so I grabbed the baby blanket and threw it around myself as I recoiled from the light. I'm not sure how many private security helicopters arrived, but it sounded like a cadre of them were flying low around the house, as they shone their spotlights in the windows and around the grounds, looking for signs of a break-in.

I waited for a while. I assumed that the helicopters were heavily armed, so when I didn't hear any gunshots, it seemed safe to leave my room to find my host.

"Oh, it's nothing. The alarm was accidentally set off. Everything's fine," she said jovially as she set off to make everyone some tea. I wondered if everything really was all right, or if she'd lived so close to potential violence for so long that the threat of it seemed almost mundane.

It took me a long time to go back to sleep. I lay in bed and thought of the relative freedom we have living in a westernized country. Even though I'd experienced upheaval in various forms throughout my life, I didn't live in the shadow of violence and political instability every day like so many other people in the world. I knew I wanted to help make the world a safer place, I just didn't know what more I could do. Several days later I had the opportunity to do something that, in my own small way, could help.

I WAS INVITED TO DO AN INTERVIEW at a large broadcasting studio near Johannesburg. When we arrived, we were asked to surrender our weapons to the armed guards at the entrance of the studio. Amber (who was my sponsor in South Africa) got a receipt for her gun and left it with the guards, and then we were escorted upstairs to the radio show on which I was going to be interviewed about reincarnation. Before the show started, Karl, the show's host, came out to the waiting room to chat with me.

"I just want you to know that I'm a total skeptic. I don't believe in reincarnation or past lives," he said abruptly. His skepticism reminded me of how I felt when Dancing Feather first told me about turning into a fox, and when I heard that Geoffrey Boltwood could exude fragrant oils from his palms.

"That's okay. Even people who don't believe in past lives can get value from past-life regressions," I replied.

"Well, I want you to try to regress me, live on the radio. I think our listeners will get a kick out of your attempt," he challenged.

Amber had warned me that this journalist had a reputation for being a hard-nosed reporter. His views were often controversial and frequently very negative. Some said his inflammatory broadcasts weren't helping the country move out of apartheid. When we went into the studio and the "Live" light came on, he asked me about past lives and then dared me to try to regress him. Normally I wouldn't regress anyone under those circumstances, but intuitively I felt it was right, and I was ready to take on his challenge.

"Allow your eyes to close, and take a few very deep breaths," I said.

Karl closed his eyes and, remarkably, almost immediately went into a trance state. I'd seen enough people in semi-trance states to know that he wasn't faking. His eyes began to flicker rapidly, which is one indication of a deep state. As I continued to talk, his body slumped down into his chair.

After a few minutes of regressing him, I said, "I'm going to count from one to three. When I get to the last number, you will be in one of your past lives. One . . . two . . . three! You are now in a past life. Tell me where you are."

"I'm in Egypt. It's morning and it's cold," he said haltingly, in a low voice.

The news that this well-known radio host was being regressed spread throughout the building that housed other radio and television shows. A crowd of people squeezed into the sound engineer's booth to view the broadcast room. They had looks of astonishment on their faces. No one could believe that Karl was in such a deep trance state.

Glancing at all the people staring through the broadcast window, I continued, "What are you aware of in Egypt?"

"There are two groups of people working for me. One group is darker skinned than the other," he said. "They don't get along with each other. I don't like one group."

"Would you like it if they got along?"

"Yes," he replied, simply.

"Would you like to help them?"

"Yes."

"Well, then, I'd like you to visualize or imagine that you're helping to create more harmony between these two groups of people."

As I talked to Karl, suddenly I thought of all the radio listeners who might also be in a suggestible state because of the guided meditation. When someone is in a deeply relaxed state, the words they hear can have lasting effects on their subconscious mind. I decided to use affirmations that were geared to the radio host's regression, but that were also appropriate for the greater audience. In my own small way, I'd been given the opportunity to contribute, over the airwaves, to the creation of more harmony in South Africa. So I repeated affirmations into the microphone.

"With every passing moment, you find a connection with all people, no matter what the color of their skin. . . . You see something good in every person you meet. . . . Every day your ability to create peace within and around you increases!"

After a while, the sound engineer indicated that it was time for a break. So during the commercial, I brought Karl back to conscious awareness. He was shivering.

"Unbelievable! I've never experienced anything like this. What happened to me? That felt so real, like I was really there. Is it possible that I had a past life in Egypt? But could it really have been Egypt, because I was cold and there were lots of plants. Isn't it always hot there?" he asked, still unnerved by his experience.

Curiously, there was a time in the far past when Egypt was cooler and had more plants than it does now, so perhaps, if he had indeed experienced a past-life memory, it wasn't historically inaccurate. When I left, he was still astounded by what had happened.

Amber told me later that, after the show, people called in to share their experiences. Evidently, all over South Africa, people had pulled their cars off the side of the road, closed their eyes, and had gone into deep, relaxed states. Homemakers reclined on their couches and were regressed back in time. Office workers stopped what they were doing, closed their eyes, and entered light trance states. I hoped that the affirmations I'd given were beneficial.

At the time, Credo Mutwa, the spiritual leader and prophet of the Zulu people, was one of many who was working very hard for peace in South Africa, and I'd been invited to visit with him. It was a long journey, and Amber and I drove miles through the open African bush to arrive at Credo's *kraal* (village or compound) in Bophuthatswana.

The sun was setting on the African plain as we arrived. Silhouetted against the setting sun, the traditional mud-and-straw huts of the *kraal* were blurred black against the blood-red sky. The constant drone of insects and the scurrying noises of a few errant chickens looking for shelter for the night filtered through the smoke of fires being lit for the evening, To the east, one lone star pierced the sky.

I had to bend over to enter through the small doorway into Credo's hut. When I straightened up inside, I was surprised to find that it was almost pitch-black. As my eyes quickly adjusted, I became aware of one flickering candle in the center of the hut. I found a place to sit in the dirt and noticed that the mud interior walls were covered with a variety of animal skins. The smell was musty and strong, like the kangaroo skins in the Aborigine's truck.

Sitting across from me was Credo Mutwa, a huge man. His presence filled the space; it was immense and palpable. Animal skins were draped over his body, and numerous talismans hung around his neck. He sat resting comfortably, with his hand lying across his drum. Slowly, he turned his eyes in my direction.

His attention felt like a laser thrust into my soul, inquiring, *Who is this woman who enters my home?* No secrets could be hidden from such a penetration of power. Although I'd met many shamans and gurus on my journeys throughout the world, nothing compared to the energy emanating from this man.

"Welcome, Little Sister. We are glad that you are here," he said sincerely.

"I'm glad to be here, Ubaba," I said, using the honorary title that meant roughly "father" or "patriarch." Amber and I were invited to share a meal with Credo and his people. Warm juices of the chicken and root vegetables rolled over my hand as I used my fingers to pick up the food off my plate to eat.

After our meal, Ubaba began to tell stories. I listened raptly as he talked long into the night, then his subject changed to talk about beings from other planets. He said that the Zulu have always been in contact with aliens.

"All you need do is look at some of our masks. Look at the

oval eyes and the small chin. These masks are representative of the aliens we have had contact with," he said, also mentioning that they'd taken him into their ships.

"Little Sister," he said, addressing me, "they have also taken you a number of times, especially when you were a child."

I didn't want to disagree with this venerable man, but the conversation was beginning to frighten me. Even though David and I had seen a UFO the night before Meadow was conceived, the idea of alien abduction seemed unbelievable.

"With all due respect, I think I would remember something like that. I'm sure that I was never abducted," I said.

"You deny it because it frightens you to remember. But you were abducted, and they are still in contact with you," he said emphatically.

I was getting *really* uncomfortable and steered the conversation away from me and aliens. I started feeling sorry that I'd ever told Heather that aliens inhabited her when she was a little girl. Maybe Credo's words were some kind of karmic payback for causing my sister to stay in bed for three days. Credo pulled out small statues that he'd crafted out of mud and clay to show us the three different kinds of aliens with whom he and his people communicated. As the evening drew to a close, he said, "When you come back tomorrow, I want to show you something."

The next day, I was astonished to be shown huge statues of various alien-type figures that the Zulu on the kraal had crafted. The statues were up to 15 feet tall. I was told that these were in honor of the relationship of the Zulu people with alien life-forms.

ALTHOUGH I WAS GRATEFUL FOR THE UFO ENCOUNTER that David and I had—it was a potent, positive sign for the outcome of my pregnancy—I didn't spend time thinking about aliens. In fact, they were the furthest things from my mind as I sat on the plane, halfway between London and New York on my return trip from South Africa. On that storm-tossed night, a loud, abrupt noise startled me. As much as I'd traveled, teaching in so many countries, I'd grown almost blasé about air turbulence, but something felt different this time. The plane began to lilt side-to-side, then leveled out. Looking to the cabin attendant for reassurance, I noticed that she looked scared.

The intercom crackled. I knew that the pilot would nonchalantly assure us that every thing was all right. He would say that we'd just touched into a little bit of turbulence . . . but it was nothing to worry about. They always do that, no matter how serious the circumstances are.

I breathed a sigh of relief just hearing the sound of the intercom. But instead of the soothing pilot's voice that I expected, I was alarmed by the frightened, halting voice that tersely said, "Fa . . . fa . . . fa . . . fasten your seat . . . seat belts!" and then said nothing more.

It's interesting to notice the thoughts that flash through your mind when confronted by the possibility of your own death. I also found myself thinking about a Korean flight that had recently gone down, killing all the passengers. As soon as the plane started having problems, a man aboard that plane wrote a good-bye letter that was found and given to his family.

In the event that we crashed, I decided to write good-bye letters to David and Meadow and to a few close friends to let them know how much I loved them. I also wrote about the great moments of my life, as well as my regrets. I was surprised to note that my greatest moments weren't things that would look good on a résumé. My triumphs were small things like my getting close enough to a stray cat to pet it, or the times when Meadow ran up to me to tell me that she loved me, or the occasion when I'd unconditionally accepted someone who'd slighted me.

My regrets filled pages of my journal. I regretted not watching more sunsets and not spending more time helping Meadow with her school projects or curling up with David on the couch. I realized that what was truly important in life wasn't what I did, but whom I spent time with—friends and family—and how I spent that time. I promised myself that if I survived that flight, I'd change my life and take more time to cherish the people I loved.

Our pilot succeeded in landing the plane. Although we were never told what the trouble was, I noticed that there were emergency vehicles standing by when we landed. When I disembarked, I was filled with a determination to stay focused on the advice of the roller-skating angel and love myself, my family and friends, and God even more deeply.

CHAPTER FOURTEEN

Am I Ready to Live?

(1998–2004)

"Denise, your dad is dying. Come back as soon as you can," a neighbor of my father said urgently.

I held the phone away from my ear and stared at it numbly. I couldn't believe what I'd just heard. My father had colon cancer, but I hadn't expected to receive that call so soon. Actually, I didn't expect to *ever* receive it. Even though he didn't play a big part in my daily life, somehow I thought he'd always be around.

Shaking myself out of my stupor, I immediately threw some clothes into a suitcase and raced to the airport. Once there, I was told that it would take three flights to get from the small town where I was teaching in central California to the small town in Oregon where my father lived with his second wife.

The first flight was bumpy, but I barely noticed the turbulence. My thoughts were far away. As I leaned my head against the window, I thought about my relationship with the man who was my father. We'd never been very close, especially after the sexual abuse in my childhood. Yet through the years, I'd visited him many times and had tried to establish deeper ties. Even though I still felt emotional wounds from my childhood,

I yearned to have a loving relationship with him. Now, maybe it was too late.

As the plane bounced around, I remembered the two times I'd tried to talk to my father about the abuse, but both times he denied it and abruptly left the room. Once I asked him if he thought that I'd made it up. Somehow it was important for me to know what he felt. He didn't answer me, so I asked him again, "Do you think I'm lying?" Again, he didn't answer me, but just looked down at the floor. It was the closest that I ever got to an apology.

After that, we had an unspoken pact of silence, but the abuse was always in my awareness whenever I was with him. It was an invisible but solid wall between us. Even when I wasn't thinking about it, my body reacted when I was around him. For example, if he gave me an innocent hug, a wave of nausea unexpectedly washed over me.

The emotional scars from the abuse just would not heal. I wouldn't be consciously thinking about the past, but it was always there, buried deep in my subconscious, ready to uncoil and strike out. However, I irrationally thought that if only my father would admit what had happened and apologize for it, then perhaps it might all get better. Maybe it wasn't too late. I had crazy visions of a deathbed apology and reconciliation.

My final plane touched down near the small local airport. A family member picked me up, but by the look on her face I knew that the news wasn't good.

"You're too late. He died a few hours ago," she said dully. Her words didn't register. I couldn't quite believe that he wasn't alive.

"He can't be dead," I said. "Where's his body? I want to see his body."

"You can't. We've sent it to be cremated."

"If he's not cremated yet, then I can still go see it," I said adamantly. I didn't know why I wanted to see his body, but somehow it seemed important.

Finally, back at his home, after much discussion, it was agreed that I could go see his body. He was being held in a warehouse-type building in the industrial area of town. At the front desk, a troll-like man scrutinized me.

"I'm here to see the body of my father," I said.

With the authority vested in people who have small jobs but who like to feel important, he informed me that it wouldn't be possible.

"I *will* see my father's body," I said, as I gave him a hard, penetrating look.

My obstinate determination seemed to shake him for a moment, but he recovered and said haughtily, "Okay, but don't say I didn't warn you."

I was escorted into a harshly lit, cold room, where it became clear why the troll at the front desk didn't want me to go in. My father, gray and lifeless, lay on a slab. He was partially covered with a sheet, but his head and the exposed parts of his body were badly bruised. He *didn't* die of head injuries, but there were gashes and nicks on his head and face. He was a big man, and I think he must have been difficult to carry, so I imagine they must have dropped him several times getting him into the warehouse.

I pulled up a crate and sat down next to him. For a while I just sat there. Then I reached up and put my hand in his. It was cold, yet strangely reassuring. It was the first time I could remember that I didn't feel nauseated when we touched.

I started to talk out loud. I didn't care if anyone else heard me; I had a lot to get off my chest.

"I'm so damn angry with you! Now that you're dead, you're never going to admit to abusing me. You're never going to apologize for what you did! And I'm angry that you died before this could be healed," I said, trembling as I spoke.

I was crying so hard that I was having trouble getting the words out, but I continued, "I don't even know why I'm saying this now, because I'm not even sure that I believe it, but I forgive you. I forgive you for taking advantage of me when I was small. I forgive you for the way you put Mother in the mental hospital. I forgive you for ignoring me when I was shot and not helping me when I was struggling to try to get to college.

"I forgive you for telling me 'good luck' when I called you and said I needed to borrow some money to fix the hole in my aorta, even when I told you I'd die without surgery. But damn it! I forgive you for that, too!" I was shouting and not thinking rationally, but everything that I'd stored up for years erupted out of me.

Even though I was saying the words, I didn't feel like I was really forgiving him, because I was becoming more and more enraged. A lifetime of anger bubbled to the surface as I continued to list all the things for which I "forgave" him.

Then I heard these words—they seemed to come from my father: "All those years *you* kept hoping that I would come forward to ask for your forgiveness . . . *I* kept hoping that you would come forward and forgive me."

Suddenly the anger and sadness dropped away. My father was dead, but I had heard his words almost as clearly as if he was still alive. All of my anguish disappeared, and I felt empty . . . now realizing that all those years that I'd been waiting for an apology, *he* had been waiting for my forgiveness.

I had to take the first step. It had to start with me! In that moment, I let go of the resentment and anger I'd harbored for a lifetime. I just surrendered, and it drained out of me. I didn't have to hold on to any of it anymore. A sense of salvation and freedom filled me, as the room overflowed with a shimmering golden light. Once again I found myself surrounded by the light I'd experienced at 17. As I squeezed my father's hand tightly, it didn't feel cold anymore. I knew that I loved him, and I knew that he loved me. Wonderful forgotten memories from childhood flooded my being—my father fixing the tire on my red bicycle, the time he pulled all of us through the snow on an old wooden sled, and the way he tossed a two-year-old Brand into the air as he squealed with delight. I loved my father . . . I truly loved him.

I stood up and fully looked at him. For the first time that I could remember, I really saw him. In the past, I usually avoided looking into his eyes, but as I looked at him, I became aware of the pain and disappointment in his life. I sensed his self-disgust for abusing his daughter. I saw all his unfulfilled dreams and heartaches. And I wept.

Gently stroking his forehead, I said, "Good-bye, Father." I hadn't called him Father since I was a kid. I always called him by his first name—"Dick"—it had seemed appropriate, but now I was saying farewell to my father.

The lightness I experienced must have followed me, because the memorial service we had a few weeks later was joyous. We created a "stage," did skits reminiscent of the Play Nights when we lived in the barracks, told great stories about Father's life, and shared photos. It was the first time that Heather, Gordon, Brand, and I had been together since we were children, and it felt like a kind of homecoming. Then later, we stood outside to cherish the enormous rainbow that splashed across the sky. Even though it was a sad event, there was a lot of joy and love shared.

IT'S BEEN SAID THAT IT'S EASIER to heal a relationship once the person has entered the spirit realm, and maybe that's true. My relationship with my father got better once he passed on. In fact, I think he even tried to contact me after his death, despite his having told me that he didn't believe that anything followed death.

"When you're dead, you're dead. That's it. End of story," he'd said to me while he was recovering in the hospital after his first cancer surgery. He believed that since heaven wasn't scientifically provable, it didn't exist.

"But Dick, there *is* life after death. I know. I experienced it," I said.

"Well, if the Mormons are right that death isn't the end, I'll put a big 'M' in the sky after I die," he said, laughing. I was curious why he mentioned Mormons and not any other faith. He said that in his 20s, he'd dated a Mormon girl. Although he didn't agree with her religion, he'd really liked her and had often wondered if he wouldn't have been happier if he'd married her instead of my mother.

Not long after my father's death, I was driving a group of my seminar participants in a van. As we meandered down a country road near Ellensburg, Washington, looming ahead in the sky was an "M." It looked like it was made by a jet trail, except that it was geometric and precise. There was no other cloud in the sky except for that perfect "M." I was so astounded that I couldn't say anything, so I just kept driving.

Suddenly, the woman next to me shouted out, "Look! There's an 'M'!"

Soon everyone else was talking excitedly about the "M" in the sky. I pulled the van off the side of the road, and everyone piled out to look at it. As I sat in the van gripping the steering wheel, I started to sob. He was okay . . . my father was okay! I knew it was his way of telling me that he was all right.

BEGINNING TO HEAL MY RELATIONSHIP with my mother was much harder. Ever since I'd left home at age 18, she'd continually refused to see me or have any contact with me. Through the years, this had brought me deep sadness. Although I was angry at the way I'd been treated as a child, I still yearned for my mother's approval and love. She had visited me only twice when I was an adult, and both times were disastrous.

The first time she visited me was shortly after I was married. David is normally a very calm, laid-back man, but after a couple of days of my mother's haranguing behavior, he took me aside to talk. I thought he was going to chide me to try to be more understanding. Instead, he said, "Denise, if I had grown up with your mother, I would have killed her. I don't know how you survived with that woman." His words sent a shudder thorough me, as David didn't say such things lightly.

The second time she visited, she came to meet Meadow, her first grandchild. My daughter, who was about five years old at that time, was very excited to show her grandmother her postcard collection that she'd tied in a red ribbon. While I was in the kitchen, my mother brusquely took Meadow into the bathroom, ripped her postcards to shreds, and then flushed the pieces down the toilet. Tears streamed down Meadow's rosy cheeks as she watched her cards swirl down the toilet. Then my mother came out of the bathroom, found me, pushed me in a corner, and began to hit me. Meadow, who had never witnessed violence firsthand, was horrified. She ran to David and asked him if the world was ending.

That was the only time she ever saw her grandmother. We never made a conscious decision for Meadow not to see my mother again, but after that traumatic experience, she had no inclination to see her anyway.

Even though my mother had been hospitalized for two years for schizophrenia when I was a child, she never again received treatment. Somehow she managed to sustain a solitary life for herself in spite of periodic severe bouts of paranoia. Although I tended to take her rejection personally, she was equally unkind to my siblings, and they, too, more or less, kept their distance in their adult years.

With the exception of those two brief meetings, I hadn't spent time with my mother in the 30 or so years since I'd left home. Over the years, however, I often longed for her, and I would foolishly pretend that things had changed and she really did love me. Ever hopeful, I would then call, but as soon as she heard my voice, she would yell into the phone, "Don't ever call me. I never want to hear from you again!" and slam the phone down. With age, she'd settled into her ways, not improving, but not worsening.

I don't know why I thought that one day it would be different. About every six months I'd call just to hear the sound of her voice, and then would softly hang up or pretend I'd gotten a wrong number. I knew that if I called too often she'd change her number, and I wouldn't be able to hear her voice anymore, so I was careful. David found me sobbing after one of my "calls" and said, "Denise, she's never going to change. She's never going to love you. Quit torturing yourself." I knew he was right, but I kept hoping that something would change. And it did.

Brand called one day to say that he needed help cleaning out my mother's house after she'd moved into a Veteran's Home. We decided not to tell Mother that I was helping. Ever since she'd returned from the mental hospital when I was 12, she seemed to have a deeper aversion to me than to my siblings, and we didn't want to upset her. So I flew to Ohio, and my brother and I began the enormous job of going through a lifetime of objects.

Rummaging through her things, I felt uncomfortable and a bit like a voyeur. However, as we sorted through her personal items, I began to discover a different side to my mother. I realized that she'd managed to carve out a life for herself in her isolated cabin on a lake.

There were photos on the refrigerator of her aged dog and cat in a variety of seasons and holidays. Sadly, she had them euthanized when she went into the Veteran's Home because she wasn't allowed to bring any animals with her. She didn't feel that she would have been able to find good homes for them. There was a photo of her dog dressed in a Santa hat for Christmas and another with it scampering through colorful leaves in the fall, and there was one of her cat curled up in the sun, next to spring flowers. There were even some photos of my mother looking happy as she nestled her animals in her arms.

I could feel the depth of affection that she had for her pets and they for her. It was strange to see photos of this woman who'd been so cruel, looking normal and happy. It was almost like the love that she could never quite find for her children, she'd lavished on her animals. I used to feel sad that my mother had never really known love in her life, but looking at the photos of her animals, I found it comforting to realize that she had.

I climbed into the small attic area and found a moldy cardboard box filled with paintings I'd done as a teenager. She had saved my paintings! She seemed to hate me so much that I thought that she would have thrown them away long ago. On her bookshelf, I even found my high school yearbooks. Was there a place inside of her that cared for me?

In another attic box, I found photos of her at various times in her life. As I sorted through them, one photo jumped out at me. It was taken before my mother had married my father. She looked like she was about 20 years old and completely happy. Her eyes sparkled, and she seemed to be full of hope and expectation for the future. I disliked the woman who'd hit me, but I could love this young woman in the photo.

As I looked at the image, I thought of my healing process

with my father's body in the cold storage room. Could it be that all those years that I was waiting for my mother to love and accept me, her soul was waiting for *me* to love and accept her?

In the photo, her eyes were so bright and loving. As I continued to look at her, something miraculous occurred—as an acceptance of my mother and my life with her began to grow within me. I realized that I had grown into the woman that I was—not in *spite* of her, but *because* of her. I doubt that I would have gone on such extensive inner voyages of self-discovery nor would I have studied extensively in native cultures had it not been for the difficulties that I'd experienced as a child with my mother. I was a better person because of everything I'd gone through.

Looking at the photo, I also felt profound grief for the emotional turmoil that my mother had experienced as a result of her mental illness. It must have been very hard to live with so much rage all the time. And it must have been so scary to be handcuffed and hauled off like a criminal when she was committed to the mental hospital. A dam of grief, past resentment, and fear burst forth, and I sobbed until there wasn't anything left inside of me except compassion for my mother.

True forgiveness is a magical force that often works in mystical ways. I decided to call my mother when I got back home, but this time I was determined to totally accept her, no matter what she said. I wasn't attached to the outcome of my call. For the first time ever, it was all right, no matter how she responded.

"Hi, this is your daughter, Denise."

"Oh! Hi, Denise!" she said. I was astounded, because our calls usually never got this far.

"I'm just calling to say 'Hi' and to find out how you are," I replied.

"Oh, I'm feeling tired lately. Thank you for asking."

"I'm wondering, is there anything that I can do for you?"

"Yes, that would be nice. I need someone to help me go through my mail," she said.

"Would you like me to fly out and help?" I asked, surprised at myself for asking, especially as I'd just been to Ohio.

"I'd like that," she said.

It took three flights and a long drive in a rental car to get to the Veteran's Home. It seemed like a lifetime had passed since the last time I'd seen her. Meadow was five then, and now she was in graduate school. I wondered how I would react when I saw my mother again. Would I instantly revert to the child who desperately wanted her mother's love, or would I still feel the unconditional acceptance that I felt as I went through her belongings?

The walk down the hallway to Mother's room seemed to stretch out for a mile. When I came to the open door, I stood just outside of it. It was so quiet. Softly, I knocked.

"Come in," I heard a quivering voice answer.

I stepped inside to see my mother sitting up in her bed. Her stark white hair hung loosely over her shoulders, the same white hair I'd been shocked to see for the first time when she returned to us from the mental hospital. She looked smaller than I remembered and somewhat frail. She didn't look like the towering, self-centered tyrant of my childhood.

When I entered, she smiled. She didn't say anything for a moment and then said, almost a bit surprised, "Why, you are so beautiful!"

I couldn't believe it. Her first words to me were loving and kind, and the amazing thing is that I'm pretty sure it would've been all right if they hadn't been. I remembered that old maxim: "If you let it go, it comes back to you." I'd let go of the need for my mother's love, and now she seemed to be expressing it.

She started to talk and talk and talk. I sat next to her bed and just listened. Then she started talking about being a mother.

"You know, Denise, I did the best I could, and I must have done a good job, because look at how well you turned out," she said.

"Well, certainly we are each a product of our childhood, and I'm sure that my childhood with you helped form me," I said diplomatically. (*Plus a lot of therapy*, I added to myself.) In addition to my quest to understand alternative forms of healing, I'd also gone to many nontraditional therapists and counselors.

After she chatted for a while, I asked her if she wanted to help me sort through her mail.

"Oh yes, I'm so glad that you came. I needed someone to help me with it," she said.

I thought there would be piles of bills to attend to and correspondence to update. However, there were only a few mail-order catalogs and advertisements.

"Yes, I'm overwhelmed with all this mail and need help sorting it out," she said with exasperation.

For about 15 minutes, I picked up a catalog from the pile and asked if she wanted it. She would think about it, and then say yes or no. I did this until we had all the catalogs sorted into the ones she wanted to keep and the ones she was discarding. I'd taken three flights, rented a car, and driven for a few hours to help her sort catalogs. I know that she didn't have a concept of how much effort it took me to get there; she just knew that she needed someone to help her sort catalogs. In a different situation, I might have been disgruntled, but the whole experience was a miracle to me. The fact that she seemed to enjoy my company was incredible. I would have done it for far less.

My siblings couldn't believe that Mother had been so kind

and loving, and I'm still amazed by what happened. I believe that simply accepting her unconditionally opened the door for healing. Now when I call her, rather than immediately hanging up, she sounds excited and happy to hear from me. She even ends her conversations with "I love you." This continues to be a miracle.

A COUPLE YEARS LATER, I received an early-morning call from Heather to say that Mother, who at the time was 87 years old, was dying. The doctors said that her congestive heart failure was so severe that she only had hours to live. I stared out the window as Heather gravely described the situation. It was very dark outside, but a sliver of the moon was peeking through the clouds. I could hear the resident wild owl hooting in the distance. Heather jolted me out of my thoughts when she said that she was going to catch the next plane to Ohio.

"I don't want her to die alone," she said simply.

"I'm glad you're going to be there with her," I replied. Heather lived closer to Mother, and I knew I couldn't get there in time, so I was grateful that she was going. "Thank you, Heather," I whispered as I hung up.

My mother was dying. No matter how painful my childhood was, she was still my mother. I felt sad for her suffering, and grief for the chasm that had existed between us for so many years. I didn't want to be alone with such an armful of feelings, but I didn't want to wake up David either. He didn't do well without much sleep.

I thought of driving to the all-night Denny's to nurse a cup of coffee until he woke up, just to be in the company of others. But somehow this didn't quite fill the hole in my soul. So I sat in my darkened office, illuminated only by a softly glowing amber lamp, staring listlessly out the window.

When I called Meadow to let her know, she didn't seem

surprised. She said she'd just woken up from a dream in which her grandmother was dying. It had occurred at the exact time that Heather had called me, so she was almost expecting my call.

When Heather arrived at the hospital, she was ushered into my mother's room. She told me that when she looked into the room, Mother was lying so still in the bed that she wondered if she'd already died. However, she saw Mother's chest rise, and she knew that she was still alive. Heather didn't want to be far away if something were to happen, so she lay on the floor, keeping vigil with Mother through the night. In the early-morning hours, she heard a long exhalation from Mother . . . and then nothing. No breath. Complete stillness. Trembling, Heather began to sob, "My mother is dead. My mother is dead!"

Then Mother inhaled raggedly and began to breathe again. Abruptly, my sister's tears stopped, and she lay down on the floor again to continue her vigil.

Then it happened a second time . . . no breath. Heather jumped up. Nothing. No breath. She waited and watched . . . and waited . . . and waited. No breath. Then she sobbed again, "She's dead. My mother is dead!"

Suddenly my mother started coughing and breathing again. After the fourth time, my sister said, "That's it! I'm waiting until the doctors say you're dead before I throw myself on you again!" And she sat in a chair with her arms crossed.

In the morning, my mother sat up and ate half her breakfast. The nurse said, "This is incredible. We were sure that she'd die last night." At lunch, Mother wholeheartedly ate her meal and even asked for ice cream.

Death, like birth, comes in its own time. The doctor said it was astounding that she was still alive. Mother regained her health quickly (attributing her recovery to "good genes"), and a few months later, she went out to a Valentine's Day party.

Confronting her death at that time was a huge blessing, because it allowed me to once again examine my relationship with her. I realized that I love her, and I'm grateful for what I gained in my life with her. Grandma was right when she said, "The roots go deepest when the wind blows strongest." My life with my mother allowed my roots to go deep.

I'D DONE A SUBSTANTIAL AMOUNT OF HEALING in my relationships with my parents; however, it was my relationship with myself that eventually needed the most attention. I had turned 50, and my vitality and joy began to wane as I found myself feeling stuck in daily routines and responsibilities. I was going through menopause and often felt tired and depleted. Self-contempt and a lack of self-esteem grew as I drudged through my life.

Pushing through my aversion to hospitals, I decided to get a series of physicals just to get a baseline on my health. Hence, I found myself in a stark, sterile-looking room at the hospital waiting for the results of a routine mammogram. A brusque doctor ushered me into a room with x-rays of my breasts clipped to the light box on the wall. She pointed to one picture of my right breast and briskly said, "In this area there's a 50 percent chance that this is cancer." And then pointed to another area of the breast. "There is at least a 95 percent chance that this is cancer . . . and that's optimistic. You have cancer."

I asked her straightforward questions, and she answered in an abrupt way, suggesting that I have surgery as soon as possible. I thanked her. It was all so matter-of-fact. I asked her if she was ever wrong. She told me that she was sure that I had cancer, because in the 12 years that she'd been at the hospital, she'd never been wrong.

I got in my car to drive home, but I couldn't start it. My hands shook and my legs trembled. *Cancer? I don't have cancer. I can't have cancer.*

My foundation was crumbling, and I couldn't think clearly. My car finally started with a jerk, and I drove out of the hospital parking lot. When the light turned green, the guy behind me honked his horn. My car lunged forward as I pressed on the gas. I felt numb and I was scared.

I also felt ashamed of myself for having cancer. How could I be a healer and have cancer? At home, I sputtered the diagnosis to David but didn't want to talk about it. I knew that David was upset and needed to talk, but I needed time to myself. Finally I fell asleep in shock and in denial, upset with myself for not being able to talk to my husband.

When I woke up the next morning, I felt dull and worn-out. I knew that I needed to take stock of my life. I asked myself if I was ready to die. Surprisingly, I felt that I was. Meadow was out of college and living on her own. I knew that David would miss me, but I also knew that he'd be okay.

The next question was more challenging: "Am I ready to really live?" In order to "really live," I knew that I needed to make some changes in my life. I was aware that many of those who contracted cancer were pleasers and caregivers—the type of people who postpone happiness and put others' needs before their own. I began my tenure as a caregiver as a child, when Mother was incapacitated, but somehow I never stopped. It was time to change, but I was scared.

I was told to come back to the hospital for more tests, but I wanted to wait a month. I needed time to ponder my options. I immediately began to learn everything I could about cancer: traditional, alternative, and psychological approaches. I also did some deep soul-searching. It was an uncomfortable process, but very revealing. I meditated, wrote in my journal, and prayed. I took long walks and found a great therapist. I knew there had to be some kind of clue to why I had cancer.

Then one day it hit me! I'd been waiting, since I was a child, for my real life to begin, but it never did. I always had some future goal to be accomplished before I could be happy, but no matter what goal I reached, there was always just one more that had to be attained.

When I was in high school, I thought that when I finally moved away from the upheaval at home, my real life would start. But when I moved out, nothing changed. Then I finally got into college, and I was sure it would happen then . . . but it didn't. I thought that when I got a job, my life would begin. That wasn't it. After that, I knew that I had to get married to be complete, and that didn't do it either.

There was always some future goal that I had to fulfill before my life turned out, such as owning our own home, having a baby, writing a book, or traveling to other countries. All the while, I kept waiting. There was always something I had to do or accomplish first. I thought that when I was done with my "to-do list in life," I could relax and do what *I* wanted to do, but I never got it all done.

I suddenly realized that my life *had turned out!* Faced with the possibility of cancer, I knew that if I didn't find happiness now, I might never get the chance. I realized that there was no better time to be happy than right now, because if not now, when? Happiness was how I experienced each moment. It was a journey, not a destination. This realization was a defining experience for me.

From that moment on, I felt more relaxed than I had in years. I knew that life would always be filled with challenges, but I didn't need to wait for everything to be perfect in order to be happy. I only needed to believe that I was on the right path. And I *was* on the right path . . . *even when I didn't know it.*

I resolved to not put everyone else's needs before mine and to cherish myself more. It was okay to be a caretaker, but I had to take care of myself before I could take care of anyone else.

A month after the first series of tests, I went back in for more. They couldn't find any cancer. They said they must have been mistaken the first time. So either the first test was wrong, or all the inner work I did had healed my body. I was relieved, but most of all I was immensely grateful for the entire experience, because I'd come to know myself more fully because of it.

After the cancer scare, I decided to continue my soul-searching. We'd just bought a home on 40 acres, nestled in the wine country of Central California. It was only a few miles from where, as a child, I'd dug my dirt hole to take refuge from my parents' arguments. David needed to stay in the Pacific Northwest to oversee the sale of our home, so I moved into our new house and spent seven weeks by myself in an empty house, surrounded by rolling hills, oak trees, and wild grasses.

It was an incredible experience to be completely alone. For furniture, I had a foam pad for a bed and a rather old rocking chair. There were no newspapers, magazines, or television. I didn't even answer e-mails, telephone calls, or mail. Even during the two years I lived in the Zen Buddhist monastery, there were other people around. For the first time I could remember, I was caring for myself instead of everyone else. I went for walks, painted, took candlelit baths, and listened to music. I lay on the grass and watched clouds and birds for hours. I sat with my back against the old oak trees and listened to their messages. I'd been so busy in my life that I'd forgotten to drink in the wisdom of the earth, the trees, and the sky.

Slowly but surely, the part of me that was authentic and real began to surface. During my seven weeks of solitude, I began to feel the emergence of a passionate, wild woman rising from somewhere deep in the murky waters of my soul. It felt as if a huge burden had been lifted from my shoulders, and the strong, sensual, sacred part of my personality—the goddess part—was being birthed.

It was during this gestation period that my new direction became clear. I had taught feng shui and space clearing for the last few years and had enjoyed it immensely, yet the aspect that gave me the most joy during those years was training people to tap in to their inner wisdom regarding their home and life. That's what I loved.

I realized that I wanted to devote the next phase of my life to training people how to find their deepest truths and hear the secret messages from their soul. "Soul Coaching!" . . . I could almost hear my guides and angels cheering when I thought of the concept. Everything I'd learned during my life could be distilled into a potent Life Coach training program. I would teach others what I knew about healing the body and the soul so they could become professional Soul Coaches. Miracles would abound! I was on fire with excitement about it!

In addition to traveling the world and teaching large groups of people in hotels, I could also teach intimate groups on our land. In this way, I could call upon the assistance of the spirit of the earth, stars, and ancient trees to empower every aspect of the training. I knew that here I could open portals for others to step through so that they too could touch the realm of golden light. I was ready to start the next phase of my life.

After selling the house, David finally arrived to find me refreshed and renewed. We then began the process of renovating our new home—a 50-year-old ranch house—and clearing some of the areas surrounding it and remodeling the outbuildings. We named our place Summerhill Ranch. The name seemed to fit. The northern part of the property has a very large hill, and it glows in the summer when the wild oats that cover it turn golden.

We're very happy at Summerhill Ranch. In the morning,

we watch the fog from the Pacific Ocean roll over the Santa Lucia mountains down to the vineyards below. Here, only a few miles from the dirt hole of my childhood, I've established my roots. Even as a child, I knew that my hole was a kind of womb of the earth, a sacred place of brooding that would give birth to dreams of my future. Maybe I planted part of my spirit here, and perhaps, sensing my wandering soul, the land had called me back. It is a retreat and a sanctuary. Whatever the reason, my connection with the earth here is intimate and timeless.

I know that I am home.

AFTERWORD

Coming Full Circle

Just as the earthquake coincided with my journey to write this book—a process that cracked open hidden, dark memories—it seemed as if the multitude of aftershocks corresponded *and sometimes even helped* splinter open my past even more. When my office walls shook violently with each tremor, it felt as if old memories were being shaken loose as well. My past, which had been so carefully veiled, revealed itself in greater and greater depth. Sometimes when an aftershock hit, I'd dive under my desk, and other times I'd just hold on to my chair and continue to type.

I had no idea what I was getting into when I agreed to write this memoir. Over the years I'd declined previous offers to write about my life. On the surface, I told myself it would be egotistical to write about myself. Subconsciously, however, I think I was afraid of what I would uncover. I was scared of being vulnerable and laying bare my soul in print. I was also afraid of exposing painful memories and having to examine myself in the harsh light of truth.

Writing this book was one of the most challenging endeavors I've ever undertaken. As I traveled deep within myself to recall the darkest moments of my life, old wounds were opened.

I ached with sadness for the child I once was and grieved for her pain. I wondered why I'd ever taken on the task of writing my life story. Yet, there were also times when I found myself laughing at some misadventure in my past or savoring some forgotten tenderness. From its earth-shaking beginning on the winter's solstice, to its completion a few weeks following the summer solstice, the writing of this book was filled with synchronicities.

One of these remarkable "coincidences" occurred in early January, just after the earthquake. David, Meadow, and I went for a vacation in Kauai, a lush Hawaiian Island. It was wonderful to get away from the clean-up and repair after the quake. We rented a condo overlooking the scenic Hanalei Bay. As David and Meadow hiked or swam, I sat on the lanai with my laptop and wrote about my mother and her experiences on the Hawaiian Islands. Smelling the salt air and the fragrant tropical flowers as I wrote, it was easy to visualize her in Hawaii before the war.

On the wall behind me was a large framed print from the '40s of a woman posed at the beach in a bathing suit. The woman in the poster had a striking resemblance to my mother. It almost seemed that she was looking over my shoulder as I wrote about her. I chalked up the similarity to my active imagination and forgot about it until, upon our return home, I came across some bathing-suit photos of my mother when she'd modeled in Hawaii in the '40s. In the photos she looked surprisingly like the woman in the poster. Then I saw written on the back of the photos that they'd been taken by the same artist from the print in the condo! Although I didn't find the exact photo of the print, the shots were so similar that it seems probable that an image of my mother *was* looking over my shoulder, silently encouraging me as I wrote.

A darker synchronicity occurred the day I began to write about the man who shot me. On that day, I decided, once again, to see if he was back in prison or if he had maybe even died. My Internet skills are rudimentary, so I called my brother Brand, and asked if he'd be willing to try to locate him. The next day Brand e-mailed me a picture of the shooter that he'd found on the Web. The photo had been *taken the day before . . . the day he had been let out of jail!* In other words, he'd been let out of jail, again—after having been imprisoned for five years—*on the exact day* that I started to write about him.

I looked at the color image of him on my computer screen. Cold chills ran up and down my body, and I had trouble breathing. Although he was much older than when I'd seen him as a 17-year-old, the sly, hooded eyes and the unctuous countenance were the same. I found myself ducking to the side of the computer so he wouldn't "see" me. I knew I was being irrational, but I couldn't help myself.

Since he'd been convicted of a sex offense, his photo and address were posted on the Internet the day he was released. The odds of him being let out of prison on the day I began to write about him were astounding.

Once again, panic filled me. Although I'd forgiven him years before, I wasn't sure that I wanted to encounter him again. What if he read the book and tried to find me? Was I going to have to look over my shoulder for the rest of my life? Could I face each day with confidence and joy, knowing that he was out there? Once again, I turned to chocolate and devoured half a cake before getting sick.

Then my inner voice spoke to me firmly and decisively: *Denise, there are no certainties in life. You have stated that you want to live life courageously and passionately, yet in the face of this uncertainty, you wither.*

You know that inner power comes from facing fear, no matter what form it comes in, so step up and face your fear! You also know that everything that occurs in your life is an important part of your destiny, allowing you to grow spiritually, so accept your life in all its convolutions.

As soon as I had this talk with myself, I relaxed. I realized that every synchronicity that occurred while writing about my life was an affirmation that some deeper force was guiding, nudging, and even shoving me forward. It was that same force that exists deep beyond the surface of life, in the place where the spirit of the wind, thunder, and clouds are born—a place divine and wondrous.

That sacred place holds the quickening of spirit. It is where endings and beginnings are born. My beginning in this life allowed me to soar into light as well as descend into darkness, yet through my journey I came to the sacred understanding that both the light *and the dark* were important parts of my journey. Each event propelled me forward and allowed me to come closer to the place of spirit and mystery—my true home.

AS I'VE SLOWLY COME TO TERMS with my life, my siblings have also struggled to overcome our past, and each has found their path in life. Heather was eventually granted a scholarship by the University of Hawaii and got a degree in biology. She later wrote a book about seaweed, and had an art exhibit of her remarkable fish prints at the National Aquarium in Washington, D.C.

The same tenacity of spirit that allowed Heather to leave home at 17 to make a life for herself got her through the incredible challenges of being a woman in the male-dominated world of the United States Merchant Marines. Through sheer will, integrity, and excellence, she got her unlimited master's license and made her career in the Merchant Marines working on ships as diverse as NOAA research vessels, to super tankers, to USMC support vessels for the Iraq war.

Brand received a doctorate in astrophysics; works for NASA at Johns Hopkins University; funded the Fortner Chair of Astrophysics at the University of Illinois; started two companies, including Spy Glass, Inc.; and wrote three scientific books. *Mensa Magazine* lists him as one of the 20 most famous Mensans in the world.

My brother Gordon never married and took a more internal path in life. He leads a quiet life working with computers in his home.

My mother still lives in a Veteran's Home in Ohio. She continues to surprise her doctors with her determination to hold on to life. Twice in the last ten years, I received a call from the hospital telling me that Mother had less than a day to live because of severe heart failure. Yet she continues to thrive despite her doctor's prognosis. She says it's her "good genes."

Sometimes, when I worry about my prospects for continued good health because of the number of organs that were removed when I was 17, I think of my mother's survival against medical odds . . . and I rally, remembering that I have her genes.

One of the joys of writing this book was to be able to reconnect with my past loves. Rich Betts lives in the small town where he grew up. He does maintenance in the local school and is married with three children. Ron Collins, now a retired academic, never married. He lives a fulfilling life in Oregon, hiking, singing in a peace choir, and helping to preserve native plants. Robin Lee is an award-winning architect and owns a successful architectural firm in Honolulu. He and his wife have been very involved with the Waldorf School educational system while raising their three children.

All in all, every one of the people who have been important in my life—both the ones I wrote about, and the ones that I hold dear in my heart yet didn't make it onto these pages—have given me so much. Sometimes what I gained was painful, and sometimes it was joyful, yet I wouldn't be who I am without what I learned from each of these individuals.

Now, as I let go of these pages and release them to the universe, the aftershocks are no longer monumental. They're just gentle rumbles now and again. The challenges in my life that seemed so earth-shaking as I wrote about them have been laid to rest, and now are mere trembles in my memory.

I don't know where the currents of my future will take me, but I do know that if I seek out that which is authentic and real within myself and live each moment as joyously and passionately as possible, I will be home wherever I am.

Yesterday I was shopping at the local grocery store, standing between the crackers and the flour, as the '60s song "Locomotion" was playing on the in-house sound system. At the end of the aisle was a gangly 12- or 13-year-old girl who reminded me of myself at that age. She was all arms and legs. Her long, skinny limbs seemed to jut out of her body at awkward angles.

She wasn't aware of me—or anything else in the store—as she danced to the music. Her hands fluttered like dried leaves flapping on the end of a bare branch. Her legs flailed to the left and right in time with the music . . . and she was in a total state of joy.

I looked at her and smiled—the slight smile of an adult bemused by the actions of a child. Then I thought, *Hey! The heck with this. I don't want to be the amused spectator. I want to embrace it all just like she's doing.*

So I started fluttering my hands, waving my arms overhead, and stomping my legs with abandon in time to the music. Life is too short not to dance in the aisles of the supermarket.

Thank you so very much for joining me on this journey. I hope that we meet sometime . . . "dancing in the aisles."

I am honored to have had you as my companion and fellow traveler.

EPILOGUE

Across the River

My book is complete. I only have to read it one last time before it's submitted to my publisher. As I'm scanning through it, the house begins to shake with a strong aftershock, and I dive under my desk. I should be used to this by now, but I'm surprised because we haven't had any aftershocks for a long time. I shouldn't be startled, however, because the earth's movements have closely followed my inner tremors as I've written this book. Somehow it seems appropriate that the earth would stir in the last moments before I send off my manuscript.

Perhaps it's a blessing.

Later in the evening, I chat on the phone with a dear friend who's also the managing director of Hay House Publishing in Australia. As we talk, the room seems to fill with golden light. It's incredible. I'm not sure why it's happening. My heart feels so open and full. When I get off the phone and get ready for bed, the light lingers.

3:15 A.M.: Something wakes me. In the next room the dogs are restless, which is highly unusual—once they're bedded down they could sleep through an earthquake. In fact, they've done just that before. I get up for a while and then decide that

3:15 is too early to wake up. As I lay down to sleep, I have an image of a tall Native American man doing a stomp dance. He's wearing a cape decorated with designs of eagles on it. It isn't a dream, but more like a vision. I feel happy to see him.

6:00 A.M.: My brother Brand calls to say that Mother has passed on in the night. He says that she died at 6:15 A.M. Eastern Standard Time, which was *3:15 A.M. Pacific Standard Time!* He didn't want to wake me, so he waited a few hours before telephoning. My throat tightens and my cheeks tingle, like when I've been crying, but there are no tears. I feel numb and it's hard to breathe. I expected this call, but now it all seems so final and forever.

A couple of days ago, my mother's caregivers at the Veterans Home called to say that she wasn't doing well. But they'd done this many times over the last few years, and she always pulled through. When they called this time, I had tried to get a flight back East to see her, but everything was booked for the Thanksgiving holiday, and there was also a big snowstorm in Ohio, which made flights difficult. So instead of being there in person, I spent hours talking to her on the phone. She was a bit disoriented, but I knew she could understand me. I talked to her about what would happen when she reached the "other side of the river."

My mother's Cherokee heritage was important to her, and when I was a child, she used to say that when Cherokees died, they went to a heavenly place where game was plentiful, fish splashed silver out of deep clear waters, and berries were plump and ripe. She called it the "Happy Hunting Grounds."

When I got older, I thought that this sounded corny and very politically incorrect, like something Tonto might have said in *The Lone Ranger.* But as she lay at the advent of death, I told her that I believed that her family would be waiting for her on the other side of the river in a place where the air was sweet and the wind swept majestically across tall, wild grasses. I said that I believed there would be a stomp dance in her honor when she arrived. I hoped it was true.

And I sang to her . . . her favorite songs and ones from my childhood. I belted out "Mr. Sandman" and "Blueberry Hill," or at least what I could remember. When I ran out of songs, I sang Christmas carols and then just made some up.

Every time I asked, "Do you want to hear another song?" she would mumble, "Yes." So I just kept singing until my throat was sore. Her nurses said that whenever I was singing, my mother's respiration slowed down and she smiled. As I always did, I ended that final phone call by singing "Happy trails to you until we meet again . . ." because I believe that we *will* meet again. And then I closed by saying, "I love you, Mother." And I meant it.

As I hang up the phone after talking to Brand, I walk outside. The sky is as dark as night, and tiny bright stars punctuate the darkness. To the west, a full moon peeks between the tall pine-tree branches. The air is sharp when I inhale. I think about the golden light that permeated the room during my phone call. I wonder if that was Mother's spirit coming to say good-bye before her transition.

An owl hoots from a nearby oak tree, and then another hoots from a pine tree . . . and then another from the orchard. In the background, I can hear owls through the canyon. They hoot and hoot and hoot loudly and repetitively . . . a dirge? A rite of passing? I've never heard owls do this before. It's amazing!

Suddenly the image of the tall Indian I "saw" at 3:15 appears in my mind, and I'm sure that my mother is dancing around a fire with friends and loved ones somewhere beyond this realm . . . happy, exuberant, and free . . . in the Happy Hunting Grounds.

ACKNOWLEDGMENTS

To Reid Tracy, my publisher at Hay House, I am deeply indebted. It was your inspiration and encouragement that allowed me to spread my wings as I wrote this book. Thank you!

To Louise Hay, the spirit of Hay House, my gratitude is boundless.

I am also very appreciative for the remarkable Hay House team: Jill Kramer, chief editor-par-excellence, your clarity and compassion are stellar. To Shannon Littrell, a genuine, heartfelt editor; Amy Gingery, a visionary in the art department; and Richelle Zizian, who could make the stars shine brighter, I am indebted to each of you. And to the Hay House "divas"—Jacqui Clark, Jeannie Liberati, Margarete Nielsen, Christy Salinas, and Stacey Smith—what a team!

And a very special thank you to Leon Nacson at Hay House Australia. Your friendship throughout the years has meant more than I can begin to tell you. You are a friend for life.

My family was wonderful in supporting me on this journey. I walked hand-in-hand with my sister, Heather Fortner, and my brother Brand Fortner, as we relived our past together while I wrote this book. With additional thanks to my brother Gordon Fortner. I am also grateful to David's family—his parents, Al and Harriet; and his sisters, Sue, Terri, Sandi, and their spouses and children—for their support through the years.

To Lynora Brooke, I am so very grateful for your grace and the depth of your understanding. To Rich Betts, Marika Burton, LuAnn Cibik, Ron Collins, Amber Dotts, Holly Foster, Sue Foster, Lynne Franks, Patti Hanmer, Debbie Kaminski, Judith Kendra, Priya Kroeger, Robin Lee, Cynthia and Shumway Poole, Kathryn McFarland, Amber McIntyre, Jayne McGuire, Elyse Santoro, Rick Schulze, Stratton Semmes and the entire Semmes clan, Delores Talbert, and the fabulous Interior Alignment® and Soul Coaching® family, thank you for being in my life.

Meadow Linn and Katie Olsen, you were my muses as well as my editing geniuses. There are no words to describe how grateful I am for your assistance. And most of all, I am grateful to David, my wonderful husband. I am so glad you said *yes* so many years ago.

ABOUT THE AUTHOR

 **Denise Linn**'s personal journey began as a result of a near-death experience at age 17. Her life-changing experiences and remarkable recovery set her on a spiritual quest that led her to explore the healing traditions of many cultures, including those of her own Cherokee ancestors, the Aborigines in the Australian bush, and the Zulus in Bophuthatswana. She trained with a Hawaiian kahuna (shaman), and Reiki Master Hawayo Takata. She was also adopted into a New Zealand Maori tribe. In addition, Denise lived in a Zen Buddhist monastery for more than two years.

Denise is an internationally renowned teacher in the field of self-development. She's the author of the bestseller *Sacred Space* and the award-winning *Feng Shui for the Soul*, and has written 16 books, which are available in 24 languages. Denise has appeared in numerous documentaries and television shows worldwide, gives seminars on six continents and is the founder of the International Institute of Soul Coaching®, which offers professional certification programmes in life coaching.

For information about Denise's certification programme and other lectures, please visit her website or write to: Denise Linn Seminars, P.O. Box 759, Paso Robles, California 93447, USA.

www.deniselinn.com

We hope you enjoyed this Hay House book. If you'd like to receive our online catalogue featuring additional information on Hay House books and products, or if you'd like to find out more about the Hay Foundation, please contact:

Hay House UK, Ltd.
292B Kensal Rd., London W10 5BE
Phone: 44-20-8962-1230 • *Fax:* 44-20-8962-1239
www.hayhouse.co.uk • www.hayfoundation.org

~

Published and distributed in the United States by: Hay House, Inc., P.O. Box 5100, Carlsbad, CA 92018-5100 *Phone:* (760) 431-7695 or (800) 654-5126 *Fax:* (760) 431-6948 or (800) 650-5115 • www.hayhouse.com

Published and distributed in Australia by: Hay House Australia Pty. Ltd., 18/36 Ralph St., Alexandria NSW 2015 *Phone:* 612-9669-4299 *Fax:* 612-9669-4144 • www.hayhouse.com.au

Published and distributed in the Republic of South Africa by: Hay House SA (Pty), Ltd., P.O. Box 990, Witkoppen 2068 *Phone/Fax:* 27-11-467-8904 • www.hayhouse.co.za

Published in India by: Hay House Publishers India, Muskaan Complex, Plot No. 3, B-2, Vasant Kunj, New Delhi 110 070 • *Phone:* 91-11-4176-1620 *Fax:* 91-11-4176-1630 • www.hayhouse.co.in

Distributed in Canada by: Raincoast, 9050 Shaughnessy St., Vancouver, B.C. V6P 6E5 • *Phone:* (604) 323-7100 • *Fax:* (604) 323-2600 www.raincoast.com

~

Take Your Soul on a Vacation

Visit **www.HealYourLife.com®** to regroup, recharge, and reconnect with your own magnificence.

Featuring blogs, mind-body-spirit news, and life-changing wisdom from Louise Hay and friends.

Visit **www.HealYourLife.com** today!

JOIN THE HAY HOUSE FAMILY

As the leading self-help, mind, body and spirit publisher in the UK, we'd like to welcome you to our family so that you can enjoy all the benefits our website has to offer.

 EXTRACTS from a selection of your favourite author titles

 COMPETITIONS, PRIZES & SPECIAL OFFERS Win extracts, money off, downloads and so much more

 **LISTEN** to a range of radio interviews and our latest audio publications

 CELEBRATE YOUR BIRTHDAY An inspiring gift will be sent your way

 LATEST NEWS Keep up with the latest news from and about our authors

 ATTEND OUR AUTHOR EVENTS Be the first to hear about our author events

 iPHONE APPS Download your favourite app for your iPhone

 **HAY HOUSE INFORMATION** Ask us anything, all enquiries answered

join us online at **www.hayhouse.co.uk**

292B Kensal Road, London W10 5BE
T: 020 8962 1230 E: info@hayhouse.co.uk